China's One-Child Policy and Multiple Caregiving

This book explores the effects of China's one-child policy on modern Chinese families. It is widely thought that such a policy has contributed to the creation of a generation of little emperors or little suns spoiled by their parents and by the grandparents who have been recruited to care for the child while the middle generation goes off to work. Investigating what life is really like with three generations in close quarters and using urban Xiamen as a backdrop, the author shows how viewing the grandparents and parents as engaged in an intergenerational parenting coalition allows for a more dynamic understanding of both the pleasures and conflicts within adult relationships, particularly when they are centered around raising a child.

Based on both survey data and ethnographic fieldwork, the book also makes it clear that parenting is only half the story. The children, of course, are the other. Moreover, these children not only have agency, but constantly put it to work as a way to displace the burden of expectations and steady attention that comes with being an only child in contemporary urban China. These "lone tacticians," as Goh calls them, are not having an easy time and not all are living like spoiled children. The reality is far more challenging for all three generations.

The book will be of interest to those in family studies, education, psychology, sociology, Asian studies, and social work.

Esther C. L. Goh is an assistant professor within the Department of Social Work, National University of Singapore.

Routledge Contemporary China Series

China's One-Child Policy and Multiple Caregiving

Raising little suns in Xiamen

Esther C. L. Goh

Routledge
Taylor & Francis Group

LONDON AND NEW YORK

First published 2011
by Routledge
2 Park Square, Milton Park, Abingdon, Oxon OX14 4RN

Simultaneously published in the USA and Canada
by Routledge
711 Third Avenue, New York, NY10017

Routledge is an imprint of the Taylor & Francis Group, an informa business

British Library Cataloguing in Publication Data
A catalogue record for this book is available from the British Library

Library of Congress Cataloging in Publication Data
Goh, Esther C. L.
    China's one-child policy and multiple caregiving: raising little suns in
    Xiamen / Esther C. L. Goh.
        p. cm. — (Routledge contemporary China series; 71)
    Includes bibliographical references and index.
    1. Family planning—China. 2. Family size—Government policy—China.
    3. Parenting—China. 4. Grandparent and child—China. 5. Parent and
    child—China. I. Title.
    HQ766.5.C6G64 2011
    363.9′60951—dc22   2010049019

ISBN 978–0–415–60250–1 (hbk)
ISBN 978–0–415–85557–0 (pbk)

Typeset in Times New Roman
by Book Now Ltd, London

For Angela Goh Chor Chin

Contents

Illustrations

Figures

Tables

Appendices

Foreword

In 2005 I was intrigued and honored when Esther Goh approached me by email to discuss the potential application of a new theoretical framework to explore the phenomenon of changing family dynamics in contemporary urban China. I had just published a conceptual framework for studying parent–child relationships with the goal of engaging mainstream western researchers in overcoming the conceptual limitations of traditional theories of socialization in the context of the family. Studies linking parent variables, conceptualized as causes, and child variables, conceptualized as effects, remain dominant in basic and applied research on parenting and socialization despite critique about the underlying assumptions from the psychological, sociological, and cultural literature since the 1960s. Very little research was devoted to the dynamic processes of parent–child interaction by which socialization comes about.

I argued that the problem was a conceptual rather than statistical one. A major obstacle to knowledge construction is that scientists are hampered by language, cultural metaphors, and aphorisms that reinforce a taken-for-granted way of perceiving parents as causal antecedents and active agents and children as passive recipients. Constructs such as *intergenerational transmission* of culture and parental values and *compliance* also implicitly define the to-be-understood problem of socialization as a one-way process of influence. The problem of perceiving the child's activity and more complex concepts of bidirectional or systemic causality exists because there are no ready-made conceptual tools to effectively perceive and describe ordinary parent–child interactions in a dynamic way. The bilateral model of parent–child relations (Kuczynski 2003) therefore proposed a series of conceptual reformulations of basic processes to help researchers re-envision socialization processes and family interactions in a more dynamic way than was possible under traditional unidirectional frameworks. The bilateral model consisted of four assumptions: causality between parents and children was inherently bidirectional; parents and children were equally human agents; the long-term interdependent parent–child relationship is a context for understanding parent and child dynamics; and the unequal power between parents and children should be conceived as an interdependent asymmetry, where even children derive power from resources such as the parent–child relationship and the culture in which parent–child relationships are embedded (Kuczynski 2003).

Esther Goh's proposed study seemed to be a daunting "first customer" for the new framework of ideas. The concepts were initially proposed with western families in mind, but her study concerned China. Moreover, Esther described Chinese culture as one undergoing unprecedented rapid change. The bilateral model concerned parent–child dyads, but her study was to include grandparents within a 4-2-1 (grandparents, parents, child) indigenous family form. In addition, there was little beyond stereotypes of Confucian precepts of hierarchical power and filial piety and the contradictory notion of "the little emperor syndrome" in modern China to guide the formulation of hypotheses regarding Chinese family dynamics. Although the idea of the "little emperor" provided an initial fit for the child as agent, it had a traditional negative connotation of the agency and initiative of the child.

It was clear from the first moment of our correspondence that Esther Goh's study would require considerable stretch and redevelopment in the theory itself before the little emperor's new clothes could be perceived and described. Ideas regarding the cultural embededness of family relationships have been much elaborated. The idea of the past history not only of culture but also of unique family relationships is now much more vivid. The idea that the human agency is universal but is manifested in distinctive cultural form now has been empirically described. I am forever grateful to Esther Goh for the opportunity to participate from a distance as she re-envisioned the bilateral model for the purpose of studying family dynamics in a culturally sensitive manner.

The research underlying this book is a remarkable example of an approach to knowledge construction known as the methodology cycle (Branco and Valsiner 1997, Valsiner 2006). Methodology is conceived as the whole process of knowledge construction involving much more than the collection of data or the testing of hypotheses. Rather, the intuitive and experienced researcher makes deliberate choices in theory, world views and methods with the central aim of understanding the phenomena of interest. The process of knowledge generation is a recursive one with new findings feeding back to change the emerging theory. In the present research, Esther Goh selected the phenomenon of rapid change in the structure and dynamics of family life in China brought about by unparalleled social experiments by the successive communist governments. The identification of the phenomena was initially guided by depictions in the popular media of the *4-2-1 phenomenon* as well as the *little emperor syndrome* whereby young children exercise unprecedented influence within an emerging new three-generational family form. A developmental world view was chosen in order to understand contemporary family dynamics as emerging from the macro structural and historical contexts that give rise to the new family dynamics and feeding back into a new emerging cultural context that extends into the future. Bilateral and social relational theories were chosen for the micro level of analysis of family interaction to understand grandparents, parents, and children as active agents who interpret, respond to, and strategize within the context of their culturally embedded close relationships. Specific methods, surveys to provide a broader context for the status of grandparents in Xiamen, and ethnographic field studies of five carefully chosen families were also selected so as to be consistent with both theory on family dynamics and also the current state of knowledge of the phenomena. These choices worked together to provide a fascinating new image of family processes in China and provide a map to guide discoveries in the future.

At the heart of this book is a set of rich descriptions of interactions among three co-resident generations of five rigorously chosen families with an only child (with the exception of the migrant family which has two children) in modern China. Each family is a study of diversity in the manifestation of universal processes of family life including human agency, bidirectional influence and dynamically changing relations of unequal power. Each family has a unique relational history, a unique economic basis, and a unique set of social relationships that form the basis of the influence agency and power of each family member. Despite their differences, together the families stand out as recognizable representatives of Chinese culture engaged in a period of rapid cultural change.

I have no doubt that this study will prove to be an important contribution to cultural theory on the family. Its focus on family dynamics is unique and will pave the way for new research on underlying processes not only of socialization but also the development of the family system. Furthermore, the rich descriptions and analyses of five families in urban Xiamen will suggest new ways of incorporating history and cultural transformation in accounts of family development.

Leon Kuczynski
Professor
Department of Family Relations and Applied Nutrition,
University of Guelph,
Ontario, Canada

Preface

Prior to becoming an academic, I worked for many years as a social worker. The bulk of my practice was at a non-profit organization in Singapore that focused on work with children and families. Parent–child relationships have always intrigued me and much as they shaped my original career choice, this fascination continues to influence the formulation of my intellectual puzzles now that I have moved into academia. Having seen many children of divorce live through the process of their parents' marital breakup, I set out with the intention of inquiring into the impact of parental marital qualities on their children's outcome. The early research design was to adapt existing Western instruments on marital qualities and children's behavioral outcome to Chinese culture so as to understand the causal effects from parents to children in the Chinese context.

A deliberate choice was made to pursue my intellectual puzzle in a cross-cultural site – Xiamen – a coastal city situated in southeastern China. The motivation for taking on a cross-cultural inquiry was two-fold. First, gaining some understanding of parent–child relationships in a culturally different yet predominantly Chinese community would provide me with material to compare and contrast with my own experience in Singapore: getting to know others is a route to understanding self. Second, in Xiamen I would be able to observe families with fresh eyes and avoid the blind spots common to local researchers. During my initial field visit to Xiamen in 2004 I realized that the way I conceptualized my research puzzle was flawed. The three key liaison persons who became my personal friends through previous contacts – a professor in the local university, a clinical psychologist, and a pre-school educator – all challenged my hypothesis-testing endeavor, which they considered too simplistic. In their view, this cause-and-effect model of associating parental attributes with particular outcomes in children could not reflect the actual scenario in Xiamen, where children are not solely raised by parents. Instead, grandparents are also integral partners in parenting who cannot be left out of the research design. This way of raising only-children in contemporary China is commonly known as the 4-2-1 phenomenon, i.e., four grandparents and two parents jointly raise one child. After much soul searching, I abandoned my original idea and decided to embark on a drastically different pursuit. The challenges posed by my key liaisons helped me realize that my chosen instruments and methods left me missing a number of the more interesting phenomena which were taking place in Chinese families.

What went wrong? First was my use of a rather global conception of parenting, which failed to capture some of these essential elements of contemporary Chinese childrearing. This is precisely what Peterson *et al.* (2004) consider an indiscriminate usage of western concepts and measurements in Chinese research. Similarly, Roopnarine and Carter (1992) warn against the danger of non-western scholars importing western intellectual technology and bending their own cultural practices to fit into these frameworks. Second, in the original conceptualization I failed to see the role of grandparents and hence, left them out of the picture. This would have undermined the trustworthiness (or validity) of the entire study. In the socio-cultural context of urban Xiamen, where grandparents are actively involved (together with their adult children) in raising grandchildren, they will prove to be of great interest in what follows. Third, the implicit assumption of unilateral, one-way deterministic influence from parents to children in my original conception was dubious. Only-children in urban China should not be treated as passive recipients of influence from their parents.

To overcome these problems and get a better picture of childrearing in Chinese families I changed my research design and used instead a bidirectional lens of investigation to examine the relationships between children and their multiple caregivers. This means that attention is paid to the understanding of how generations influence each other in the intergenerational family system and considers children, parents, and grandparents simultaneously as agents. Readers will see how interactions within these long-term relationships both enable and restrain the exercise of agency and assertion of power of influence on fellow family members. Moreover, grandparents are now a core component of the project. This not only avoids the imported, Western "parent/parenting" duality but also underscores the indispensable role grandparents play in caring for grandchildren in urban Xiamen. Also, throughout, my focus is on the possible tensions, contradictions, conflicts, and possible solutions (or lack thereof) across the three generations, notably between the two older generations who are collaborating closely in caring for the youngest generation. To achieve these purposes, I took up the challenge by switching to a method that was more flexible in the face of surprises and complexities in the field – ethnography.

Methods

Ethnographic research enables the researcher to learn about people's lives from their own perspective and from within the context of their own lived experience (O'Reilly 2005). This is done through interacting and conversing with the researched but also through participating in, and observing, the everyday life of your research subjects over an extended period of time. In addition to building a rapport with the research participants, time enables a researcher to observe changes as they happen and to gain a first-hand understanding of the processes involved, understanding which helps to answer the "how" research question. This is information that is not typically accessible through surveys or one-time interviews. My hope is that the results of my ethnographic research will provide, even in a modest way, a culturally relevant conceptualization for understanding and researching childrearing in China.

For much of its history, research in parent–child relations has been a theory-testing enterprise. Socialization theories, with roots in psychoanalysis, behaviorism, and structural functionalism were especially important in providing early research questions, variables, and causal hypotheses (Kuczynski and Daly 2003). There is awareness among contemporary researchers of the need for conceptual innovations that could shed light on the parent and child processes which are neglected by theory-testing studies. The ethnographic method, though time consuming and labor intensive, is proving to be useful for achieving this goal.

To complement my ethnographic findings, I also surveyed a non-random sample drawn from 39 primary schools from two zones, namely Huli 湖里 and Siming 思明, within the main Xiamen island. This was done to compensate for the lack of published statistics on the subject of grandparents and parents raising children together. These quantitative statistics provided a broad, though shallow, context for the narrow and deep ethnographic analysis.

Negotiating entry, recruiting participants, and building relationships

An initial field visit and a pilot study were carried out between 2004 and 2005. The main field work was conducted between March and September of 2006. Although one professor strongly urged me to stay with her and her family, I politely declined. After much bargaining, we compromised by making sure that I stayed a stone's throw away from her so that she could "keep an eye" on me. Having this professor as an anchor in a strange community was vital to my field work. Not only could I consult her for daily activities, but I often needed clarification on matters that had direct implications on my research, like culturally appropriate modes of expression, customs, habits and practices of the local people. With her help, my pace of blending into the community was hastened.

Tapping into the networks of the three key liaison persons, I spelled out the criteria for my sample population and requested their help in recruiting potential research participants. The criteria for selecting the five families were in accordance with the various types of grandparental involvement in providing childcare seen in the survey. These variations included: lineage (childcare provided by patrilineal or matrilineal grandparents) and living arrangements (grandparents staying close by or under the same roof, and whether grandparents split up to take care of grandchildren from different adult children). A divorced family was selected because there is a rising divorce rate in urban China (Liu 2006). A migrant family with a pair of siblings cared for by their paternal grandparents, with marginal involvement by the parents, was included as an outlier or deviant sample (Marshall 2006) to contrast with the other samples so as to provide possible disconfirming data during interpretation.

Over the first month there was a gradual process of recruitment. During introductory meetings with the families, I provided a narrative of myself to the potential participants. In the session I made a conscious effort on my part to capitalize on my Chinese ancestry. Although Chinese by ethnicity, I was born and raised in Singapore, a much more westernized society. I described myself as a *huaqiao* 华侨 (overseas Chinese) who had a keen interest in Chinese culture and society. I also noted my ancestral roots in the neighboring province, Shantou 汕头, which was the place from which my father emigrated. This narrative seemed to be welcomed by the participants, as they perceived my purpose was to learn from them. In my self-narrative, I also disclosed to the participants my professional background as a social worker in Singapore. When I explained my research goal to them, most of the participants were in agreement that it was an area that needed attention. The meetings were attended by a key liaison person, myself and the anchor person in the families. In each case, except the migrant family, the anchor person was the adult son/daughter. Once the anchor person agreed to participate in the research, he/she would introduce me to other family members including the grandparents and children. For the migrant family, it was the paternal grandmother who was the anchor person for the family.

To thank the participants for allowing me access into their families, I offered myself as an English tutor, free of charge, to their children/grandchildren. Having received such a valuable gift – access into the families – it made sense that I would offer them something in return (Eder and Corsaro 1999). This strategy of reciprocity was also used by Fong (2004) in her ethnographic work in Dalian, a city in northern China. The ages of the six children in the five families ranged from five to ten years old. I designed different curricula for the children according to their age and language competency levels. I visited each family once a week. During the visits, I would tutor the child and stay back to chat with the adults at home. The families often invited me over for dinner. This was the way the Chinese families expressed their appreciation for my tutoring their child. I did not usually decline those invitations as they were opportunities for observation and participation. I also learned from my key liaison person that it was *keqi* 客气 (polite) to bring fruits or dessert to share with the hosts during these dinners.[1]

My language proficiency was not an issue as Putonghua (which is known as Mandarin in the west and is the *lingua franca* in China) is my mother tongue. Moreover, I am familiar with the Minnan dialect spoken in Xiamen and southern Fujian as my ancestors migrated from Shantou which speaks a variant of Minnan, Caozhou. These two dialects are mutually intelligible. Despite some cultural differences, the language fluency enhanced my ability to participate in the field. However, I found myself occasionally having to clarify certain colloquial points with the key liaison person. Also, more effort had to be put into communicating with the elders as most of them spoke Putonghua with the accent of their dialect tongues. For instance, one grandfather spoke with a heavy Shandong 山东 accent. I had to politely clarify his meaning or ask him to repeat so that I could under-stand him better. Through the six months in the field I also picked up many expressions in Putonghua which were new to me.

All the participants, except the newly divorced single mother, addressed me as "*Wu lao shi*" 吴老师 (teacher Wu). Initially I felt uncomfortable with this term, as "teacher" might put me in a one-up position. However, the key liaison person told me that I should just accept the name because it gave credibility to my role. The single mother saw me as a peer and called me by my Chinese name. Knowing I am a social worker by training, this single mother often confided in me her pain of marital breakdown. Friendships began to develop with most of the participants midway through the field work. One pivotal breakthrough in my relationship with the migrant family was responding to their invitation for lunch in their tiny quarters in the slum. I remember going through hard struggles within myself and reflecting in my field diary my fear of having lunch in the slum. I was concerned with the hygiene standards. Besides, cooking a meal for me might exhaust a large portion of their food budget. But when I overcame my own inner hurdles and went to have lunch with the family, they were visibly happy. From then on, I often ate with them and would take supplies like rice, oil and food items as gifts.

Organization of this book

The book starts with an overview of the socio-political and cultural factors which brought about significant transitions in the Chinese families and how children are raised. This is followed by a discussion of the need to closely examine the one-child-many-caregivers phenomenon of grandparents and parents raising only-children as joint projects in three-generational families. Chapter 2 discusses the importance of reconceptualizing the way child-rearing is being studied in China and presents the case for shifting from the unidirectional model to bidirectional perspective in understanding parent (grandparent)–child relationships. Chapter 3 moves from the macro forces to mezzo level discussion of the city where the study was conducted, drawing on the results of a survey conducted in 39 primary schools. The results of the survey both contextualize the work and provide concrete evidence of the prevalence of multi-generational parenting in Xiamen. In doing so, it provides a useful background for the ethnographic stories that follow. Chapter 4 presents the micro-dynamics between the grandparents and parents in caring for grandchildren within the five participating families. Chapters 5 and 6 describe the children's point of view in being surrounded by multiple adults on a daily basis. Both the power and plight of these "little suns" are presented. The concluding chapter proposes a shift in the conceptual framework in researching childrearing in China. Based on the empirical findings from this study, it offers an indigenous theoretical framework for future research.

Endorsement

The topic of this work is a most timely one. China has adopted a "one child per couple" policy since the late 1970s and childrearing is thus an entirely different matter in modern-day China. As a consequence, not only are most families in urban China having only one child, boy or girl, but the task of childrearing is being shared between two generations, that is, the child's parents and grandparents. Although grandparents in China have always shared in the care of their grandchildren, this has never been studied, so far as I know, by examining how the different parties play their roles, and the dynamics involved in the process. This book is trying to answer these questions.

In doing so, the author is breaking new ground. She has employed an ethnographic method for understanding the dynamic process among children and their caregivers. The approach implies a direct involvement of the researcher herself in understanding the process and what roles the different parties, including the children themselves, play and how they interact with one another. Although only five families have been included in the ethnographic portion of the study, it means six months of hard work by the researcher in order to get acquainted and accepted by the five families. Only this type of approach could yield the information that gives us a true picture of childrearing in urban China. Complementing this, she has also developed a very rich set of survey data, with responses from over a thousand parents.

Dr Goh offers us new insights into Social Relations Theory as well as a considerable amount of original data. This is not an easy task, as it takes into account that every party involved in childrearing could be an agent and they are influencing each other in a dynamic way. Her theory could prove extremely useful in the development of social work practices that take every party as an agent and the process to be one that is cybernetic rather than linear. This approach provides us with a lot of information on the interactions between generations, not only between children and their parents, but also that between children and their grandparents, as well as between their parents and their grandparents. After all, childrearing is now an extremely complex task shared among generations.

Before closing, I want to note that the manuscript is written so beautifully that I was touched by some of the verbatim reports. I am sure that Dr Goh enjoyed the research for this project, though rather difficult at times. The final results show that she has clearly benefited from the experience of conducting it, as the reader will from reading this book.

Nelson Chow
Chair Professor
Department of Social Work and Social Administration
The University of Hong Kong

Acknowledgments

To the most important person in my life (you know who you are), you have given me energy, passion and meaning to persevere in this project. Without your support this book would not be possible.

My heartfelt appreciation goes to Professor Leon Kuczynski of the University of Guelph, Ontario, for his intellectual advice, generosity, and constant encouragement. Words alone cannot express my deep gratitude. I wish to express my sincere thanks to my three key liaison persons in Xiamen. To maintain confidentiality, their names will not be mentioned. Many thanks for your warm friendships and invaluable help throughout the duration of my field work there. I am deeply indebted to each of you.

Special thanks go to Edyth Banks and Peter Wissoker for reading and re-reading many versions of the draft manuscripts. Without your help, it would be difficult for me to discover my own blind spots as a writer. Lisa Khoo, your eyes are as sharp as laser beams detecting even small misalignments in the references, figures and layout. You have spared me time and energy by attending to these important details so that I can devote myself to writing the text. Thank you.

To the reference librarians of the University of Hong Kong, thank you for your help in the library research phase of my work. I have also to mention the three excellent reference librarians of the National University of Singapore Library, Hayati Bte Abdul, Herman Felani M. Y., and Aaron Tay. I cannot thank each of you enough for all the assistance in references, endnotes and all kinds of "problems" I encountered in the process of manuscript preparation. Thank you so much for the countless times you performed onsite "rescue missions" in my office. Hayati, thanks for answering my emails even in the middle of the night. My life as a researcher would be miserable without able and kind librarians like you.

The five families who participated in my study, they are now friends. Your generous acceptance has provided me a close-up glimpse into family dynamics. Your trust and friendships are so precious to me. Thank you.

Figure 7.1, "Contemporary Chinese intergenerational family relationship system," in Chapter 7 was first published online in the *Asian Journal of*

Social Psychology. Part of Chapter 5 first appeared in *Culture and Psychology*, Volume 15, Issue 4. These two articles were co-authored with Leon Kuczynski. Part of the analysis of conflicts and dialectics between parents and grandparents in Chapters 3 and 4 was presented in the Fourth International Consortium for Intergenerational Programmes in Singapore between 26 and 29 April 2010.

Esther C. L. Goh
National University of Singapore

1   Introduction

Only-children in China are often affectionately referred to as "little suns" by their parents and grandparents. From the term "little sun" it is not hard for the reader to imagine the central position these only-children occupy in the hearts and minds of their caregivers. Just as planets in the solar system orbit around the sun, grandparents and parents revolve their lives around caring for the little sun. Although in the popular imagination each only-child is a "spoilt little emperor," the story of one such child, Tian Tian, reveals that the experience of growing up as a little sun is more complex than what we think.

Tian Tian, a 10-year-old girl, lives with her parents and maternal grandparents in a four-bedroom apartment located in the prime area of Xiamen Island. The apartment is tastefully renovated with a contemporary Zen style. A 50-inch flat-screen television set sits in the living room with matching furniture and parquet flooring. It is obvious that the family is financially comfortable. One room is used as a study, the grandparents occupy a room, and the master bedroom is occupied by her parents. As an only-child, Tian Tian has her own room. It is equipped with an air-conditioner, a computer, an electronic piano, a cassette player, and lots of books. When examined closely, the calendar on the wall turns out to be made from studio portraits of a "post-makeover" Tian Tian printed onto an oversized calendar.

Tian Tian says she loves having her grandparents stay with her family because she feels less lonely when they are around. Her maternal grandparents, a dignified looking older couple in their seventies, shuttle between their home in Nan Ping 南平 and Xiamen to help care for their grandchild. Usually the older couple will spend one-third of the year in Nan Ping and two-thirds in Xiamen. Tian Tian claims that her parents often fight. When her grandparents are around, she can run to them for refuge or hope that they will intervene in the fight. When her grandparents are back in their home town, Tian Tian has to face these conflicts on her own and often she feels frightened, lonely, and anxious. She also feels powerless to stop the heated quarrels. Sometimes she gets caught between her parents when they fight and becomes the innocent victim. Her grandparents also buffer the harsh punishments Tian Tian sometimes gets from her father.

Of course, it doesn't hurt that Tian Tian's grandparents are good cooks. According to Tian Tian, every meal is delicious when her grandparents are in Xiamen. She describes her parents as amateur cooks and she dreads eating the meals they prepare. Her grandparents take care of the household chores, including repairs, and do the grocery shopping. Her mother plays a supplementary role in doing the chores on weekdays but does more on weekends and her days off. On the other hand, her father does no work around the house. Although Tian Tian occasionally helps run errands to the grocery stalls down the street for her grandparents, basically she thinks her main job at home is to study, read books, sleep, watch television, and play the piano.

Being an only-child, surrounded by four adults on a daily basis, is not always a bed of roses. No doubt Tian Tian feels treated like the precious one, but she also recounts that she is often the first to be blamed for things. She will be the first one to enjoy the best food on the dinner table or receive a gift. However, parents and grandparents often turn on her when things go wrong because she is the only child around. Tian Tian feels this is very unfair and says that she is often the *shou qi bao* 受气包 (a person upon whom anyone can vent his spite). Her dilemma is that she simultaneously wishes to grow up quickly as well as wanting to always remain a child. According to Tian Tian, growing up quickly will allow her to be independent from the adults around her. But she confesses that she also enjoys the love and attention she receives as the only child in the home.

Tian Tian's story is not an isolated case. In many families, grandparents from either or both paternal and maternal lineage (ranges from one to four grandparents) and two parents are actively involved in the joint project of raising the one child. As noted in the Preface, this is commonly known as the 4-2-1 phenomenon. That is, four grandparents and two parents caring for one child. In reality there may not always be four grandparents caring for one grandchild, sometimes there are only two or even just one. However, the term "4-2-1" used in this book refers to the phenomenon of a single child with multiple caregivers. Many of the children being raised in these families have similar stories. I heard them in Xiamen, and it is likely that things are similar in many urban cities in China.[1] To have a deeper appreciation of the experience of little suns growing up in contemporary China, we need to first understand the drastic transition from the traditional family form that Chinese families are undergoing and how these transitions have influenced the way children are raised today in China.

Chinese families in transition

Childrearing values and practices are the most conservative aspect of a culture and generally persist over time unless a society undergoes critical changes (LeVine 1982). The one-child policy put in place by the Chinese government in 1979 can be considered one of the most drastic forms of collectivization of childbearing (White 2006) – it has turned out to be the longest campaign ever implemented in China. Together with other socio-political and economic policies introduced in Deng's era, this policy has resulted in a generation of only-children in China being raised in a time of rapid and dramatic social and cultural change. This has altered both the structure and dynamics of family life in a manner not attempted anywhere else in the world.

Historical background

Prior to 1949, the "traditional" Chinese family was an ideal type with deep foundations in the classical injunctions of Confucius and Mencius. Families were patrilineal, patrilocal and patriarchal and were governed by rigid norms regarding appropriate hierarchical interactions between the generations (Levy 1949). Traditional Chinese parents followed a unidirectional, father-to-son, model of transmission of socialization, guided by Confucian teachings. Generations of scholars prescribed exemplary ways to raise children and manage households, known as *jia xun* 家训 (family precepts). The exacting rules governing parent–child relationships included mutual obligation, appropriate modes of communication, social interaction, and etiquette (Kim 2006). A rigid, hierarchical power structure within the family was reinforced by these teachings. Fathers, in particular, had total control over sons and were enjoined to maintain an awe-inspiring and psychologically distant relationship with them (Ho 1996b, Tu 1985, Wang 2004). The concept of *xiao* 孝 (filial piety) served as a guiding principle and governed Chinese patterns of socialization (Ho 1987). Parents had the obligation to instruct children, and children to be unconditionally respectful and obedient, provide for aged parents and conduct themselves so as to bring honor and avoid disgrace to the family name. This framework of ideals came under attack after the Chinese Communist Party (CCP) took power in 1949 and traditional Confucian values were derided as hindrances to the communist ethos.

The landscape of Chinese families changed dramatically after the CCP's ascension. The Party introduced a number of social engineering efforts to alter the family, and these took two forms: direct and indirect. The enactment of new family laws and regulations (such as the 1950 Marriage Law and later revisions) aimed to reduce the power of the traditional patriarchal families, promote gender equality, discourage arranged marriages, encourage simpler weddings and funerals, and so on. Indirect family change came about as state social engineering produced alterations in other institutions and thus indirectly fostered changes in family patterns and attitudes. The socialist transformation launched in 1955 indirectly affected Chinese families in profound ways, particularly by depriving them of meaningful property and family businesses and by making all citizens more completely dependent upon the bureaucratic structures of state socialism (Whyte

2005). This abolition by the state of the family as an economic unit shifted parental power within families. After the liberalization of the economy began in the 1980s, the family underwent another change, into a unit of consumption. Yan's (1997) long-term ethnographic work in China led him to conclude that the decline in the family as an economic unit brought about a democratization process within the Chinese family in which power and authority shifted from senior to junior generations. According to his observation, the leadership role of *dangjia* 当家 (family manager) now rests with the younger generation. We will see later the implications of this power shift for the collaboration between parents and grandparents as they jointly raise the grandchildren.

Two policy initiatives that directly affected Chinese households were the attempts to broaden the participation of women in the labor force and the instituting of a one-child policy. In traditional Chinese society (that is to say, prior to the revolution), women's "proper" place remained within the "inner" realm of the family and household, while the proper place for men was linked to the "outer" world of labor and public affairs (Hershatter 2007). The policy of liberating women from housework to participate in the labor force began in the early years of the People's Republic of China. Women's labor was regarded as an integral part of the state development strategy. Campaigns to publicize working women in the 1950s emphasized women's enthusiasm for labor, their farming skills, and their strong bodies. During the Mao years (1949-76) paid employment became a standard feature of urban women's lives (Wang 2003 cited in Hershatter 2007). The CCP downplayed gender distinctions. Hence, men and women maintained rough wage equity for the same kind of work (ibid.). Today, Chinese women's participation in the labor force is among the highest in the world (United Nations 2000). The unique situation in China is one of limited flexibility in work arrangements, especially in waged jobs. Recent surveys conducted in eight provinces in China (Short *et al.* 2002) found that women attach a high priority to their work, even after childbirth. One of the reasons that mothers in China are able to maintain outside work despite the inflexible and long working hours, shortage of childcare facilities, and a general mistrust towards domestic helpers (Goh 2006), lies in the availability of grandparents to serve as alternative childcare. This results in grandparents from either or both sides of the lineage, together with a pair of parents, forming a coalition of caregivers to the precious single child in urban China.

The one-child policy was first implemented in 1979 and it has dramatically altered urban family life and the way children are raised. The fertility rate dropped from 6 births per woman before 1970 to below the replacement rate of 1.8 in 2003 (UNICEF 2005), and 1.55 today (Greenhalgh 2008). China introduced stringent and coercive family planning programs to curb population growth, and as a result fewer children are born to each family. Although in recent years minor readjustments have been made by some local governments to the one-child policy, according to family planning officials, a proposed abolishment of the one-child policy is not likely to be effected anytime soon (Yan 2006). On the other hand, it seems the Chinese people have internalized this policy and accepted the norm of having only one child. Findings by Nie and Wyman (2005) show that the younger generations in Shanghai deem having one child as the ideal. They believe parents who have only one child are able to spend more to cultivate that child. Hence, even with the possible relaxation of the one-child policy, many urban couples may still choose to have one child.

Parents of only-children are found to have a greater tendency than other parents to underscore the importance of having children and ranked having children as the most meaningful aspect of life. They consider having a child a major life aspiration or fulfillment and many saw children as embodying the only hope in life (Chow and Chen 1994). This child-centered orientation calls for family members, including grandparents, to channel and pool resources so as to ensure that only-children receive the best possible care.

The shrinking number of children in each family has also brought about a shift in the way children are valued in China. Recent empirical research across many countries (Trommsdorff 2009) has shown that the economic value of children drops and the emotional value increases as a society becomes more affluent. China is experiencing a similar shift. Thus, the traditional ideal of *yang er fang lao* 养儿防老 (children as old age insurance) with its economic value focus, for instance, has become *yang er pei lao* 养儿陪老 (children as companions for old age) an emotional and psychological value (Ye 1996, Zheng *et al.* 2005).

Other new values were emerging as well with the advent of a generation of parents of only-children. Parents no longer supported the idea that children should obey and not talk back when being disciplined (Ho 1996a). Researchers are also seeing mothers being less strict and more affectionate to their offspring, as noted in some recent research that compares parenting in mainland China with that in Chinese societies such as Hong Kong or Taiwan. Lai and Zhang (2000) found that Beijing mothers controlled their children less and expressed affection towards their children more frequently than the Hong Kong mothers. They are also more expressive in emphasizing their children's achievement, compared with their Hong Kong counterparts.

Dependency of the middle generation and the prevalence of three generational family types

The parental desire to provide the best for the only-child means the cost of raising this child can only be sustained by both parents working full-time and working hard. Work in contemporary urban China has changed from how it used to be in the era of secured life-long employment with state-run enterprises. The declining role of state enterprises has led to structural unemployment and fierce competition in the job market within the private sector. Individuals now fend for themselves against unemployment, accidents, disabilities, old-age maintenance and other risks (Shen et al. 1999). These macro market-oriented economic reforms have significantly changed the ways households arrange their livelihood strategies (Zhu et al. 2010). Family is now the most important safety net for providing mutual help and support among family members. This help takes many forms, but two important ones are the provision of childcare and financial support. The need for these has strengthened intergenerational family bonds in a way that is magnifying the role of grandparents in contemporary Chinese families.

Limited day care for preschool children (Chen 1985), expensive private baby sitters, and mistrust towards domestic helpers all make grandparent care a cheap and trustworthy alternative. These types of reasons are used as culturally acceptable justifications for the middle generation to expect childcare help from the senior generation. According to the venerated Chinese sociologist Fei (1992), unlike their Western counterparts, Chinese adults continue membership in their parental family even after they have formed their own nuclear family units. This continued membership functions at the structural, organizational, and interpersonal level (Chen and Sun 2006). At the structural level it solves problems posed by external constraints, for instance, the shortage of urban housing and lack of affordable childcare facilities (Whyte and Parish 1984). At the organizational level, the family household is viewed as a "corporate group" for both generations. It becomes a common enterprise in that each member has a vested interest in maintaining its existence (Chen 2006, p. 235). At the interpersonal level, the seniors' unreserved devotion to the children encourages their adult children's sense of continued family membership. Pan (2002) describes this dependent tendency of the middle generation as *ji bu wan nai de niu zhang bu da gao yang* 挤不完奶的牛, 长不大的羔羊 ([treating the senior generation as] cows with inexhaustible milk and [seeing themselves as] lambs that never grow up). Since it takes two hands to clap, one should note that this dependency is reinforced by the senior generation. Chinese parents uphold the ideology that they have to persistently render help and support to their children until they can give no more (Goh 2009, Li 2003). Not only do the middle generation look to their parents as default child caregivers for their "precious only-children," but, as in Tian Tian's family, they are expected to do household chores, grocery shopping, and meal preparation as well (Pan and Lin 2006).[2]

Reconceptualization of childrearing in China

It is a good time to reconceptualize childrearing research in China as the rapid changes in the macro environment discussed earlier are reshaping the dynamics of childrearing within individual households. Given the scope of changes taking place in Chinese families, I offer three ways to reframe parenting research in urban China that may yield insights which are closer to the lived experience at the empirical level: First, a dynamic view of parenting where adult caregivers *and* children are considered as active agents and seen as bidirectionally influencing each other. Second, grandparents should be treated as an integral part of the parenting team in raising children. Finally, the popular image of only-children as spoilt emperors needs to be given a second look.

The need for a dynamic caregiver–child perspective

Traditionally, both sociology and developmental psychology have used a unidirectional perspective in research relating to both parent–child relations and socialization (Kuczynski *et al.* 1999). Parent variables typically are conceptualized as antecedents and child variables are conceptualized as outcome, with little consideration to the processes in between (Kuczynski *et al.* 1999). By subscribing to a unidirectional perspective (parent to child), both disciplines treat children as passive recipients of socialization.

Since the middle of the twentieth century, there has been a proliferation of theories, methodology, and empirical research based on more dynamic ways of conceptualizing children. For parenting research in developmental psychology, a new era was marked by the seminal work of Bell (1968), who reinterpreted the direction of effect from children to parents, and the landmark chapter by Maccoby and Martin (1983) which outlined an interactional and process-oriented perspective which they argued ought to be adopted by the research community. That latter chapter seemed to signal the beginning of a new era in which it was acceptable to see parent–child relations as ambiguous and nondeterministic as well as truly interactive (Kuczynski 2003, p. x). Likewise, in sociology, scholars are advocating the need to recognize children as social agents who have a part in shaping their own childhood experience (this will be further discussed in the next chapter).

Over the past three decades, researchers in the West have accepted the more dynamic process for studying parent–child as an inevitable trend. That said, a close read of the literature reveals that the unidirectional way of conceptualizing research remains influential (Holden 1997, Kuczynski 2003, Holden and Edwards 1989).[3] And, in China, the research on parenting by and large remains within the unidirectional paradigm (refer to Appendix E). Here, I will use a bidirectional conceptualization of parent–child dynamics grounded in social relational theory (Kuczynski 2003, Kuczynski and Parkin 2006). This perspective is one that is similar to the better-known theory of social construction, and will be used to guide my understanding of only-children raised in the 4-2-1 context. This bidirectional perspective takes a strong position on the agency of the three generations involved: namely, grandparents, parents, and children. Agency refers to adults and children as actors who bring interpretations, intentions, plans, and strategies into their interactions with each other (Kuczynski 2003). For example, rather than viewing Tian Tian as passively receiving information from her parents, the bidirectional perspective enables me to be sensitive in picking up how she actively selects and interprets her interactions with adult care-givers. The idea of bidirectionality also assumes an interdependent though asymmetric power of influence in the relationship between parents and children. This model facilitates the discovery of dialectical interactions between children, parents, and grandparents within the context of their long-term relationship. This enduring relationship both enables and restrains them in exercising agency and asserting the power of their influence on each other. I will discuss this dynamic bidirectional model in greater details in Chapter 2.

A call for considering grandparents as integral partners in raising children

Mainstream childrearing studies both in the West and in China have focused their research lens on the dynamics between parents and children. Over the past two decades there has been a proliferation of research on grandparenting in the West. That research focused largely on grandparents who have custodial care of their grandchildren owing to drug abuse, marital break-down or incarceration of the adult child (Hayslip *et al.* 1998, Goodman and Silverstein 2006). These studies examine the demands and responsibilities placed on grandparents who had to parent their grandchildren (Smith and Drew 2002). Unlike their counterparts in the West, it is commonplace for grandparents to provide childcare on a full-time basis in urban China even when their adult children's families are intact (Goh 2009). Most provide regular childcare while their adult children take on full-time jobs outside home. Existing parenting studies in China focus mainly on parent–child relationships; the indigenous research on childrearing practice is lagging behind the reality. Only a few studies have taken grandparents' role into consideration.[4] To this point, then, grandparents have not been thoroughly studied as integral partners in raising children, although in practice they are active childcare givers in Asian societies.

In this book I will offer a novel approach with which we can organize our understanding of grandparents and parents as joint partners in raising children within the 4-2-1 family. The ideas are grounded in my numerous family visits and prolonged immersion in the field, as well as analyses of both the in-depth ethnographic data and the survey data. In watching the many tensions, contradictions, conflicts and possible resolutions or lack of resolutions between the two older generations collaborating closely in caring for the youngest generation I have observed that they form what I term *kua dai yu er zu he* 跨代育儿组合 (intergenerational parenting coalitions – IGPC). It is my assertion that, as a sizable portion of Chinese children (this will be demonstrated in Chapter 3) are raised jointly by parents and grandparents (refer to Note 1), analysis of the dynamics of the IGPC which is embedded in the overarching intergenerational family system, is crucial to under-standing childrearing in urban China.

Despite the Chinese culture's tendency to uphold the notion of *yi he wei gui* 以和为贵 (harmony is supreme), my ethnographic data and survey results show that challenges, contradictions, and conflicts between grandparents and parents within the IGPC are commonplace. Two sources of tension within the IGPC were identified: differences in childrearing philosophies and methods; and difficulties in coordinating disciplinary measures among adult caregivers. Examining the dialectical interactions within the coalition is especially relevant in contemporary China as the traditional norms governing intergenerational relationships are in transition. The once clear and accepted way of the Confucian teaching, *wu lun* 五伦 (five cardinal relations), which stipulated the hierarchical form of relationships in traditional Chinese families, has largely been abolished by the CCP's effort to reform the "old China." For instance, according to tradition older persons occupied powerful positions in the family. However, the ethnographic data show the weakened position of the grandparents today, as is made clear by their unwillingness to execute discipline for fear of displeasing their adult children or their grandchildren. The grandparents are the ones spending the most time with children because both middle-generation parents are busy working. But when there are disciplinary issues they tend to resort to giving in to grandchildren or lodging complaints to their adult children with the hope that the latter will discipline the children instead. There are unintended consequences in these actions which invariably fuel tensions and conflicts within the IGPC as well as between the IGPC and the children. The complex and intricate dynamics of the IGPC will be elaborated in Chapter 4. It illustrates the point that parent/grandparent–child interactions are far from linear in nature. This book hopes to provide initial sketches of the dynamics within IGPC, of which there is very little written in the scholarly literature.

Rethinking the popular notion of "spoilt little emperors"

The third key concept is one that takes issue with the dominant view of children in urban China as "little emperors," who are spoiled and self-centered. It is undeniable that this label reflects the phenomenon of only-children who inevitably receive the best resources from their families. This stereotype does, however, project a deterministic view of children as passively molded by their indulgent caregivers into "little emperors." But the stereotype needs to be re-examined and understood from a fresh perspective. Children should be seen as agents with ability to interpret and influence the behaviors of people around them, using intentional actions to achieve their goals. The ethnographic data shows how they relate individually to each member of the coalition and assert different levels of agency. The extent to which children's behavior influences their caregivers' behavior and thereby affects subsequent circles of interaction depends on the sociocultural conditions. In Chapter 5 I offer a sketch of the bidirectional influence between adult caregivers and children in Xiamen embedded in the intergenerational family system.

Using the bidirectional perspective to view the family one can quickly see that those who use the label "little emperor" are misinformed in their depiction of the only-child as the sole seat of power in the three-generational family. The popular notion colors our perceptions of these urban only-children and causes people to overlook another equally important but little explored dimension of the phenomenon. Being an emperor also entails huge responsibility, given the parents' sacrifices and hopes. Fong (2004) has pointed out the enormous amount of pressure adolescent only-children in Dalian city face to excel academically, academic success being the key to upward social mobility not only for the children but for the whole family. As we shall see, though, there are many pressures on "only-children" in their day-to-day interactions with their multiple caregivers, ranging from daily monitoring by their caregivers, which can be rather suffocating, to being sacrificed as victims to bring about or maintain peace within the intergenerational parenting coalition.

Rather than being "spoilt little emperors" I will argue that most only-children are more realistically described as a "lone tactician" in their intergenerational family system. The choice of the term "tactician" encapsulates how the intergenerational family relationships system enables (and provides leeway for) the child's expression of agency and power, and how this family system offers many relational resources that ensure the child is rich in possibilities for accomplishing many things. On the other hand, the word "lone" reflects the notion of how only-children born into the situation of a multigenerational one-child system – through no choice of their own – are constrained by the system. As only-children, they have to handle not only the multiple caregivers individually but also the intergenerational parenting coalition as a whole. It is in this light that I will present the two dimensions of the dynamic bidirectionality between the lone tacticians and their intergenerational parenting coalitions: the "power" and "plight" of the lone tacticians like Tian Tian, will be discussed. Let us turn first to a detailed discussion on the necessity for a dynamic, bidirectional perspective in examining childrearing in contemporary urban China.

2 Contemporary Chinese childrearing

A new lens

We don't see things as they are, we see them as we are.

(Anais Nin)

Introduction

A review of the extant literature on childrearing in China shows that parents' traits were constantly being conceptualized as antecedent variables, with the characteristics of their children serving as outcome variables. This static view of both parents and children was governed by theories that assumed a unidirectional influence from parent to children that was fundamental to the conceptualization of their research. When studies are framed in this light, they limit their ability to shed light on the childrearing processes. Most notably, grandparents were not part of the conceptualization. In addition, the extant research's tendency to treat children's outcomes as dependent variables do not take into account children as agentic beings in dynamics relationships with their multiple caregivers. Diverging from mainstream parenting research in China, this book reports findings where parents, grandparents, and children are all agents that exercise power of influence over each other despite an apparent asymmetrical power distribution among them. The members of these three-generational families are all interdependent in many ways. These dynamics are not documented by previous studies.

It is my belief that conceptual limitations have constrained the way Chinese researchers looked at parent–child relationships. In this chapter, I urge researchers to examine the 4-2-1 phenomenon with the dynamic, bidirectional lens instead of the deterministic, unidirectional perspective. I will first trace the evolution of the unidirectional model and the reasons some researchers in the West have moved away from this perspective. This will be followed by a discussion of the persistent popularity of this approach among Chinese researchers. An argument will then be made for the shift in this study to a conceptual underpinning of parent (grandparent)–child dynamics and a bidirectional frame and how this can be fruitful in capturing findings closer to the ground with the implication that it is likely to then yield new discoveries.

The unidirectional model

Why hasn't the research community, particularly the research community in China, paid more attention to the rich, dynamic relationships between grandparents, parents, and grandchildren in China? I attribute it to the overuse of the unidirectional model of socialization. Much of the research on family life in China was undertaken using models that offered only a limited view of what transpired in the family. This was a result of both the choice of methods and theoretical approaches. For instance, survey methods based on self-reported assessment by parents are popular as they have many advantages, including being time efficient in the data collection process. However, such methods have constrained the discovery of new insights.

Reliance on a unidirectional model for conceptualizing parent–child relationships, especially in psychology and the early work in sociology and anthropology, led Western researchers to assume that parents possess pre-existing traits, attitudes, goals, and childrearing behaviors which were transmitted to them from their own parents and through their culture. The parents, in turn, were expected to transmit these qualities to their children and thus determine (to some extent) how the children turned out (Kuczynski 2001, Bell 1979). For instance, the learning theories, which dominated the research scene from the 1950s to 1970s, emphasized the role of parents as teachers and disciplinarians in shaping their children's development and as role models for children to copy; psychodynamic theory held that children were socialized by internalizing their parents' values and characteristics. Likewise, attachment theory argued that the level of nurturance and responsiveness provided by parents to their infants and toddlers determined the quality of attachment the child formed to the parents, which in turn would carry over into the child's subsequent relationships through lasting internalized representations (Maccoby 2002).[1]

Despite explicating different aspects of the effects of parenting, these theories share a common set of underlying assumptions. The first, as has already been noted, is that causality is unidirectional – from the parents to the children. Parents' traits were considered independent variables and the outcome on children the dependent variables, and research questions in these paradigms often involved identifying the products of parenting that are associated with particular outcomes in the children. The second assumption concerns the unit of analysis for studying parent–child relations. Parents and children are implicitly conceptualized as discrete individuals engaged in a social interaction rather than as persons who are involved in a long-term interdependent relationship (Lollis and Kuczynski 1997). Treating parents and children as individuals prevents formulation of intervention designs that take the long-term relationship into account. A third assumption found in this literature pertains to the nature of agency in parent–child relations. When children are deemed passive recipients of parental inputs (as noted in the first assumption), parents are then conceptualized as agents of socialization who have goals and strategies and exhibit different parenting styles, while children are denied agency. In this model, studies of children's compliance to parents' commands will tend to consider submission to be a form of competence, whereas non-compliance is a form of deviance or failure, rather than an expression of the agency of the children (Kuczynski and Kochanska 1990). That agency is simply not considered. In the same vein, parents are also treated as passive with regard to their own socialization and cultural acquisitions under this unidirectional model. The fourth assumption in this model views power relations between parent and child as asymmetrical and vertical. Parents are assumed to have more power to fuel the relationship. This conceptualization of asymmetrical power offers a static, unidimensional and mechanistic view of parent–child relationships (Kuczynski 2001, Bugental *et al.* 1997, Eisenberg 1992, Russell *et al.* 1998). In doing so, it neglects the different discourses of power balancing that change over developmental stages and as well as the sociopolitical and cultural contexts of parent–child relationships.

Represented by Talcott Parsons (1902-1979), early functional sociologists were basically unidirectional in their conceptualization of children. In his major work on the family, Parsons (Parsons and Bales 1955) posited two main important functions of family namely: socialization of children so that they can truly become members of the society and stabilization of adult personalities. The child acquires competence at social interaction within the family. In this view children are passive in regard to being socialized. Recent sociologists pursuing new childhood studies (Corsaro 2005, Mayall 1994, 2001, Alanen 2001, Punch 2001, James 2001, Ahn 2010, James and Prout 1997, Wyness 2006) have conceptualize parent and children and their relationships in creative ways beyond the unidirectional model. These sociologists have begun to pursue multifaceted understanding of children as social participants (Edwards 2002, Alanen and Berry 2001, Hutchby and Moran-Ellis 2001, Pole *et al.* 2001, Christensen and O'Brian 2003, Jensen and Mckee 2003, Hallet and Prout 2003).

Classical anthropological studies on childhood (Mead 1961, 1962, Malinowski 1927, 1929, Benedict 1989, Whiting 1963, Whiting and Whiting 1975) described how cultures (largely in non-Western societies) are transmitted from generation to generation.[2] They therefore saw a process of unidirectional influence where culture is communicated to individuals through families. According to LeVine (2007), since the 1990s, linguistic anthropologists inspired by the sociolinguistics movement have begun to study the child's acquisition of communicative and development of the self. Instead of viewing the child as merely passive recipient of cultural transmission, they studied the co-construction of cultural narratives between mother and children that contribute to the child's sense of shame, self-esteem and other culturally organized aspects of self (Miller *et al.* 1996, 2001, Fung 1999). Some developmental psychologists in the West have also moved away from the unidirectional model to examine the interactions between parenting styles and possible genetic attributes of children (Kochanska 1997 cited in Maccoby 2002, Bates *et al.* 1998). However, the unidirectional model remains largely popular with contemporary researchers in China.

Extant Chinese parenting studies

Although developmental psychology began in China since the early 1900s, it has gone through a complex series of starts and stops in the past 90 years (Lin and Chen 2009, Tardif and Miao 2000). Systematic academic inquiry into childrearing in China, however, is a relatively new scholarly endeavor (Quoss and Wen 1995). A recent search for research articles captured by the China National Knowledge Infrastructure (CNKI) database using keywords including *qin zi guanxi* 亲子关系 (parent–child relationship), *er tong fa zhan* 儿童发展 (child development), *jiating guanxi* 家庭关系 (family relationships), and *fumu yu hai zi* 父母与孩子 (parent and child/children) found 22 empirical papers (excluding literature reviews and parenting articles in popular magazines).[3] Although the collection of journal papers in the CNKI database started in 1995, only one article was published in 1997. The other papers were all published after the year 2000. Appendix E presents a summary of these research methods and measurements employed. Findings from this database search demonstrate the influence of the unidirectional model in empirical studies on childrearing in China. Much like the older Western studies, which were governed by theories that assume unidirectional influence, these studies set out to test the associations between particular parental traits (as antecedents) and outcome factors on children. The antecedent factors include parental styles (Zeng *et al.* 1997, Wang *et al.* 2006, Liang *et al.* 2007, Yin *et al.* 2009, Qin Liu *et al.* 2009, Du and Su 2009, Guo *et al.* 2008, Yang and Hou 2009), attitudes (Li *et al.* 2006), practices (Chen *et al.* 2003a, Chen *et al.* 2003b, Niu *et al.* 2004), parents' educational attainment (Zhou and Yang 2009), influences of parents' undesirable habits (Chen and Zhang 2010), and family environment (Shen and Chen 2009, Ye *et al.* 2006). Child outcomes tested in these studies were school adjustment (Liang *et al.* 2007, Zeng *et al.* 1997), academic performance (Yin *et al.* 2009), psychological health (Baiqiao Liu *et al.* 2009, Yang and Hou 2009, Zhou and Yang 2009, Chen and Zhang 2010), and pro-social behavior (Niu *et al.* 2004). The Chinese researchers, however, were not entirely monolithic in their approach to the subject. Thus, a few studies by Chen and his associates (Lu *et al.* 2002, Chen *et al.* 2003a, Chen *et al.* 2003b, Hou *et al.* 2003, Shaung *et al.* 2004) hint at the need to consider children's influence on parents (Chen *et al.* 2003b) and bidirectional influence between parent and children. They also made tentative mention of culturally specific findings in comparing these findings to their Western counterparts (Shaung *et al.* 2004, Hou *et al.* 2003). Undoubtedly, the extant childrearing research findings in China illuminate some aspects of children's outcomes, based on various parental inputs. But there are clearly limitations to this dominant tendency subscribing to the unidirectional approach.

The use of Western-developed instruments by Chinese researchers

Some attempts have been made by Chinese researchers to validate Western-developed scales for use in understanding the Chinese population.[4] Overall, however, the tendency for researchers to borrow Western instruments is cause for concern, and we can see this reflected in the work of Peterson *et al.* (2004), among others, who criticized the indiscriminate usage of Western concepts and measurements in Chinese research. The problem is that Western measurements tend to be based on rather global conceptions of parenting which fail to capture essential elements of Chinese childrearing. The authoritarian style, for example, is composed of several parental behaviors, expectations, and emotional qualities which do not appear to be exactly the same in China and in the West. For instance, Chao (1994) asserted that Chinese parenting has often been described as "controlling" or "authoritarian." These styles of parenting have been found to be predictive of poor school achievement among European-American parents, and yet the Chinese are performing quite well in school. She believed the concepts of authoritative and authoritarian are somewhat ethnocentric and do not capture the important features of Chinese childrearing.

The tendency to apply Western definitions to Chinese families was confirmed in a recent literature review by Xu, Zhang and Zhang (2009). They observed that since the 1980s, most parenting research in China utilized Baumrind's parenting styles typology (authoritarian, authoritative permissive, and uninvolved) to conceptualize their research. The few studies on childrearing in China published in Western (English) journals (Andrew *et al.* 2004, Chao 1994, Huang and Prochner 2004, Quoss and Wen 1995, Zhou 2004, Chen *et al.* 2000a, 2000b, 2001), although similar to the native Chinese researchers' unidirectional orientation in examining parental antecedents on children's outcome, were more sophisticated in their measurements. The authors tended to avoid the indiscriminate use of Western-developed measurements. Huang and Prochner (2004) for instance, introduced a new dimension to capture the unique Chinese parental "training" (*guan* 管) style, drawn from Chao (1994). Although their approach overlaps with Baumrind's authoritarian parenting style, it involves a more "family-based" control that is not meant to dominate the child but instead aims to maintain family harmony and the integrity of the family unit. According to Peterson and associates, multi-dimensional parental style instruments developed in the West may fail to generalize effectively from one cultural setting to another and, at worst, may simply be a reflection of cultural bias that masks subtle differences in meaning (Peterson *et al.* 2004). Researchers have to exercise care in adopting scales developed in a different culture. Translating and back-translation procedure is a common methodology employed by researchers in utilizing Western scales in cross-cultural contexts (Werner and Campbell 1970). The difficulties, however, lie in ensuring conceptual equivalence, scale equivalence, and norm equivalence (Koh *et al.* 2007).[5] In a prior decade we find Roopnarine and Carter (1992) also warned against the possible challenges of non-Western scholars importing Western intellectual technology and bending their own cultural practices to fit into these frameworks.

Methodological concerns

Most Chinese studies utilized surveys of self-reported assessments as the data collection method. There is a tendency for Chinese parents to report themselves as adopting the authoritative parenting style (high control and high warmth) and to see a causal link between this style and a positive outcome in their children (Zhou 2004). Some inconsistencies between parents' self-reported style and how their children perceived them were found by Quoss and Wen (1995). Chinese parents perceived themselves to be democratic, while their children rated them more authoritarian (high control and low warmth).[6] These inconsistencies are useful as they can be used to juxtapose different dimensions and perceptions of parenting. The concern here, however, is the over-reliance of extant research on only one source of data, i.e., self-assessments by parents (Chen *et al.* 2000a).[7] A noteworthy limitation in relying on survey methods to access parental attitude is the underlying assumption that once you understood the core philosophy (parental attitude) that guides a parent's childrearing you could then understand both parental behavior and the child's development. This unidirectional deterministic relation, however, has been questioned (Holden 2002). As early as the 1950s and 1960s, researchers (Zunich 1962, Gordon 1957) have cast doubts on the links between attitudes and behavior. Wicker (1969 cited in Holden 2002) reviewed 42 studies and concluded that little support could be found for the idea that stable attitudes influence overt behavior.

A related limitation pertains to the heavy reliance on two main methods of data collection used by indigenous Chinese researchers: laboratory observations and the already-discussed self-reported assessment. Chen *et al.* (2000b) have correctly pointed out that laboratory situations might impede spontaneous expression of affective communication between parents and children. They have advocated for the need to investigate parent–child interaction in other settings, such as the home. The homogeneity of existing methods has limited access to different aspects of parent–child relationships (as described in Appendix E). For instance, parents are usually the data source, especially when a survey questionnaire is utilized. Perspectives from children are rarely considered. Hence, it is difficult to access how children actually play a part in influencing parenting style. Zou *et al.* (2005) in their overview of the research found that uniformity in research method, small sample size, and lack of valid instruments are some of the more important shortcomings in the current studies. She urges researchers to use larger sample sizes, multiple methods, and multivariate research to access the different facets of family dynamics. Xu *et al.* (2009) mentioned in their literature review paper that psychologists in China need to move away from laboratory work and survey methods and enter into the natural environments where children live to understand how environmental factors interact in influencing children's development.

One example of work that goes beyond mainstream methods is that done by Chen Huichang and his collaborators (including students). Like most developmental psychologists, survey and laboratory observations are part of their repertoire in data collection. But they also use other methods as well. They were among the first few to conduct qualitative and in-depth observations in the homes of their research participants on evenings and weekends. They used methods commonly used in Western research but still rare in China, such as interviews, video taping, and vignette discussions with both parents and children.

Need to contextualize research

Finally, a third concern I have with the extant Chinese research on childrearing is the lack of attention to cultural context, beyond a small set of truisms about Chinese culture both (broadly defined) and how it manifests itself at the level of the family. Zou *et al.* (2005), after reviewing Western and Chinese research on family functioning and youth crimes, noted the lack of research that seriously considers Chinese culture as context. She questioned whether the empirical results found in the West could be used to explain phenomena in Chinese families. The research lens has been focused mainly on transactions between parents and children, which are examined without adequate attention to specific family, social and cultural contexts. One important contextual dimension to consider is the dramatic change in the economic structure. Within a short span of less than three decades, China has moved from a planned economy to a market-oriented one. Prior to economic reform in 1978, China did not have a labor market in the conventional sense (Xin 2000). Instead, the central government exercised total control over every aspect of labor arrangements. Much has been written about the inherent problems of this job placement system. But despite its problems, it did provide workers with a sense of stability and security as housing, pension, medical care, and even children's schooling were linked to one's work unit (ibid.). As the economic reform efforts intensified, the central government had to downsize state-owned enterprises so as to give way to a competitive labor market. Workers no longer benefited from the security of the "iron rice bowl" once promised them and they were forced to face the uncertainty and stress of unemployment (Price *et al.* 2007). The rapid and otherwise unsettling transitions of the economic reforms have created powerful demands on individual workers and their families who cope with economic stress and uncertainty. In this study, I report my observations of one consequence of this heightened sense of anxiety. This unstable job market has been used by adult children – sometimes unintentionally – as a justifiable reason for enlisting help from the senior generation with childcare and house chores, which might in turn be creating an unbalanced relationship between the two generations, one which seems to favor the adult children. In the following chapters, the reader will see how these imbalances are enacted and their influence on childrearing practices in some families. In short, then, too few researchers are attending to the cultural underpinnings of human behavior.[8] China is experiencing rapid change at the macro level, as discussed in Chapter 1. These changes need to be taken into consideration when studying childrearing and parent–child relationships.

Too much information is lost through the use of the current paradigm. Let us turn to the bidirectional framework which I believe will facilitate access to different dimensions of childrearing dynamics and provide a richer understanding of the 4-2-1 phenomenon from a position that is closer to ground.

The bidirectional model

In social science research as in life, "we do not see things as they are, we see them as we are," so it is said.[9] Our assumptions and theories govern what we look for in the data (or in our lives) and consequently guide the design and choice of methods for any piece of social research. Central to the bidirectional model I am proposing is a shift away from viewing children as passive recipients of socialization to seeing them as actors and agents in their family life – just like their caregivers. Different disciplines vary in the speed with which researchers have warmed up to the bidirectional model in the face of decades-long dominance by the unidirectional approach. In psychology and sociology, ontological and epistemological developments have led to the gradual emergence of some types of bidirectionality, including new perspectives for viewing children (Shehan 1999). Historically, the dominating ontology of childhood considered children to be inferior to adults. It was grounded in the assumption that influences flow from adults to children.[10] Epistemologically, researchers privileged objective accounts of events that understand adults' experiences as objective reality and children's experiences as illusory and unreliable (ibid., p. 6). In recent decades, a number of scholars conducting parenting research in the disciplines of psychology and sociology have begun to embrace less deterministic and more constructionist theories of childhood, where children are seen as negotiators and co-creators of their own worlds (ibid.). As a consequence, children are increasingly being viewed in terms of who they are, not just in terms of what they will be (Orleans and Overton 1999).

In developmental psychology, the unidirectional point of view embodied by classical unidirectional theories has come under attack for overemphasizing the role of parents in determining how a child will turn out (De Mol and Buysse 2008, Valsiner *et al.* 1997). The strongest critique comes from researchers who believe that genetic make-up, experience with peers, or even a chance life event will have more influence on a child's development than the parents (Rowe 1994, Harris 1998). Thus, psychology as a discipline, as least in the West, has gradually shifted from treating parenting as a top-down (from parent-to-child) influence to examining a set of interactive processes whereby parents and children react to each other and influence each other from the moment a child is born (Maccoby 2002, Bugental and Goodnow 1998). In sociology, on the other hand, the paradigm shift from objectivism to social constructionism and other interpretive theoretical perspectives has encouraged increased attention to the marginalized in society. As sociological attention to women and minority groups has gained ground, so has the attention given to children (Corsaro 1997). Not surprisingly, the manner in which children are considered agents has taken different forms in the two disciplines.

Developmental psychologists have taken the lead in investigating the idea that causality is inherently bidirectional in parent–child relations, and many models of bidirectionality have been proposed (Sameroff 1975a, 1975b, Lerner 1993, Holden and Ritchie 1988, Riegel 1976, Valsiner *et al.* 1997, Bronfenbrenner 1979).[11] However, references to bidirectionality between children and parents are often generic and researchers tend to only pay lip service to this concept in their research questions and design (Kuczynski *et al.* 1999). That is, despite the wide endorsement of the bidirectional concepts, such ideas often remain unimplemented in the actual, empirical research (Kuczynski *et al.* 2009). In sociology, tension between structural narratives and individual resistance within the structure have become access points for understanding agency (Scott 1985, Fine 1992). In terms of children's agency at the micro level, sociological researchers are trying to explore children's meaning-making activities. In examining children's agency within family, social constructionist perspective provides a promising theoretical framework for a sociological perspective of bidirectionality and mutual influence (Jenks 2005, James and Prout 1997).

To reiterate, then, the idea of seeing children as active agents has been evolving for several decades. In conducting the current study, I have found the relationally based, bidirectional model – social relations theory (Kuczynski and Parkin 2006), developed by Kuczynski and his associates over the past three decades – helpful as a framework for understanding the micro dynamics of single children and the relationships they have with their multiple caregivers in urban Xiamen. Drawing from psychology, sociology, and behavioral genetics, this model is a comprehensive framework with which to study the child, as well as parents and grandparents, as agents in family life. Unlike bidirectional approaches that consider immediate, reciprocal exchange of behaviors between parents and children (Sameroff 1975a, 1975b) social relations theory understands bidirectionality to be a dialectical process in which human agents construct meanings out of each other's behavior from which they produce qualitative changes (ibid.). The usefulness of this bidirectional framework lies in the alternative web that fundamentally challenges the unidirectional way of looking at parent–child relationships through a set of interconnected assumptions regarding the nature of agency, context of relationships, power, and dialectics. It makes sense at this point to elaborate each of the key assumptions of this bidirectional perspective, beginning with the nature of agency.

Agency

The bidirectional model of parent–child relations takes a strong position on the agency of both parent and child during interaction. This view of agency understands parents and children to be actors with the ability to make sense of their environment, initiate change, and make choices. The three dimensions of agency are autonomy, construction, and action (Cummings *et al.* 2000, Kuczynski 2003). Autonomy is the universal motive for self-determination and self-protection. Construction is the capacity of parents and children to create new meanings from their interactions with their environments. Action emphasizes the capacity of individuals to express agency behaviorally through action, irrespective of their social power (Giddens 1984).

Agency in the bidirectional model takes on both behavioral (Skinner *et al.* 1988) and cognitive aspects (Damon and Hart 1988). In this study, children were not treated as passive recipients of input from their adult caregivers. By recognizing agency in both parent (grandparents) and child the bidirectional frame facilitates movement away from an agent (parent/grandparent)–object (child) relationship to an agent (parent/grandparent)–agent (child) perspective on interaction. Taking this approach allowed me to recognize that one of the key research questions in three-generation families was how Chinese children interpret and make sense of the dialectical relationships among the caregivers and how they in turn exercise their agency in interacting with the web of adults around them. In the same vein, agency exercised by grandparents and parents in their collaborative efforts, the division of labor of childcare tasks, and the resulting tension and conflicts were also brought to the fore.

Agency in relationship contexts and embedded within culture

According to the bidirectional framework, parent–child interaction should be understood as taking place within a relationship context. Parent and child are bound by a specific enduring and close relationship in which both participants have an investment (Hinde and Stevenson-Hinde 1988). Their relationship has a past and they anticipate that the relationship will continue into the future. Interactions between people who have a close enduring relationship follow different dynamics than interactions between adults and children who are unfamiliar with each other (Dawber and Kuczynski 1999). These relationship dynamics provide a basis for understanding the motivational issues underlying mutual receptivity to influence, conflict, and negotiation in parent–child relations. In what follows, the reader will see how the agency of each member is exercised within the relationship context. This is crucial for understanding the high degree of mutual influence in the Chinese family and it clearly has implications for how agency and power are enacted by grandparents, parents, and child in multigenerational families in Xiamen. The dynamics of parent (grandparent)–child agency relationships are located within the context of an urban, three-generational family relationship system which in turn is embedded within the rapid macro socio-cultural changes in contemporary urban China. The approach provides some initial insights into the intergenerational dynamics otherwise lacking in extant childrearing literature in China. As such, it represents a notable shift away from the current Chinese empirical studies with their focus on the antecedent or outcome of parent–child interactions while taking the context of relationships for granted.

Interdependent asymmetrical power

Conventional parenting research accords more power to parents than children: since parents possess more power, the direction of power influence is deterministic, from parents to children. A bidirectional model of parenting takes a more dialectical perspective on power. Power is conceptualized as "interdependent asymmetry" in the dynamic processes of parent–child relationships (Kuczynski and Hildebrandt 1997, Bugental *et al.* 1997, Eisenberg 1992, Dumas *et al.* 1995, Perlman *et al.* 1999). The idea of interdependent asymmetry shifts the focus from the traditional question of who has more power to a new question of what powers and resources parents and children can draw on in their relationship together. The accumulated research on parent–child social interactions indicates that seeing these interactions in terms of a "top-down" or vertical difference in power is not a useful way to understand many of the ordinary phenomena of everyday family life (Russell *et al.* 1998). It is necessary to construct a model of power that considers important horizontal, that is to say, peer-like, features in contemporary power relations between parents and children. These include mutual conflict and cooperation, child assertion, negotiation, parental compliance with children's requests, mutual responsiveness, and friendship-like qualities in parent–child relationships (Kuczynski *et al*, 1999). Parents and children interact in an interdependent, intimate relationship where each is both

vulnerable and powerful with regard to the other. The resources that constitute power include: individual resources, for instance physical strength,
expertise, control over rewards; relational resources, an important source of
power for children which derives from ceded power granted by parents
and which can be deployed in their interdependent relationships with
their parents (Dawber and Kuczynski 1999, Emerson 1962, Harach and
Kuczynski 2005, Maccoby 2000); cultural resources consisting of the
constraints, rights, and entitlements conveyed to parents and children by
the laws, customs, and practices of a culture (Kuczynski 2003, p.17). Mayall
(1994, 2002) found that children experienced very different power arrangements in interactions with adults in the intimate relationship context of the
family, particularly when compared to the institutional context of school.

Children experience a greater sense of power of influence in the parent–
child relationship context, compared with a teacher–student school environment. With parents, children generally experience more room for
negotiation. Hence, there are looser standards of accommodation to, and
negotiation of, parental wishes. Teachers, on the other hand, are more
steadfast in their authority and less challengeable than adults at home.
Compared with life at home, life at school offers less scope for negotiation.
This means that children are likely to experience more power in their relationships with parents or grandparents than in any other adult–child
relationship. In the current study we will see that single children drew
power of influence from an intimate relationship with each adult caregiver.

Another source of leverage the children have when exercising their
power of influence in the family milieu is the shift of Chinese families from
being aged-centered to being child-centered. The three-generation one-
child family form affords several routes for children's expression of power
and influence. Children are few in number, which, in contrast to larger
families of previous generations, allows the child to have one-on-one relationships with each of his or her caregivers. Each adult caregiver has
relationships in which caregivers have an emotional stake with the child.
The child's relationships with multiple caregivers increase the child's
relational resources which can be exploited to meet the child's goals (Goh
and Kuczynski 2009).

Dialectics as integral in bidirectionality

In the unidirectional model, outcomes such as children's compliance and
intergenerational transmission from parents to children are indicators of
successful socialization. Dialectical processes such as contradiction and
conflict in parent–child dynamics, on the other hand, are not seen in a positive light. The bidirectional frame adopted here captures these realistic and
complex dialectical interactions. The use of a dialectical approach is
compatible with this bidirectional perspective since both parents and children are conceptualized as interacting with each other as agents (Hinde

1997, Lawrence and Valsiner 1993, Valsiner *et al.* 1997). Parents must constantly balance their needs with their child's needs and reconcile the contradictions and differences. The task of parenting is by definition to raise a rapidly changing organism and therefore adaptation to change, rather than stability, is an essential element of successful parenting. Contradictions are inherent in any relationship, but especially between parents and children, as they frequently come into conflict because of their needs for autonomy and exercise of agency while at the same time being united by the bonds of their mutual relationship (Kuczynski *et al.* 2009). Given this, an understanding of contextual dialects as postulated by Riegel (1976) has been found to be useful in parenting research. Holden and Ritchie (Holden 1997, Holden and Ritchie 1988) claim that Riegelian dialectics is particularly well-suited to many of the contradictions, ambiguities, and indeterminate answers that are inherent in the lived experience of parents and children. A dialectically framed understanding of context implies that there is no "ideal" state toward which parent–child relations progress. Instead, new contradictions continually lead to both favorable and negative new syntheses (Adams *et al.* 1992). In the current study, the dialectical lens opens up attention to the micro-dynamics between grandparents and parents as joint caregivers to the grandchild. The intimate collaborations between the two generations of caregivers inevitably lead to tension, conflict, resolution, and continuous change. On the other hand, we note that as much as children are impacted by the tension and conflict among their multiple caregivers, they contribute to escalating or easing these dialectics. Through shedding light on the dialectics among the multiple caregivers and between them and the children, this study offers an initial understanding of the under-explored, dialectical facets of the way children are being raised in Chinese families.

A note of caution

I have thus far discussed the advantages and potential rewards that emerge from utilizing the bidirectional frame in viewing parent–child relationships, mostly because it facilitates the asking of new questions and in doing so yields new findings not accessible through the unidirectional perspective. It is important to recognize the challenges of applying this more sophisticated perspective in conducting empirical research. These methodological challenges include prolonged direct naturalistic observations which would facilitate descriptive analysis of parent–child interactions (Crouter and Booth 2003) and using theory-qualitative methods so as to understand process rather than product (Crockenberg and Leerkes 2003).

In his strong advocacy for a more dynamic process (instead of outcome) model, Holden (1997) acknowledged that such an approach is both conceptually and methodologically more difficult to investigate. Likewise, Peterson in his early writing (Peterson and Rollins 1986) was cautious of the then relatively new bidirectional model. In his opinion, the greatest obstacle to research within a bidirectional orientation was the overwhelming complexity that confronts the investigators. It is, however, interesting to observe that Peterson himself in recent years has shed his reservations and adopted a more dynamic perspective in his parenting research (Peterson *et al.* 2003).

Throughout my research I have made a conscious effort to avoid the blanket application of the bidirectional model. Instead, the assumptions underlying the bidirectional model were employed cautiously as sensitizing tools in aiding discoveries which have proven fruitful. In the last chapter of this book I propose a contextualized conceptual framework for future research on how children are raised in China. Before that, however, let us turn to the context – the research site where this study was located – the city of Xiamen in China.

3 The 4-2-1 phenomenon in Xiamen

One child, many caregivers

Xiamen city, also known as Amoy in the local Minnan 闽南 dialect, is an important gateway to the southeast coast of China. Sitting on the estuary of the Jiulong River 九龙江 opposite Taiwan, Xiamen is an old port city whose recorded history can be traced back to the Tang dynasty (AD 600–900). During the Ming (AD 1300–1600) and Qing (AD 1644–1911) dynasties Xiamen served as a strategic political, economic and military base. Later it became a gate for Chinese migration. As one of the most rapidly modernizing cities on the southeastern coast of China, Xiamen facilitated China's links with the global forces of commerce and colonialism during the late nineteenth and early twentieth centuries. The trade, imperialism, and pull of opportunity in the colonial settlements of Southeast Asia were especially pronounced in Xiamen, as it was a city that had thrived on international trade since its birth in the late fourteenth century (Cook 2006). Xiamen itself was also the place of origin for many of the Chinese who emigrated to Southeast Asia. Many of these emigrants, known as *huaqiao* 华侨, later contributed actively to the building and development of Xiamen, their ancestral home.[1]

Like New York City, Xiamen is a mixture of land and islands at the mouth of a large river. Comparatively small by Chinese standards, at the end of the year 2009, Xiamen's resident population was 2.5 million. 1.77 million of the population were *Huji renkou* 户籍人口 (registered population[2]) and the rest were *zang zhu renkou* 暂住人口 (temporary residents from other provinces). Xiamen (Figure 3.1) comprises Xiamen Island (longitude 118°04′04″E, latitude 24°26′46″N), Gulangyu 鼓浪屿 Island, and a larger region along the mouth of the Jiulong 九龙江 River on the mainland, including Tong'an 同安区, Jimei 集美区, Haicang 海沧区, and Xiang'an 翔安区. Huli 湖里区 and most of Siming 思明区 (except Gulangyu) are on Xiamen Island while the other four districts lie on the mainland. Xiamen Island is located very close to the island of Kinmen 金门, which is governed by Taiwan (Xiamen Shi Di Fang Zhi Bian Zuan Wei Yuan Hui 2004). Because of its unique geographical advantages Deng Xiaoping, the then Premier, chose Xiamen as one of five earliest Special Economic Zones (SEZ) in 1980.[3]

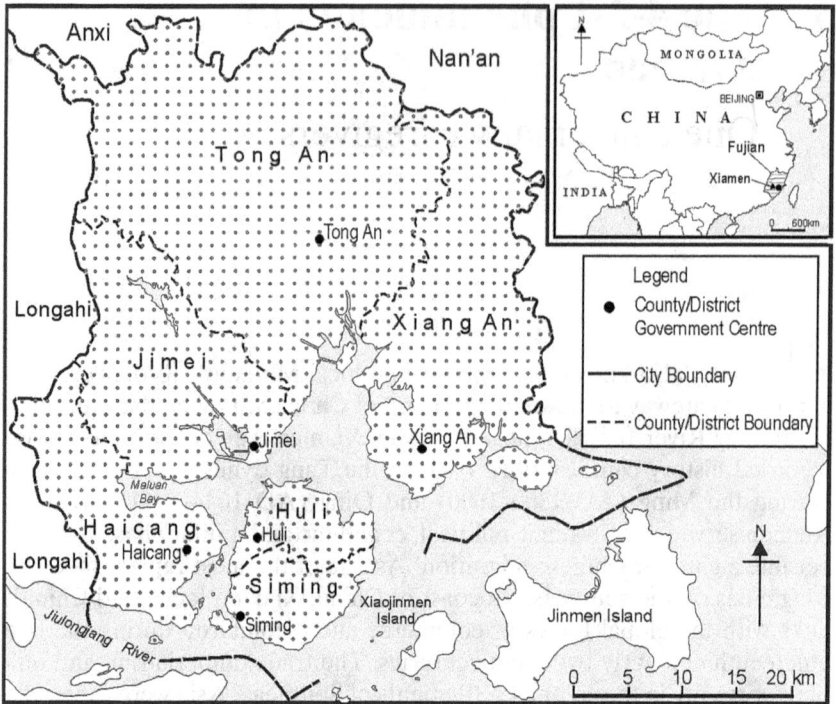

Figure 3.1 Map of Xiamen.

Since being designated as an SEZ, Xiamen has undergone a remarkable period of growth both in terms of its economy and infrastructure. To attract foreign investment, the five SEZs were designed to be the leading edge of China's transition to a market economy (Wank 1999).

To achieve that goal, the government invested heavily in both the physical and human infrastructure of the city.[4] This was done both to facilitate economic development of the southeastern coast and to enhance collaboration with Taiwan. Although the SEZ was originally confined to the Huli district in Xiamen island, in February 1984 Deng Xiaoping visited Xiamen and decided to hasten the speed of its development into an SEZ. As part of this process the SEZ was expanded to the whole island. A direct investment of 700 million *renminbi* (RMB) went into the construction of Xiamen international airport, four deepwater berths, telecommunications, water and power supplies, transport, and other infrastructure (Zheng and Huang 1988). Seven institutions of higher learning were set up to train technical and managerial personnel as employees in foreign investment companies.

Although a city within the Fujian province, Xiamen was granted a sub-provincial class, or municipality status, in its economic governance. This provided Xiamen city government special economic zone privileges, including lower import duties and the authority to approve direct foreign investment not exceeding US$30 million (Howell 1993).

To this point, the investment in Xiamen has been a wise one. Despite the global economic down turn in 2009, Xiamen achieved an annual GDP of 162.3 billion RMB at a growth rate of 8 percent.[5] In the first quarter of 2010, Xiamen's economic performance continued to show steady growth, attaining a 17.7 percent increase in GDP compared with first quarter of the previous year, highest amongst the nine counties in Fujian province.[6] GDP per capita for the year 2009 in Xiamen was equivalent to US$9,476.13,[7] compared with an overall GDP per capita of US$3,678 in China.[8] It has been ranked the fourth most livable city in China in the year 2009 by the *China News* online (www.chinanews.com.cn) behind Qingdoa 青岛, Suzhou 苏州, and Taizhou 泰州. With the liberalization of market and economic development, investments and speculation in stocks and shares have also gained popularity in Xiamen as in other modern cities in China. The total value of transactions for the year 2009 in Xiamen city alone was 35 trillion RMB.[9] In addition, businesses from Taiwan, Hong Kong, and Macau invest substantially in building their plants in Xiamen.

Little suns raised by intergenerational parenting coalitions in Xiamen

To get a sense of the extent of the intergenerational parenting in Xiamen my colleagues and I undertook a survey that was administered through the school system. The survey involved a non-random sample drawn from 39 government-run primary schools located in two zones of Xiamen Island,[10] Huli and Siming. The students involved in the survey were between 6 and 12 years old. A total of 1,743 questionnaires were distributed and 1,657 were returned. The response rate was about 95 percent. After invalid and suspicious forms were excluded the total sample was 1,627. The 30-item questionnaire was designed to collect demographic data on the families as well as documenting the collaboration between parents and grandparents as joint caregivers (refer to Appendix A for details). With 45.4 percent (N = 738) of the sampled households (N = 1,627) having grandparents involved in one way or another in providing childcare, it seems clear that the phenomenon of raising grandchildren as a joint project between two generations was commonplace in Xiamen.

The adult children who had their older parents helping with childcare and housework had slightly higher income than those who did not (Table 3.1): 54.3 percent had household income above RMB2,000 (approximately US$290) per month ($\chi^2$ = 29.66, d.f. = 1, p < 0.1). A higher proportion also had diploma (23.3 percent) and tertiary (14.4 percent) education, compared with only 15.6 percent and 8.2 percent of the households without grandparent caregivers (Table 3.2).

Table 3.1 Income levels of middle-generation parents with or without grandparents helping in childcare

Mean RMB/month	With grandparents helping		Without grandparents helping	
	Frequency	*Percent*	*Frequency*	*Percent*
No income	75	10.10	157	17.60
500	89	12.00	155	17.40
1,500	252	34.10	306	34.40
3,500	231	31.30	198	22.20
7,500	71	9.60	55	6.18
10,000	20	2.70	18	2.00
Total	738	100.00	889	100.00

Table 3.2 Education levels of middle-generation parents with or without grandparents helping in childcare

Education level	With grandparents helping		Without grandparents helping	
	Frequency	*Percent*	*Frequency*	*Percent*
Primary	63	8.5	139	15.6
Secondary	388	52.5	527	59.2
Diploma	169	22.8	139	15.6
Tertiary	105	14.2	73	8.2
Missing	13	1.7	11	1.2
Total	738	100.0	889	100.0

The subgroup of children whose grandparents were actively caring for them showed a large increase in grandparents' involvement at age seven and reached a peak (18.2 percent) at age eight, after which it started to decline gradually (Table 3.3). It is suspected that the increased involvement of grandparents during the initial years in primary school may be because of developmentally specific caregiving tasks such as preparing lunches and taking children to and from school.[11] With regard to the gender of the children, it seems grandparents were equally likely to care for grandsons and granddaughters – only a negligible gender difference was observed (50.1 percent boys; 49.9 percent girls).

A total of 1,301 grandparents were involved in caring for grandchildren from the 738 households. Paternal grandmothers and grandfathers jointly caring for grandchildren together with the middle generation constituted the largest group (22 percent),[12] followed by paternal grandmothers providing care together with parents in the intergenerational parenting coalition (IGPC) (18 percent). Maternal grandmothers and grandfathers

Table 3.3 Age distribution of children with grandparents providing childcare

Age (years)	Frequency	Percent
< 5	22	2.8
5	5	0.6
6	23	3.0
7	81	10.6
8	138	18.1
9	122	16.0
10	112	14.7
11	100	13.1
12	80	10.5
> 12	75	9.8
Missing	3	0.3
Total	761[a]	100.0

Note
a Total no. of children is > N (N = 738) as there were families with more than one child.

jointly providing care made up the third largest group (17 percent), while maternal grandmothers alone made up the fourth largest group (14 percent). About 9 percent of the households had three grandparents of different combinations from both lineages involved in the IGPC. It was not unexpected that more grandmothers (62 percent) than grandfathers (38 percent) were involved in providing childcare. The modal age of all the grandparents fell within the range of 61-70 years old, all of whom were retired, as per China's employment regulations of retirement age of 55 for female and 60 for men (Leung 2010). The most common type of living arrangement in the IGPC was three-generational coresidence (40 percent), followed by grandparents staying close by (23 percent) (Table 3.4). Grandparents providing *ad hoc* care (19 percent) was the third most common type.

The grandparents that helped tended to do so for a long period of time; 31 percent (N = 308) helped for between 6 and 10 years. In addition, more than 70 percent (N = 743) of the parents in these families said that the grandparents would be extending their service indefinitely. This high rate may indicate the absence of a sense of time limitation when receiving services provided by grandparents. On the other hand, it may also be a hint that grandparents generally do not explicitly state an ending time for their service provision. I suspect it may mean that once grandparents start to get involved, they are not likely to quit, in part because they may not see a socially acceptable way to opt out. This question will be explored further in the discussion of the ethnographic data in subsequent chapters.

Among the 738 middle generation surveyed, more than half reported that the grandparents prepare meals and do the household chores (Table 3.5). Additionally, slightly more than one-third of the middle generation stated

Table 3.4 Types of childcare help and living arrangements of grandparents

Living arrangements and types of help	Frequency	Percent
Grandparents coreside under one roof with adult children to care for grandchildren	296	40.1
Grandparents stay near adult children	168	22.8
Grandparents provide *ad hoc* help	140	19.0
Grandparents stay with one adult child while providing childcare to other adult children	92	12.5
Grandchildren stay with grandparents during weekdays and return home on weekends	37	5.0
Grandfathers and grandmothers stay with different adult children to care for different grandchildren	30	4.1
Other forms of help	90	12.2

Note
Frequencies > *N* as some families had more than one living arrangement.

Table 3.5 Distribution of work load between parents and grandparents

	Grandparents (N = 738)	Parents (N = 738)
Groceries	272 (36.9%)	301 (40.8%)
Take/fetch child	280 (37.9%)	316 (42.8%)
Meal prep	427 (57.9%)	394 (53.4%)
Housework	391 (53%)	464 (62.9%)
Daily care	346 (46.9%)	513 (69.5%)
Other tasks	41 (5.6 %)	36 (4.9%)

Note
Percentage exceeds 100 due to multiple responses.

that the grandparents do the grocery shopping, as well as taking children to school and bringing them home. Slightly less than half reported that the grandparents contribute to daily childcare (which included supervision of meals, disciplining children, and taking children to and fetching them from extra-curriculum activities). Furthermore, when similar questions were asked about their own contribution, around two-thirds of the parents stated that they carried out household chores and daily care of the children. With regard to grocery shopping and taking/fetching the children, there seems to be little difference between the parents' and grandparents' load.

Although the results show little difference in the frequency with which housework is performed by parents and grandparents, we have to under-stand that grandparents are in fact significantly reducing the burden of parents by taking on housework, meal preparation, and childcare. Some caution should be exercised in reading these results as they were self-reported by the adult children. It is possible that they may over report their own contribution while underreporting that of the grandparents. During the ethnographic phase of my research I observed grandparents doing the lion's share of housework and childcare duties in at least some of the families I was studying.

Benefits and challenges of IGPC

The middle generation clearly benefited in a number of ways by bringing the grandparents into the household. The advantages indicated by the middle generation included: helping them to focus on their work (32.5 percent); reducing overall family expenses (27.5 percent); enhancing intergenerational ties (24.5 percent); and superior domestic help provided by grandparents rather than engaging domestic help (14.3 percent) (Table 3.6). The middle generation perceived several benefits of this arrangement for grandparents, including: facilitating closer bonds between grandparents and grandchildren (55 percent); helping to occupy the mind of the grandchild (29.7 percent); and keeping grandparents occupied (13.3 percent).

The middle generation also indicated difficulties both for themselves and the senior generation in caring for the grandchildren jointly. A high proportion reported difficulties in collaboration due to differences in childrearing methods between the two generations (54.4 percent) (Table 3.7). This is followed by problems of interaction between the senior and junior (grandchildren) generations (29.4 percent), which probably meant the middle generation had to mediate between them. Difficulty in getting along with the senior generation was ranked third with a fairly low frequency (8.2 percent). It is important to note that despite awareness of the difficulties

Table 3.6 Advantages of IGPC as perceived by the middle generation

Advantages to	Frequency
Middle generation	
Helped them focus on work	546
Reduced the overall expense in the family	462
Enhanced intergenerational ties	411
Grandparents were superior to domestic helpers as caregivers	240
Other advantages	17
Senior generation	
Facilitated closer bonds to grandchildren	567
Occupied their minds	306
Helped grandparents kill time	137
Other advantages	19

Note
Frequencies > N ($N = 738$) as multiple responses were allowed.

Table 3.7 Difficulties in collaboration between middle and senior generations within IGPC

Difficulties to	Frequency
Middle generation	
Differences in childrearing methods	408
Problems of interaction between grandparents and grandchildren	221
Difficulties in getting along with senior	62
Others	59
Senior generation	
No personal time	300
Lack social activities	238
Physical fatigue	225
Others	54

Note
Frequencies > N ($N = 738$) as multiple responses were allowed.

grandparents faced in providing childcare, including depriving the older person of personal time (36.7 percent) and social activities (29 percent), and causing physical exhaustion (27.5 percent) – 29 percent of the middle generation considered it an obligation for grandparents to provide such care.

Expectations and rewards for grandparents in IGPC

The middle generation was asked whether they considered providing childcare an obligation on the part of the grandparents. As mentioned earlier, 29 percent of the respondents either fully agreed or agreed that it was an obligation. One-third indicated they had no opinion. Slightly more than one-third of the respondents (36.8 percent) either disagreed or fully disagreed that grandparents were obliged to provide childcare. Interestingly, this relatively high level of expectation placed on grandparents to provide childcare and household assistance does not correspond with the level of reciprocity they showed to the senior generation. When asked in what ways they would express their gratitude to their older parents when rewarding them, slightly more than half of the respondents (53.7 percent) said there is "no need" because grandparents are part of the family. Only about one-quarter of the adult children (26.8 percent) said they made regular monetary contributions to their parents. An even smaller number made *ad hoc* monetary contributions (17.9 percent) or used verbal affirmation (16.2 percent) as forms of expressing their gratitude.

To understand if the financial status of the grandparents affects adult children's tendency to reciprocate, we differentiated between grandparents with and without pensions. Not surprisingly, a greater number of adult children wanted to give regular contribution to the grandparents without pensions (32.1 percent) than to those with pensions (23.4 percent) (χ^2 = 5.68, d.f. = 1, p = 0.01). We also wanted to know if there was any difference in income among the 53.7 percent of adult children who said there was "no need" to reciprocate. Statistical test results show no association between adult children's income and the attitude of "no need" to reward. Hence, neither low nor high income played a part in influencing the general lack of reciprocity. These findings seem to indicate the relative dependence of the middle generations, compared with their counterparts in the West. Unlike in Western families, where adult children leave and start an independent nuclear family, Chinese adult children, even after forming their own nuclear family unit, continue their membership in their parental family. The extended family household is viewed as a "common enterprise where members from both generations have a vested interest in maintaining its existence" (Chen 2006, Stack 1975).

The survey results show that an IGPC where grandparents and parents are considered as a unit that jointly raises children is an appropriate framework for studying childrearing in urban Xiamen. Almost half (45.4 percent) of families surveyed had grandparents actively providing childcare. These joint efforts brought advantages and challenges for both grandparents and parents. A key finding is that the IGPC is complicated by differences in childrearing methods between the generations. In addition, while grandparents residing under one roof and providing childcare was the most popular living arrangement (40 percent), it is clear that the close proximity and intimate interactions across the three generations inevitably bring conflict and tension. The data from the survey provide a strong measure of the general status of the IGPC in Xiamen. It is within that context that we can begin to understand the lives of the families with whom I did ethnographic work. To introduce them, the following section presents a sketch of these five families which will provide a context for the analysis of the in-depth ethnographic data in later chapters (Table 3.8).

Sketches of research families

We begin with the Jiang family, a family with one child and a live-in grandmother (for a detailed discussion of the recruitment process for research participant refer to Appendix B).

The Jiang family (Figure 3.2)

Jie Jie, a seven-year-old boy, was cared for by his 70-year-old paternal grandmother and his parents, who are both in their thirties and work in the education sector. The adult son is a professor at a local university and the daughter-in-law, a secondary school teacher. The grandmother, a retired accountant, lived apart from her 76-year-old husband so that the two of

Table 3.8 Bird's eye view of five participating families

Name of family unit	Name of middle generation	Age	Age/ sex of child	GP(s)[a] involved/ living arrangements	Marital status of middle generation	Educational level of middle generation	Occupation of middle generation
Jiang	Mr Jiang	34	7/M	PGM/ coresidence	Married	Graduate degree	Professor in university
	Mrs Jiang[b]	32	Ditto	Ditto	Married	Diploma	Secondary school teacher
Wang	Mr Wang	32	7/M	1. MGM/ coresidence 2. PGM/ vicinity	Married	Degree	Engineer
	Mrs Wang	33	Ditto	Ditto	Married	Post-secondary	Bank teller
Tian	Mr Tian	43	10/F	MGM+MGF/ ad hoc coresidence	Married	Degree	Insurance agent
	Mrs Tian	42	Ditto	Ditto	Married	Masters degree	Hospital administrator
Bai	Mdm Bai[c]	36	5/F	MGM/ Coresidence	Divorced	Masters degree	Accountant
Fu	Mr Fu	33	10/M 7/M	PGM+PGF/ coresidence with grandsons	Divorced and remarried	Primary	Migrant factory worker

Notes

Pseudo names in Chinese characters: Jiang (蒋); Wang (王); Tian (田); Bai (白); Fu (符).

PGM = paternal grandmother; PGF = paternal grandfather; MGM = maternal grandmother; MGF = maternal grandfather.

a For easy identification, all grandparents within the same family, regardless of lineage, will be addressed with the same surname, e.g., maternal Grandmother Wang, paternal Grandmother Wang, maternal Grandparents Tian.

b In actual fact, married women in China do not take their husband's name, they retain their maiden name. Like their male counterparts, women are addressed by their own family name with the prefix *xiao* 小 (junior) or *liao* 老 (senior) to indicate their seniority in age. But for convenience of discussion, I use Mr and Mrs throughout the chapters so that readers can identify them as a couple.

c "Madam" is a title unique in Chinese culture to address an older woman regardless of their marital status. In Chinese the term is *nu shi* 女士.

them could take care of different grandchildren. After her retirement, Grandmother Jiang and her retired husband started to care for their elder son's daughter. When their younger son had a new-born of his own, he naturally assumed that his parents would be fair and provide childcare for this new grandson too. When the request was made to the older couple, Grandmother Jiang was hesitant, as it meant that she would have to move to the other end of Xiamen Island and live apart from her husband. It did

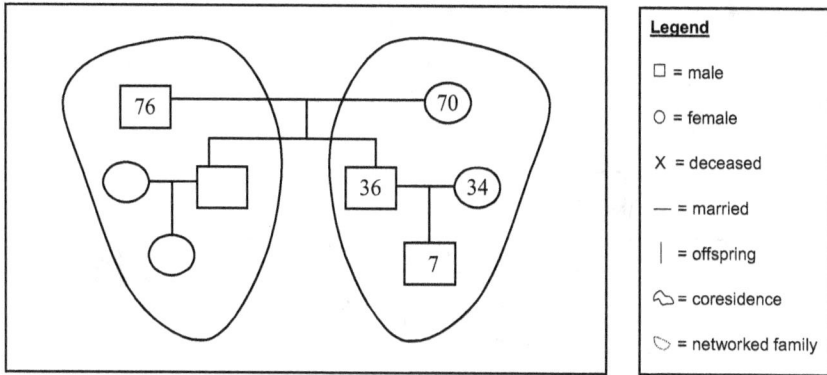

Figure 3.2 Left: Genogram of Jiang family.
Right: Legend for figures in Chapter 3.

Note: only the three-generational Jiang family on the right participated in this study. This figure reflects the extended family.

not help that she thought her younger daughter-in-law was rather difficult to get along with. However, she did not want to disappoint her son and convinced herself that she should support the young family as they were just starting out. Despite walking with a limp, she took the child to and from school on foot every day. She did the meal preparation and the household chores. Jie Jie's father coached him with his school work every evening and was also the disciplinarian. His mother stood in as academic coach when father was not available, and often buffered her son from the father's strict punishment and grandmother's constant complaints about the boy's misbehavior. The daughter-in-law thought that Grandmother Jiang was too strict and felt that she complained too much about the child. Yet, although both parents thought the daily complaints were unnecessary, the young couple had to handle them carefully so as to "give face" to the grandmother, acknowledging that what she wanted was respect from the younger members of her family.

The Wang family (Figure 3.3)

Seven-year-old Wei Wei's family was typical of a network family (Unger 2000) in Chinese cities, in that Wei Wei's father, Mr Wang, and his brother chose to reside within the same estate and formed a network in providing mutual support as well as tapping into help from grandparents for childcare. Wei Wei's maternal grandmother, an 80-year-old, illiterate widow, resided under the same roof. She had been caring for Wei Wei since age two. As in Jie Jie's situation, the grandmother prepared meals for the family and performed household chores. The paternal grandmother (59 years old), also illiterate and retired from a state-run factory, lived close by with her

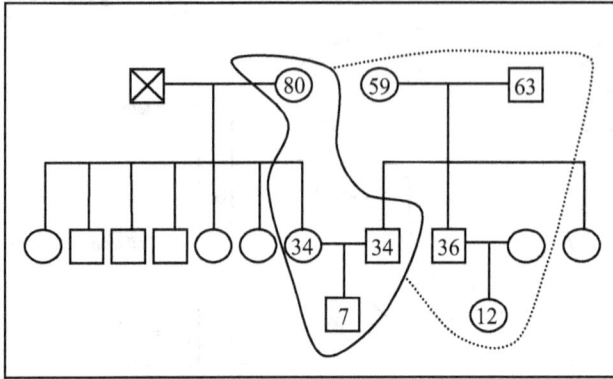

Figure 3.3 Genogram of Wang family.

husband and their elder son's family, and helped to care for the elder son's 12-year-old daughter. The paternal grandmother's role with her seven-year-old grandson was to ensure his safe travel to and from school every day. This responsibility involved eight trips to and from school per day.

These two grandmothers believed that caring for grandchildren was the best thing they could do after retirement. The paternal grandmother acknowledged that caring for Wei Wei brought her much joy and a sense of self-esteem, but it also brought some concerns, such as how to discipline the child when he pestered her to buy snacks and toys on the way home from school. She "did not dare" to administer discipline, feeling her daughter-in-law and son might not like it since they were much more educated. She would call her son at his office to complain about the grandson's misbehavior or vent her frustrations. The maternal grandmother, on the other hand, seems to have had a blissful and rather intimate relationship with the child. The child shared the same bed with *ah ma* 阿嬤 (maternal grandmother), and *ah ma* would always accede to Wei Wei's request to cook his favorite food. Wei Wei's father, a civil engineer, coached his son on his school work every evening at the expense of his own work and social life. Wei Wei's mother had a secondary school education and worked as a clerk with a bank. She deemed herself incapable of coaching the child in his academic work and left it to her husband. Her main task was to supervise Wei Wei's piano practice.

The Tian family (Figure 3.4)

Ten-year-old Tian Tian was cared for by her maternal grandparents, who shuttled between Xiamen and their home town in Nan Ping 南平 every three months. They were retired high-ranking government officials with

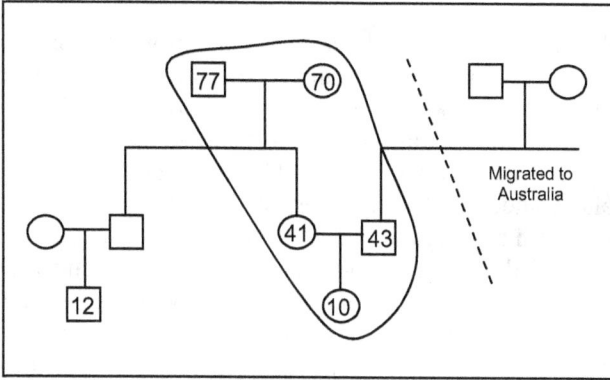

Figure 3.4 Genogram of Tian family.

comfortable pensions; both had tertiary education, which was rare for their generation. They had their own apartment in Nan Ping (about three hours' bus ride away from Xiamen), but alternated their stay between the two locations in order to help their adult daughter's family with childcare. Grandmother Tian described herself as a person who needed something to keep her occupied. Coming to her daughter's family in Xiamen made her feel useful, as she and her husband relieved her daughter of much of the housework and cooking, as well as providing childcare. Grandfather cooked for the family and grandmother did household chores. The parents, in their early forties, received tertiary education and had reasonably stable incomes. The father was a self-employed insurance agent and mother an administrative director with a local hospital. As in the two previous families, the father was responsible for coaching the child in her school work. It was not uncommon for him to use harsh physical punishment on Tian Tian. The grandparents overtly disagreed with his way of dealing with the child. The mother, though, was a rather weak figure at home. She could neither protect the child from her husband nor discipline Tian Tian when she misbehaved. Grandmother Tian was unhappy with the way the house was being run. Both her daughter and son-in-law were college graduates and earned a comfortable combined income, yet the son-in-law, who was in charge of the household's finances, left the elder generation covering the everyday costs of the house more frequently than one might expect. The grandparents were not expecting monetary rewards, as they were financially independent. Nevertheless, they wanted to feel appreciated for their efforts.

Tian Tian ranked her grandmother as her most liked person at home, followed by her grandfather. The child also used her relationship with her grandparents to mitigate her father's attempts to punish her.

The Bai family (Figure 3.5)

Bei Bei's mother, Madam Bai, was a successful accountant with a foreign investment company, and newly divorced when the fieldwork started in March 2006. Maternal Grandmother Bai was relatively young. At 50 she had asked for early retirement from her lower management job in a state-run factory after her granddaughter was born, and had since coresided with her adult daughter and granddaughter to provide childcare and assistance with housework. Along with helping her daughter in her time of need, this caregiving role also provided an escape route from her strained marriage. As a grandmother she felt obliged to continue the caring role after the divorce, out of pity for her adult daughter. Grandmother took the child to preschool, cooked, and did housechores.

The relationship between the mother–daughter dyad was, however, characterized by tension and strain. Madam Bai wanted her privacy and chose to keep the reasons for the marital breakdown to herself, whereas the grandmother felt excluded and unappreciated for her efforts. Both the grandmother and adult daughter assessed their relationship as strained. The daughter also confessed that sometimes she would vent her frustrations on her mother. An examination of the interactions between the adult daughter and her mother within the relational context showed that she seemed unappreciative at times. The permanent, long-term, and involuntary nature of parent–child relationships, coupled with the norm of prolonged dependency of the adult children, made it easy for the middle generation to take their parents for granted. It is my suspicion that the ambivalence of both parties might persist indefinitely in this intergenerational dyad, as each did not anticipate that the other would leave the household. What sustained this otherwise conflictual dyad was probably the joint mission of raising the granddaughter. The tensions between maternal grandmother and mother did not usually interfere with their care for Bei Bei, as both always put the welfare of the child at the center of their attention.

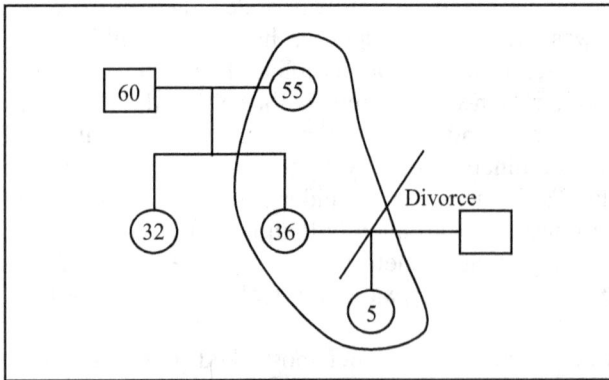

Figure 3.5 Genogram of Bai family.

The Fu family (Figure 3.6)

In contrast to other families discussed thus far, the Fu family was a low-income migrant family from rural Sichuan. Such migrants, known as *liu dong ren kou* 流动人口 (floating population), are a common phenomenon in China where a substantial portion of the rural population seeks employment in the cities. This family is intentionally included as a deviant sample. Its profile is different from the other four families in three ways: socioeconomic status; the compositions of the caregivers, and the fact that there are two grandsons in this family rather than the usual one. As an outlier sample, this family serves as contrast to the other four families so as to produce rich findings that would not be generated without its inclusion in the study.

The paternal grandparents and father of these two boys migrated to Xiamen more than 10 years ago. All were unskilled laborers: father worked in a factory, grandfather was a security guard in a factory, and grandmother a part-time cleaner at the sports complex. Three years ago the father was divorced and could not cope with caring for the two boys, and hence requested help from his parents. Both grandparents, then in their mid-fifties, took in the children gladly and considered it a "heaven-given-duty" to care for their grandsons. Since then, the father has been only marginally involved with the boys, visiting them once a fortnight. During the second half of the fieldwork, the father remarried, to a woman who had migrated to Xiamen from the same village. The two boys resided with their paternal grandparents in a tiny migrant quarter in a slum. The houses in the slum were old, disorganized, and dilapidated. Children played between crumbling walls. Migrant workers were hanging around or visiting the small eating stalls. During my first visit, Grandmother Fu held my hand throughout the 10-minute walk from the bus terminal to their quarters. She led me along twisting and turning paths of sand, without street signs to mark our way, fearing that I might get lost.

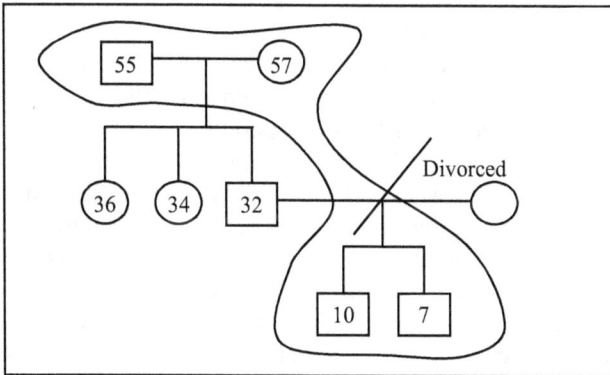

Figure 3.6 Genogram of Fu family.

The Fus lived on the second floor of a small brick building. There were three or four similar-size rooms on the same floor, inhabited by different families. All these residents shared a public toilet. When grandmother opened the door, it was a small room just sufficient to put two double bunk beds, one multi-purpose table, one stool and two chairs, and a stove for cooking. The grandparents slept on the lower deck of one bed and the two boys on the other. The upper decks of the beds were use as storage space for clothes, phone, and other miscellaneous items. The walls looked old and dirty. There was a TV set beside the cooking stove. Two big bags of bottles were lying on the floor. They were collected by grandmother for recycling, which could fetch 200 yuan of supplementary income to the family.

The grandparents, despite their own lack of education, had the clear goal of sending their grandson to university. The family was from rural Sichuan and their *hu kuo* 户口 (registration) remained in Sichuan. The kids were treated as *wai lai ren kuo* 外来人口 (migrants), which meant that the two boys were not entitled to attend state-run primary school. Instead, they could only enroll into *min ban xiao xue* 民办小学 (private primary school). The fees were double that of state-run primary schools. They wanted the 10-year-old to be enrolled in the top Tsinghua University in Beijing, and were diligently putting their savings (RMB20,000 was the target) into an educational fund toward this goal. The combined family income was only RMB1,100 (equivalent to about US$140) per month, but Grandparents Fu told me they would rather eat preserved vegetables in order to save money on food. The elder grandson won many awards from school, and his grandparents' aspirations for him were very high. If he managed to enter university, it would be a first in their entire village, the highest honor. Grandfather Fu enjoyed the powerful role of a traditional male authoritative figure. His grandsons as well as his adult son would accede to his demands. He was treated as the *yi jia zhi zhu* 一家之主 (head of the household), a traditional role that comes with cultural power.

Participant observation

To observe the intergenerational dynamics in the different families, I scheduled contact time with each family at different times of the day. For instance, during the day I could reach the grandparents, since they were retired. In the late afternoon, the grandchildren would be at home with the grandparents. In the evenings and weekends, the middle generation would be at home and I would have a chance to observe the whole family. I engaged in the discipline of taking mental notes during conversations over dinner, casual chats over afternoon tea, or any encounters with the participants. These mental notes would be transferred into my recordings as soon as possible when I got a chance to retreat to my apartment and have access to my computer. Three types of recordings were kept during the six months' field work: contact summary sheets, field notes/diary, memos. The contact summary sheet was a form that I filled up after every contact with the families. It was a discipline for me to note the date, time/duration, people involved, key and brief impressions of the session, missing links in the data puzzle, and ideas to pursue in future contacts. It also served as a form of process recording, documenting the movement of the field work in progress. Another type of recording consistently kept was memos. Memos do not just report data, they tie together different pieces of the data puzzles into a recognizable cluster to show that those data belong to a general concept. Keeping memos was a way of interacting with my data so that I did not get bogged down at the ground level. It was an analytical tool to help me make sense of the data collected, gleaning issues pertaining to methods, theories and research practice (Miles and Huberman 1994).

A total of 67 home visits/contacts were made over the six months (excluding impromptu encounters and frequent outings with participants – refer to Appendix C for contact schedule details). Each home visit lasted between 30 minutes and several hours. On average, I made 13 visits/contacts with each family. After each contact time, I logged a contact summary which recorded the nature of the encounter and salient points of observation (detailed observations were kept separately in the field notes). Since these unobstructed observations took place in natural settings, contact summaries were helpful in guiding me so as to ensure that information on different subsets of the family dynamics were gathered.

Two methods were utilized to collect data from the children. Observations were conducted each time I gave English lessons in their respective homes. Research conversations were also carried out with all six children in the sample. With the four younger children, aged between five and eight, I improvised a participatory board game and used it to engage the children in conversation. I engaged the two 10-year-olds in conversation without the game. I was aware of the power difference involved as I was their English tutor. In an attempt to lower my position the following measures were taken: First, the children were invited to have a chat with me and play the board game. Although permission from their parents was sought first, they were given a chance to reject me if they did not wish to participate. Second, permission was sought from the children for recording the session. Since all of them were curious and had never seen a digital voice recorder, I demonstrated to them how it worked and played back their voices for them. This was done to remove the possible sense of intimidation by technical tools. Third, I was seated on the floor together with the child while "playing" the board game, so as to create a casual and playful atmosphere. Fourth, I thanked each of them for helping me with the interview by participating in the game and presented a range of small gifts from which they were entitled to choose one. The board game, similar to *Monopoly*, was purchased from the local stationery store. The eighteen questions that I wanted to understand from the child's perspective were planted at different stations in the game. The children moved by throwing dice. When the child arrived at a particular station he/she would answer the question before proceeding to the next station. They could also decline to answer the questions. The three younger boys were intrigued by the game and it managed to hold their attention for the whole span of the "interview." The five-year-old girl, however, could not answer some of the questions and told me she either "did not have an opinion" or that she "had not thought about it before." Ten-year-old Tian Tian was the most articulate and could elaborate on her views without much prompting. (For a detailed discussion of the analytical strategies for ethnographic data refer to Appendix D.)

Much effort was spent in building rapport with the different generation members within the families. The grandparents were the most accessible as they were usually at home. I would sometimes just drop by to chat with them, walk with them to pick up their grandchildren from school or have lunch together with them. It was through these informal contacts that rapport was built over time. By the ending phase of my field work, friendships with most of the participants became rather strong and I had to mentally prepare both myself and the participants for termination. For instance, I would count down the remaining number of sessions to the children each time I went to their house to tutor them. Many of the mothers and grandmothers called me on the phone during the last week of my stay to express their *bushede* 不舍得 (separation anxiety) and urge me to return to Xiamen to visit them in the future. Let us turn to some of my findings about those relations. We will begin with the relationships between the two sets of caregivers – parents and grandparents drawing upon my observations and interactions with them.

4 Grandparents and parents

Who is in charge?

> But relationships, like life, are complex and our attempts to categorize,
> synthesize and capture them intellectually are, by definition, insufficient.
>
> (Wilmot 1995)

Introduction

Forty-five percent of the families in our survey had at least one grandparent
helping to raise their child. In order to clearly articulate the nature of the
intergenerational parenting coalition, we first need a clear understanding of
how it works in individual families. Toward that end we now turn to how
grandparents and parents raise the single child as a joint project, the ways
childcare tasks are shared, coordinated, and carried out across generations.
In doing so, areas of possible conflict in childrearing values and practices
will become clear. An important aspect of understanding the intergenerational parenting coalition will be to learn how (and if) caregivers resolve
their differences.

To guide the understanding of the dynamic, bidirectional relationships
between the parents and grandparents, the sensitizing tools of "agency,"
"interdependent power," and "contradictions" proposed by Social Relations theorists (detailed in Chapter 2) can be utilized to examine the
dynamics of the two generations. The dynamics within the intergenerational parenting coalitions will be presented through a recounting of my
observations of the five participating families described in the previous
chapter. During analysis of the possible contradictions and conflicts in the
coalition, an unexpected theme of "ambivalence" surfaced from the
in-depth ethnographic data. Ambivalence happens when two polarized
emotions exist simultaneously (Luescher 2004), and these emotions might
be temporarily or permanently irreconcilable. Although both positive and
negative emotions were observed in the middle generation, the negative
emotions about the collaboration with adult children in intergenerational
parenting coalition were more prominent among some grandparents, and
that produced greater ambivalence about the situation as a whole.

The Jiang family

The participants in the parenting coalition in the Jiang family were the father, mother, and paternal grandmother. These three caregivers resided under one roof and jointly cared for Jie Jie, a seven-year-old boy. As we saw in the brief description of the family in the last chapter, the grandmother struggled as to whether to offer childcare help, in part because of the way childcare tasks and housework were distributed among the caregivers. This case will provide a glimpse into both her sense of her own agency (and those in a similar situation) and offer insight into the manner with which agency is exercised in the intergenerational parenting coalition. In what follows we will see how the interactions between the grandmother and the middle generation regarding childcare practices, the execution of discipline, and decision-making help structure their relationships as these three adults exercised interdependent power over each other. We will see, too, how the Jiangs handled the contradictions and conflicts that were inevitable considering the close collaborations and the daily interactions among the adults.

After retiring from her accountant's job, Grandmother Jiang and her retired husband started to care for their first grandchild. She told me that they were both very happy, their elder daughter-in-law being both sensible and appreciative. When her second grandchild, Jie Jie, was born, Grandmother Jiang was uncertain as to whether she should oblige her younger son's request to provide childcare. Some of her contemporaries warned her that providing childcare will be physically exhausting. She was also reluctant to live apart from her husband. Still, Grandmother Jiang made the move four years ago. Every weekend she travelled several hours to visit her husband and returned on Sunday evenings to be with her younger son and his family:

Grandmother Jiang:	These few years I have this feeling, that is, taking care of grandchildren is more tiring than working.
Researcher:	Yes, indeed very tiring.
Grandmother Jiang:	Very exhausting, but *I don't have a choice* [emphasis added], I have two sons, in two places. Sometimes my old man [referring to her husband] would blame me for insisting on helping with the younger son. Now we are stuck, divided between two locations, one in the east and one in the west … yes … he resents it.

(Pilot study April 2005)[1]

From grandmother's narrative, we can see her self-imposed sense of obligation to help with childcare overcoming her deep-seated hesitations. She felt she "did not have a choice." It was no wonder she lamented to me, "This is the life of having children, non-stop giving of oneself; it is very tiring" (Field notes 16/5/06). After becoming part of the intergenerational parenting coalition, Grandmother Jiang had no time for herself. A typical day revolved entirely around her seven-year-old grandson.

Jie Jie slept in the same bed with his grandmother. At seven in the morning she would wake him and get him ready for school. She would then fix his breakfast. After breakfast, she would walk Jie Jie to school, about ten minutes away. At the time of my fieldwork, Grandmother Jiang was approaching 70 years old. She had considerable pain in her knee joint and walked with a limp in her left leg. Oftentimes she could not catch up with Jie Jie and had to resort to yelling at him when he jaywalked. On her way back from the school, she would do grocery shopping for the day at the neighborhood stalls. The rest of the morning was spent cleaning the house and doing chores. Grandmother Jiang claimed that because her son and daughter-in-law were working full time the load naturally landed on her.

At noontime, she would walk to school to pick up her grandson. (It was the practice for school children to go home for lunch before returning for another half-day's schooling in the afternoon.) It was not uncommon for her to have to wait for a long time (from ten minutes up to an hour) at the school gate before her grandson was released from class, as the teachers would detain children to complete any unfinished school work. Grandmother Jiang said that standing all that time at the school gate was very tough on her legs. After fixing herself and the boy a simple lunch, she looked forward to a short siesta. Her energetic seven-year-old grandson, however, did not care for siesta and wanted his grandmother to play with him. At about 1:30 pm, she would walk the child back to school. A peaceful couple of hours in the afternoon were the only time she could catch her breath before starting to prepare dinner for the family and getting ready to pick the child up from school at 4 pm. When her adult children returned from work, they would supervise the boy's school work and grandmother would do the dishes after dinner. In the evenings, the older lady would watch some TV programs before retiring.

Grandmother's account of the division of childcare tasks and housework corresponded with the description provided by the middle generation. Mr Jiang acknowledged that initially there had been no clear communication or negotiation in the family as to how the tasks should be shared among the senior and middle generations. He described the division of labor as "a naturally evolving process." This "natural process" meant that his mother was loaded both with childcare tasks as well as the bulk of the household chores. It was not until Grandmother Jiang could no longer endure it and voiced[2] her difficulties, that the middle generation was alerted to the unbalanced load of housework that she bore. Mr Jiang explained:

> Actually my mother helps me a lot. In addition to caring for the child, she does the marketing, prepares meals for us, and does the bulk of the housework. Of course when we come back from work we [he and his

wife] will share some of the tasks. For instance, my wife will do laundry and tidy the rooms, I will be in charge of supervising the child's school work. My mother cooks, does marketing, washes the dishes, etc. To be honest, it was not divided this way at first. When we [he and his wife] were busy [with work], the *lao ren* 老人 (older person) did most of the housework. Later, my mother had some complaints and I realized that I was in the wrong about this, because she is here to assist us. After letting the domestic helper go we probably pushed most of the jobs onto her. I reflected on it and made some division of labor among us … after I came back from working in Beijing I had all three of us sit down and draw up a clearer plan. Perhaps I assumed that my mother would not mind helping us, I supposed she would do anything for us. But from the *lao ren*'s standpoint, she is getting older, and also she might feel she has no obligation to help so much since we have set up a family of our own. She feels that by helping to do grocery shopping and preparing meals, she is already providing sufficient help. That is why I came up with a more detailed division of tasks.

(JJ-F 25/7/06)

Over the two years I knew the family the middle generation made considerable adjustments, not only in terms of a more equitable sharing of the housework but also in their attitude towards the help they received from Grandmother Jiang. Juxtaposing what Mr Jiang told me with the information collected from the paternal grandmother during my first field visit in December 2004 and the six months of field work in 2006, it seems that grandmother felt the attitude of the middle generation did improve over time, and she felt quite comforted by this (JJ-PGM 13/8/06). The middle generation had come to realize that they needed to change their "take it for granted" attitude towards grandmother's help with household chores.

It is interesting to observe the interplay of relational power and agency between the generations in the Jiang family. Despite the reallocation of household chores, Grandmother Jiang was still the caregiver who spent the most time with the child. She was the one who picked him up from school and had to face first-hand his teachers' grievances about unfinished homework or undesirable behavior in class. Grandmother felt much stress having to face all these complaints, but said she did not have the power to punish her grandson, and felt her daughter-in-law did not like her strict ways with the boy. Hence, to avoid conflicts, she refrained from disciplining the child. Instead she achieved the desired outcome by influencing her son to act on her behalf. If Grandmother Jiang's complaints were heard and translated into disciplinary action by her adult son, this would mean that her position in the home was acknowledged. However, her way of exercising indirect power of influence often seemed to backfire as it strained her relationship with her daughter-in-law as well as her grandson.

According to Mr Jiang, his mother loved to complain. He attributed this to the fact that she needed something to complain about and Jie Jie's noncompliant behaviors not only gave her a basis for her complaints, but also drove her crazy. He described her as "always finding fault" with the boy in any situation. Her complaints revolved around the child's lack of respect for his grandmother, his teacher's negative comments about him, other parents' comments about him, his fights with other children in school, etc. In Mr Jiang's mind, many of these complaints were trivial, but he still needed to listen as any complaints from Jie Jie's schoolteachers were deemed important and so warranted attention and a sign that he might need to take action to deal with the child. However, he found his mother's complaints about the boy's disrespect to her burdensome. Although he had given his mother the authority to discipline the child by spanking him on the buttocks if he misbehaved, as mentioned, however, she refrained from executing any physical punishment. When asked separately how they responded to the complaints and how they felt about being stuck between grandmother and son, Mr and Mrs Jiang had the following responses:

> The effects of these complaints for me [Mr Jiang] is that I need to respond to them, as she [paternal grandmother] is doing it for the good of my son. She has stricter demands on the child, although I don't think much of some of her complaints. She expects me to discipline the child, I feel quite frustrated!
>
> (JJ-F 25/7/06)

> I [Mrs Jiang] have once indirectly and very subtly requested her [paternal grandmother] not to complain in front of the child, I did it very indirectly and carefully. She can complain about almost anything. If the child has completed his school work and behaved well, she would pick on other things like [the grandson] eating too slowly or too quickly, spilling food on the floor, etc. I know my child is not perfect, but *nai nai* (paternal grandmother) has very high standards. It is so much easier with a domestic maid ... with *nai nai*, the situation is very different. Many times we need to show our respect to her by responding to her complaints. If her son [Mr Jiang] does not do anything about it, I need to somehow do something [to appease grandmother].... That is why I feel the child is both the lubricant [of the intergenerational relationships] as well as the victim ... sometimes he gets a spanking from us after we have listened to all these complaints.
>
> (JJ-M 1/08/06)

It seems the middle generation was sandwiched between the senior and junior generations in these situations. The pressure they received from the grandmother directly influenced how they handled their son. Although Mr Jiang claimed that he felt frustrated and tired from handling these complaints on a daily basis, he thought he had never over-punished his son under pressure. He was worried that overpunishing the child might cause the child to hate him or leave him one day (JJ-F 25/7/06, p. 6). Still, according to Mr Jiang, some spanking that he inflicted on his son was not due to the grandmother's complaints. Instead, he undertook the spanking because he felt that the child deserved it. Mrs Jiang felt quite differently, however. Her remark that her son was both the lubricant and victim provides an intriguing and perhaps enlightening reflection on the unique characteristics of the Chinese parenting coalition of multiple caregivers. The need to "save grandmother's face" sometimes drove her to actions which she later regretted or felt were unwarranted.

It can be seen that Grandmother Jiang often struggled with her own ambivalent feelings. On the one hand, she thought she should altruistically render help to her adult son; on the other hand, she felt unfairly treated and exhausted. Grandmother said that her dream of retirement was as a time of freedom. She had hoped to enter the *lao ren da xiu* 老人大学 (university for elders) and to spend more time with her husband, as they had lived apart for many years owing to work commitments (Field notes 16/5/2006). But these dreams could not be realized. Also, the exhaustion from caring for her grandson and doing house chores had taken a toll on her health. From my interactions with Grandmother Jiang and analysis of transcripts, field notes, and memos I realized that in addition to this physical exhaustion there was another source of exhaustion: the feeling of being taken for granted. She told me that she felt her daughter-in-law and son treated her like a domestic helper when she first came to live with them:

> It sounds awful, but when I first came to help them, I was treated like a *bao mu* 保母 (domestic helper). In fact my life here is exactly like a *bao mu*. Of course, I know I should not think this way as I am helping my own child and grandchild. But in reality, am I not like a live-in helper? I do all the chores in the house.
>
> (JJ-PGM 13/8/2006)

It was not uncommon for Grandmother Jiang to well up in tears when talking to me. Her ambivalent emotions were evident. On the one hand, she felt she could not disappoint her adult son; on the other hand she felt her son and daughter-in-law neither appreciated how tough it was for her to shoulder all these responsibilities nor helped to relieve her of the load. Grandmother Jiang felt she had suffered a great deal of emotional pain during the first two years of helping to care for her grandson. As much as she tried to suppress these feelings, they inevitably manifested themselves in her daily interactions. Although not verified, it is my hunch that one of the channels through which she expressed her ambivalence was the constant complaints she lodged to her son. Instead of overtly expressing her negative emotions about being treated unfairly, she tried to get her son and daughter-in-law's attention by complaining about the trouble her grandson gave her.[3]

Contrary to the image portrayed by the popular media that grandparents are the ones "spoiling" the grandchildren, the Jiang family experienced the reverse. It was the paternal grandmother who was the strictest and most demanding of the three adult caregivers at home. According to Mr Jiang, his mother lacked patience with the child. The middle generation felt she was constantly finding fault with her grandson in areas like cleanliness, respect for elders, and manners. They thought the older lady forgot that children need time to grow. Mr Jiang's own father was strict and authoritative, hence, he vowed to be a very different father. His wife, Mrs Jiang, on the other hand, had grown up in a very liberal family where her parents openly showed affection and indulged her as she was the youngest child. Mrs Jiang deemed her mother-in-law's expectations of the child unrealistic.

> I tend to let him [her seven-year-old son] be spontaneous and have some freedom ... as long as he does not hurt himself or others. For instance, if he sings or plays little games on the public bus, it is fine with me. To me, it is okay to let the child have some fun. I will not restrict him too much. But *nai nai* (paternal grandmother) is stricter. In her eyes, the child has to sit still all the time, otherwise she will keep nagging and scolding him.
>
> (JJ-M 31/7/2006)

Mrs Jiang often felt frustrated by these demands and could only keep the tension at bay by suppressing her own annoyance with the grandmother. When asked whether she had tried to communicate with her mother-in-law, Mrs Jiang told me that "talking" was a dead-end. She believed it was inappropriate and ineffective to have open communication in Chinese families. She consciously lowered her voice during this portion of the interview so that her husband, who was in the next room watching television, could not hear our conversation:

> In China, many daughters-in-law and mothers-in-law cannot get along; I would say 80 percent of them are not on good terms. When I first got married, I was young and naïve, I was direct with her (mother-in-law). But after so many years of weathering this relationship, I have learned this is a dead-end. Many things are just too deep rooted, there is no point talking. When there are *mao dun* 茅盾 (conflicts), I will choose to compromise or try to please both sides [child and grandmother] ....
>
> (JJ-M 1/08/06)

Bird's eye view of the Jiang parenting coalition

From the analysis presented above, it can be seen that although the middle generation was dependent on grandmother providing childcare so that they could work, both parents acknowledged there were challenges and difficulties in the coalition. On the other side of the coin, grandmother's self-imposed obligation to help with the childcare consigned her to a situation marked by great ambivalence. The middle generation loaded the grandmother with an unfair amount of housework along with the childcare, causing her to feel taken for granted, physically exhausted, and bitter. Fortunately, after enduring for two years she exercised her agency in voicing her unhappiness, and her son took positive steps to redistribute the housework load among the three caregivers. The parenting coalition of the Jiang family demonstrates the dialectical nature of bidirectional influences between the senior and middle generations. Although all three adults tried to suppress their sense of ambivalence and minimize contradictions in the coalition, these hidden tensions and undercurrents found their way to bring about antithesis in the system. The Jiang family was the only one among the five families that showed some overt qualitative change at the end of the six months of my fieldwork in Xiamen. Owing to Grandmother Jiang's fast-deteriorating health condition, she was instructed by her doctor to undergo major orthopedic surgery. It was owing to this impending operation that she finally mustered her courage to relinquish the caregiving role and move back to her husband's place (Field notes 13/8/06). This health problem enabled her to relinquish her role as childcare giver and in doing so relieved the ambivalence. Grandmother Jiang confessed that it would have been very difficult for her to find an excuse not to continue in the role without being ill. Hence, we can see her exercising agency through employing the culturally acceptable construct of "a natural consequence owing to ill health." This was able to serve as an excuse that allowed her to exit the coalition in a way that maintained an amicable, long-term relationship with her adult son and daughter-in-law. We also see that the extent to which agency could be exercised by the three adult caregivers was constrained by the dynamics within the intergenerational parenting coalition. This is reflected not only in Grandmother Jiang's sense of obligation to come and help and her limited ability to improve her situation but also the middle generation's need to take the grandmother's complaints about Jie Jie seriously, albeit with much reluctance.

The Wang family

The Wang family had a more complex configuration of the parenting coalition than the Jiang family. The multiple caregivers included the father, mother, the maternal grandmother (who lived under the same roof), and the paternal grandmother (who lived a stone's throw away). These four adults were all caring for one seven-year-old boy, Wei Wei. Unlike Grandmother Jiang, who experienced a great deal of ambivalence, the two grandmothers from the Wang family showed no signs of ambivalence about the parenting arrangement. Not surprisingly, then, the dynamic of this coalition was quite different from that of the Jiangs.

Both grandmothers were illiterate and had been rendering childcare since they retired. The maternal grandmother, an 80-year-old widow, was still active, healthy, and mobile, and helped with meal preparations for the family. The paternal grandmother's role was to ensure the seven-year-old grandson's safe travel to and from school every day. To these two grandmothers, caring for their grandchildren was the best thing they could do after retirement. In fact, the 80-year-old maternal grandmother had been caring for the children of one or another of her other adult children since her retirement 30 years ago. She had seven adult children, two of whom were grandparents themselves, so she was a great-grandmother. To these two grandmothers, "grandparenthood" was a status symbol signifying the fulfillment of the sacred duty of *chuan zong jie dai* 传宗接代 (passing down the family line). Paternal Grandmother Wang talked about how she derived a sense of esteem and pride from this role. For instance, she attributed the fact that her grandson had begun to walk at 11 months to her careful attention to his nutritional needs. Unlike Grandmother Jiang who had a retirement plan before the grandchildren came along, these two grandmothers construed providing childcare as the only meaningful thing to do after retirement. Their agency was expressed in the way in which they constructed the meaning of their "caregiving role" so as to gain a sense of worth from their responsibilities.

As with the Jiangs, the Wangs had no explicit communication as to how the housework was to be shared among the three adults residing under the same roof, namely Mr and Mrs Wang and the maternal grandmother. The middle generation, however, always took the initiative in sharing housework and tried their best not to let either grandmother do too much. They seemed to adopt the attitude that housework and childcare were their responsibility and both the grandmothers were only there to *kan tou kan wei* 看头看尾 (keep an eye) and assist them. Mrs Wang recounted to me the following:

> No, we have never discussed what you want me to do or what I should do: Never! It is a kind of habit. In terms of supervising the child's school work, I feel I should let him [her husband] be responsible. I will keep an eye on the child's piano practice; in terms of coaching school work, he is the one doing it. If he is not at home, I will stand in. I am always at home. To me, the *lao ren* (old person) is just here to *kan tou kan wei* (keep an eye) [while the middle generation is at work]. I do not have expectations of them [the grandmothers].
>
> (WW-F 24/7/06)

Although there was no explicit discussion or communication about role division, the initiative taken by the middle generation to lighten the older person's load made the workings of the coalition rather smooth. It is therefore my suspicion that the middle generation's proactivity (exercising

agency to help) in sharing housework and showing care for the older generation through action, rather than taking them for granted, is a significant
factor influencing positive collaboration and the workings of the parenting
coalition.

Although the four members of the Wang intergenerational parenting
coalition were all content with the arrangement, this does not mean that
power was equally distributed among its four members. Mr Wang seemed
to have the strongest power of influence among the four. He exercised his
relational power of influence with each of the coalition members so as to
ensure smooth coordination within it. Both the grandmothers and his wife
would all confer with him in matters relating to the child. He would usually
make the decisions and the other adults execute them. But, as can be seen in
the analysis, this parenting coalition was not without problems.

Although paternal Grandmother Wang was happy providing childcare,
she had some concerns about disciplining the child, who constantly pestered
her to buy snacks and toys on the way home from school. She "did not dare"
to administer discipline as her daughter-in-law and son might not like it,
since they were much more educated than she. Nevertheless, she would call
her son at any time of the day at his office to complain about the grandson's
misbehaviors or vent her frustrations. Like Grandmother Jiang, this was
possibly a channel for her to validate her role as a caregiver.

I had the opportunity to witness an episode during an unplanned home
visit (Field notes 30/4/06). One afternoon, after visiting another family, I
was walking back to my apartment. As I passed near her apartment,
paternal Grandmother Wang could be seen rushing back to her home in
fury. She gestured to me to come along with her to her apartment on the
sixth floor. As we climbed the stairs, she recounted to me how her grandson
had wasted her money by misplacing a brand new yo-yo which she had
bought him the day before. The moment she stepped into her apartment,
she headed for the phone and called her son (Mr Wang). She huffed and
puffed while complaining to her son, using their dialect which I could not
understand. But her expression and volume made it unmistakable that she
was conveying her fury to him. She told me afterwards that she had asked
him to punish the grandson and said she would be physically present that
evening (they live only a stone's throw apart) to make sure that the child
received the spanking he deserved. This kind of bombardment from the
paternal grandmother seemed to be common. Mr Wang had to handle it
alone, at the same time working out how many of these complaints to filter
away. He saw himself as a buffer between his mother and his son. To Mr
Wang, harmony should be maintained within the family at all cost.

To avoid any complications in handling the complaints from her mother-
in-law, Mrs Wang retreated from the scene as much as possible. Hence, Mr
Wang bore the brunt of the unpleasant complaints. Since the paternal
grandmother was the one who took the grandson to and from school, she
was naturally the one who would report in detail to her son about the child's

little misbehaviors: how he pestered her to buy snacks and toys for him along the way from school, how he refused to cooperate with his grandmother, etc. When relating these incidents to me, Mr Wang's facial expression was one of helplessness. He felt he could not stop his mother from complaining, as he deemed that as being disrespectful, so he would just have to endure them.

> From my perspective, these [little misbehaviors] are a normal part of growing up. But she [paternal grandmother] feels they are wrong, the child should not do this or that. I feel I cannot argue with her. I just tell her I would take note of what she said. But whether I will actually discipline the child, she would not know [because they do not live under the same roof]. I find these complaints quite a headache. In my workplace I have enough headaches. When I come home I have to handle all this nagging from my mother, and I feel very frustrated. In the past, I would transfer these frustrations to the child by overly reprimanding him. But these days, I have adjusted myself. I filter what she tells me. I will think through what she said, and decide for myself whether what the child did was right or wrong or just part and parcel of growing up. I will try my best to protect my mother's interest. I will not convey everything she complained about to my son so that the child does not have ill feelings for *nai nai.*
>
> (WW-F 24/07/06)

Mr Wang always performed this balancing act very attentively. He acted as a buffer and filtered out content he assessed as unfair or unnecessary, finding ways to communicate with Wei Wei on issues that he thought warranted attention. He would consider the interests of the adults as well as the child. Moreover, Mr and Mrs Wang did make an effort to put up a united front for the coalition so as to lend power to the grandparents. When asked what would be his response if the grandmothers disciplined Wei Wei, he said:

> We [he and his wife] have this practice that no matter who disciplines [the child], we will show our support. Whether the discipline was warranted or not, we will deal with it later. We will not side with the child against any adult.

Mr Wang, being the adult with most power of influence, used this method of allocating some of his power to the other coalition members. The middle generation took care to share the work load, show appreciation and accord power to the grandmothers.

As mentioned earlier, these two grandmothers considered providing childcare to be the only option left for them after retirement. But this perceived lack of choice did not lead to a negative experience. In fact there was no apparent tension between these grandmothers and the middle generation beyond that mentioned above. Although both grandmothers were illiterate, they felt respected and appreciated. Unlike Grandmother Jiang who had difficulty coping with the heavy house chores, this 80-year-old maternal grandmother who resided with the family thought that doing housework, cooking, and caring for the grandson was good for her as these activities kept her active and healthy. Besides, she reported that her daughter and son-in-law were proactive in sharing the load. In the evenings, the middle generation would take over the house chores and supervision of the child. When asked her motive for caring for grandchildren, the maternal grandmother remarked, "Parents cannot leave their children and children cannot leave parents, it all begins with breast feeding (父母离不开儿女, 儿女也离不开父母. 从吃奶开始就是这样)." She also felt comforted that her son-in-law was easy to get along with and showed her due respect. Moreover, she was glad that her son-in-law would give her pocket money on his own accord, although she had a pension and did not need the money, and her daughter would take her shopping for clothes during spring festival (WW-MGM 4/8/06). She felt appreciated. The relationship between maternal grandmother and the middle generation under one roof seemed blissful.

The analysis presented thus far should not give the reader a wrong impression that this parenting coalition was free of problems. In fact, the age-old sensitivity between mother-in-law and daughter-in-law existed in the Wang family too. Mrs Wang told me she would avoid any communication with her mother-in-law as far as she could.

> Not everything can be discussed between daughter-in-law and mother-in-law. It will be lucky if the communication goes well. Anything that is not pleasant, I will not say. I will let my husband talk to her. I usually will not talk much to my mother-in-law. Even when she comes over to my apartment, I will not tell her anything.
>
> (WW-M 21/07/06)

It is well documented that the relationship between mother-in-law and daughter-in-law is one of the most difficult in Chinese families (Logan *et al.* 1998, Hu 1995). Hence, it is no surprise that the dyad experiences struggles and perhaps discomfort with each other. However, Mrs Wang chose to tolerate the slight tension that came with this somewhat fraught relationship. To manage it she created both physical and emotional distance between herself and her mother-in-law so as to maintain a cordial relationship. The paternal grandmother on the other hand commented that she would communicate with her son and rarely with her daughter-in-law. She claimed that her Putonghua 普通话(Mandarin) is not fluent (she speaks a variant of the Minnan dialect) and thus that she has difficulty communicating with her daughter-in-law. Acknowledging there were some differences in childrearing methods the paternal grandmother said she would readily give in to her daughter-in-law and son since they were more educated than she was. She did not seem bothered by the lack of communication (Field note 24 Jul 2006).

Bird's eye view of the Wang parenting coalition

The Wang family was rather successful in maintaining a relatively cohesive coalition among the four adult caregivers. Mr Wang, the person who held the most power, played a pivotal role in coordinating all the members and attending to the interests of each party involved. He was an effective head of the team and the caregivers all ceded leadership to him. It was obvious that Mr Wang led the coalition through his relational power. Also noteworthy was the function of distance in this family. Unlike the Jiang family, where the grandmother who tended to complain was residing under the same roof, paternal Grandmother Wang, who often lodged complaints against her grandson to Mr Wang, was off the premises, albeit nearby. Although the apartments of Mr Wang and his elder brother (where paternal grandmother resided) were within the same estate and approximately three minutes walking distance apart, this short distance provided a breathing space where Mr Wang could filter and buffer the complaints about his son. In addition, this space also gave him the liberty to calibrate the degree of discipline he deemed most appropriate without having to be put under the type of pressure that Mr Jiang experienced. Hence, it seems the Chinese ideal distance of *duan yi wan re tang bu liang* 揣一碗热汤不凉 (a bowl of hot soup will not turn cold when taken between two households) served this family well.

The Tian family

The composition of the Tian family's parenting coalition is again different from either the Jiangs or the Wangs. The members of the coalition were the maternal grandparents, and the father and mother. The maternal grandparents shuttled between Xiamen and their hometown in *Nan Pin* every three months. Hence, they periodically resided under the same roof as their adult daughter, son-in-law, and 10-year-old granddaughter. Unlike the grandparents in the previous two families, this pair of grandparents exercised a fairly high level of agency and power of influence but they also experienced an intense sense of ambivalence. Yet, there was no sign that they intended to quit their caregiving roles.

Both of the Tian grandparents were retired high government officials who enjoyed comfortable pensions. They had their own apartment in Nan Ping (about three hours' bus ride away from Xiamen). It was their choice to help their adult daughter's family with childcare periodically, hence the arrangement whereby they stayed alternately in the two locations.

Grandmother Tian described herself as a person who needed something to keep her occupied. Spending time with her daughter's family in Xiamen made her feel useful as she relieved her daughter of much of the house chores and cooking. Besides, the older couple thought it their duty to "lend" strength to their "weak" daughter against her sometimes violent husband. The grandparents construed their giving as "altruistic" as they saw their daughter as needing help. Unlike Grandmother Jiang, who had to deal with expectations imposed on her by an adult son to provide childcare against her will, this pair of grandparents chose to provide help of their own accord.

Unlike the two grandmothers in the Wang family, the Tian grandparents took part in many social and recreational activities after retirement. For instance, Grandfather Tian loved to dance and often travelled back to *Nan Ping* for dancing classes and competitions (Field notes 4/8/06). Grandparents Tian were very conscious of the sacrifices they made in providing help to their daughter in Xiamen. Not only were the Tian grandparents self-motivated in their decision to join the intergenerational parenting coalition, they did not allow their daughter or son-in-law to dictate their comings or goings. They decided for themselves when to come to Xiamen to help out or return to their hometown to rest, when to be with their adult son's family. Grandfather Tian frequently returned to his home town to take part in senior dance competitions. Clearly they retained a good amount of autonomy in their caregiving role.

Although they took on many of the household chores when in Xiamen, the grandparents did not feel overburdened as their adult daughter often took the initiative to help. Moreover, the family was financially comfortable and engaged an hourly rated domestic helper to do the heavy chores. Hence, the grandparents' role was focused on meal preparation and light housework.

Mr Tian, the son-in-law, acknowledged that his in-laws were a great help in relieving the family of the housework load and making their lives much more relaxed:

> They [maternal grandparents] come to stay with us because they think we need their help. *Lao ren jia* (old people) would sometimes feel lonely, so they can chat with their daughter and interact with their granddaughter. I think it benefits both sides. They are most welcome to stay with us because it reduces our load. House chores are a big burden. When my parents-in-law are here, we don't have to worry about meals … washing the vegetables or preparation. Once we come back from work the meal is ready. When they are not around, there are many things to attend to. But when they are here, we feel very relaxed.
>
> (TT-F 31/7/06)

Mr Tian's narrative reveals his interpretation of the help he received from his parents-in-law and how he responded to his own interpretation. In spite of acknowledging their (middle generation's) dependence on the senior generation, he chose to think that it was also for the benefit of the older couple. From his perspective, "old people sometimes feel lonely" and coming to stay in Xiamen periodically allowed the grandparents to ease their loneliness by having their adult daughter and granddaughter to chat with. The grandparents, by contrast, felt they were making sacrifices to play the caring role and perceived themselves more at the giving end of the relationship. There is an obvious discrepancy in how the two generations perceived the giving and receiving of help. This might have contributed, at least in part, to the lack of explicit expression of gratitude on the part of the son-in-law and consequently the feeling of being taken for granted by the grandparents.

It was interesting to observe the turf Mr Tian carved out for himself from the range of childcare tasks and housework. He took on the role of academic supervision for the child, which he deemed as the most important of the whole range of tasks performed by the parenting coalition. He believed that the other adult members did not have the ability to supervise the child. In addition, he frequently did the daily marketing for the family early in the morning. However, the maternal grandparents did not appreciate this as he did not consider their dietary preferences, which left them having to buy what they wanted to eat. Other than these two tasks, Mr Tian washed his hands of other duties.

The way interdependent power was played out among the four adult members of the Tian family's coalition was very different from the earlier families. In contrast to the unanimous deference given to Mr Wang, who had assumed the headship of the Wang family coalition, the parenting coalition of the Tian family was one of competing power.

Compared with the grandparents discussed earlier, this pair of grandparents seemed to assert more influence and power in their relations with the middle generation. This assertiveness could also be seen in the way the grandparents openly and sometimes indiscriminately criticized their daughter in front of me, an outsider. During my visits the adult daughter readily submitted to their criticisms and took the "one-down" position. For instance, during one visit, Grandmother Tian criticized her daughter's child-drearing methods as inferior in front of me. I felt somewhat embarrassed for the daughter, but to my surprise Mrs Tian smiled in agreement with her mother (Field notes 5/05/06). The Tian grandparents also interfered regularly when their son-in-law disciplined his 10-year-old daughter, and protected the child from punishment. Grandmother Tian commented:

He [son-in-law] is worried that we will protect her [granddaughter] ... it is not unreasonable for us [grandparents] to side with her. He hits the child so severely, don't you think we have to do something? Marks [from spanking] all over the body [of the child], bruises all over .... Yes, she [child] is very mischievous, she does not *ting hua* 听话 (obey). Children are like a piece of blank paper, we adults can paint them green or red, it is up to us. We should not blame the child.

(TT-MGM 1/08/06)

This disagreement with the way their son-in-law punished the child physically came in part from their own history. In their experience as parents during the era of political upheaval between the 1960s and 1980s, they felt that their two children had grown up without much parental attention and supervision and yet turned out fine.[4] The grandparents also blamed their son-in-law for setting a bad example to his daughter, and hence they aligned themselves with the child against her father. The power this brought them within the coalition was derived also from being a couple. That this pair of grandparents formed a dyad within the coalition made them more powerful, unlike Grandmother Jiang who had to live apart from her husband in order to render care. Also, Grandparents Tian exercised their personal power in the sense that they believed that, being highly educated and having a wealth of life experience, they knew what was best for their grandchild.

The Tian family fit the popular image of strict parents and lenient grandparents. Mr Tian believed his seemingly harsh parenting strategies were working well, as reflected in the improvement in the child's school results. During my participant observation of the family dynamics, I noticed that the maternal grandparents often sabotaged Mr Tian's tactics for handling Tian Tian by criticizing their son-in-law in front of their grandchild. The grandparents did not hide their displeasure and disagreement with their son-in-law's parenting style (Field notes 5/5/06). Hence, in the Tian family, the clashes over childrearing values were overt, rather than hidden or covert as was the case with the Jiang family. When asked if he felt his in-laws interfered with his parenting efforts, interestingly Mr Tian said he did not think there was a problem. He commented:

I don't see any complications. Everyone [the four adults] plays his own role. I am in charge of Tian Tian's academic work. If they [grandparents] think I am too harsh and want me to change, I will make some adjustments. Maybe sometimes I would reduce the use of ... [physical punishment]. But I do not deliberately change myself just because the grandparents are around. I take things naturally.

(TT-F 31/07/06)

As can be seen from Mr Tian's narrative, although he would occasionally heed the grandparents' appeals, in general he was oblivious to the protests they staged. He was confident that the concrete school results would speak for themselves and ultimately prove that he was right.

Mrs Tian, like her parents, did not see eye to eye with her husband about the way he dealt with the child. However, she felt powerless to change his style. Hence, she tended to form an alliance with her parents against her husband. The difference in childrearing philosophies was not only intergenerational but also intragenerational in nature. As a researcher I could feel the subtle undercurrents of tension and strife as grandparents and their adult daughter aligned against Mr Tian. Nevertheless, Mrs Tian did sometimes feel her parents were overindulgent towards her daughter and wished they could be more firm with the child.

> I sometimes wish that my parents can be more firm with the girl [Tian Tian]. They tend to gave in to her whims and fancies. I am trying to teach her [Tian Tian] how to budget. When they give her money on demand, it spoiled my plans. Sometimes when I am discussing ways to handle Tian Tian with my husband, my parents will barge in and give their opinions. I don't quite like that. Although I told my parents about how I feel, they disregarded what I said.
>
> (TT-M 31/07/06)

Interestingly, although the Tian grandparents exercised a high level of agency in their decision to participate in this coalition, they did experience a rather high level of ambivalent feelings in their relationship with the middle generation, especially with their son-in-law. They often vented their unhappiness about him to me when I visited them. For instance, the grandmother revealed the following:

> *Wu laoshi* 吴老师 (referring to me as "teacher" as I was the English tutor for the grandchild), since we know you very well,[5] I am telling you about this. My son-in-law is calculative until the last cent. If there is money left from the grocery shopping, he expects me to return the change to him, even though it can be just one yuan. Usually he does not give me enough and I have to fork out money from my own pocket. I was a senior engineer, yet he treats me as less than a domestic helper. With a helper you have to pay her a salary. I come here to help for free and yet I have to supplement the household expenses!
>
> (Field notes 11/08/06)

Grandmother Tian was unhappy that her son-in-law (who was in charge of the household's finances) was explicitly skimming off the elders even though the middle generation earned a comfortable combined income. The grandparents were not expecting monetary rewards as they were financially independent. Nevertheless, they wanted to feel appreciated for their efforts and did not expect to receive this kind of calculative treatment from their son-in-law. They were also disappointed that the middle generation did not remember their birthdays, and that although their son-in-law paid lip service to the idea of taking them for trips these never materialized.

The other factor which contributed to Grandparents Tian's sense of ambivalence about their caregiving roles was the lack of a social network in Xiamen:

Grandmother Tian:	Whenever I go back to my home town, all my friends say they missed me ... when I go back I get to play badminton or poker games with my friends.
Researcher:	When you are in Xiamen you don't have time for all these?
Grandmother Tian:	Oh, no time at all, I am so busy fixing three meals a day for the family here ... also, there are so many chores to attend to. I used to go for exercise back home, but I don't get to do it in Xiamen.
Researcher:	It is a big sacrifice!
Grandmother Tian:	Over here [Xiamen] I feel very lonely, alien to the environment. I can't speak the language [the local dialect is Minnan]. Two years ago I tried to join in a dance group in a neighboring primary school, but I could not make it. During that time, Tian Tian [the granddaughter] was in kindergarten and I had to take her to and from school. I am a very optimistic and sociable person, I love to have activities, but now my lifestyle is very different. Well, since I am old now, I have to accept it.

(TT-MGM 1/08/06)

Despite this intense sense of ambivalence, Grandmother Tian showed no signs of withdrawing her help. She told me she would help until her physical health did not permit it. In a sense, the Tian grandparents chose to tolerate their situation instead of resolving their strong sense of ambivalence. Their adult daughter and son-in-law, on the other hand, experienced little or no ambivalence in their collaboration with the grandparents in the parenting coalition. The adult daughter, for one, was always grateful for the support from her parents. And, despite all the overt displeasure that his parents-in law showed toward Mr Tian, he claimed he did not feel any difficulty about having the grandparents around.

Bird's eye view of the Tian family

In the Tian family, differences in childrearing philosophy created a "battle-field" where members of the intergenerational parenting coalition sought to gain the upper hand for their power of influence. The coalition was split into two opposing forces, one composed of the relatively powerful grandparents, sometimes together with their adult daughter, the other, the son-in-law. Although in the Jiang family there were also hidden tensions and undercurrents within the coalition, the scenario in the Tian family is slightly different. Here the conflicts were more overt. However, it is interesting to observe that this coalition continued to function despite these disagreements. Mr Tian seemed to cope by turning a blind eye to the opposition. Even though the unhappy and ambivalent emotions were real to the grandparents, they chose to continue as part of the coalition because they saw it as their duty to support their daughter.

The Bai family

Unlike the other three families discussed, the intergenerational parenting coalition in the Bai family was composed of only one member from the two generations (senior and middle). This small coalition was made up of the maternal grandmother and her adult daughter, who was recently divorced. Together they jointly cared for a five-year-old child, Bei Bei.

Maternal Grandmother Bai was the youngest among all the grandparents in the study. After her granddaughter's birth five years ago, she took early retirement at age 50 from her lower management job in a state-run factory, and relocated to Xiamen to provide childcare. Since then she has coresided with her daughter and granddaughter. This caregiving role's main positive aspect was that it provided an escape route from her own strained marriage. However, Grandmother Bai did not get along well with her daughter. According to her, her agency and initiative in providing help had evolved into a kind of entrapment. As with Grandmother Jiang, Grandmother Bai's life now basically revolved around her five-year-old granddaughter's schedule and she had no time to herself. She had endured it for five years, and often asked herself how much longer she would remain tied down. However, this older lady could not see herself leaving the coalition as she had the typical Chinese grandparents' sense of "self-imposed obligation" where she thought she could not leave her adult daughter, especially after the latter was divorced and needed help. An understanding of the relationship between the two caretakers can be seen in Madam Bai's unapologetic (if not condescending) attitude when she told me that she left most of the housework to her mother:

> To be honest, there is no clear division of work. But...hmm, my mother is that kind who does not think or plan things. She can't handle anything that requires thinking. Of course I will not push everything to her and go out to enjoy myself. But I will let her do the simple tasks. I am lazy sometimes and let her do such chores as doing the dishes, or some other things that do not require too much skill. Besides, I really dislike doing dishes, so I hardly do it. But things related to the child, I will do more. These kinds of things you need to think about. You see, after I come home from work there are things I still need to think about ...sometimes, she [grandmother] will complain about me looking so

tired ... she has been out of the working world too long, she is kind of outdated, she does not understand.

(BB-F 30/7/06)

This account of a lop-sided division of housework corresponded to my observations during several home visits made when the grandmother was busy doing laundry by hand, or cooking (Field notes 7/5/07, 14/5/06). Madam Bai exercised her agency at the expense of her mother. At the cognitive level, Madam Bai constructed for herself a rationale to justify her lack of motivation to do the menial housework: she felt tired after a day's work in the office; house chores were "simple tasks that did not require skills" and thus suitable for grandmother as the latter is a simple-minded person. It is interesting to note that the grandmother's exhaustion after caring for the child, doing housework, and preparing meals the whole day was not taken into consideration. Madam Bai neither showed appreciation (at least not explicitly) for what grandmother did nor actively helped to relieve her load. Instead, she sometimes blamed her for not understanding a working person's tiredness after a day's work in the office. The grandmother sometimes threw tantrums at her daughter, protesting her heavy housework load or retaliating for her daughter's rude attitudes. Madam Bai's "take-for-granted" attitude can partly be explained by the involuntary nature of parent–child relationships where neither partner can easily leave the relationship (Kuczynski 2003). This problem could be more prevalent in Chinese society as the middle generation's dependence and the senior generation's need to give are deemed socially acceptable and make it possible for these two hands to clap.

Data collected separately from the grandmother and adult daughter converged as they both assessed their relationship as strained in part because: the household chores were unevenly distributed; Madam Bai kept her mother out of her personal problems; and they had frequent conflicts based on various differences of opinion. The adult daughter thought her mother was a simple-minded person and did not want to disclose her own struggles and pains of divorce to her. Grandmother, on the other hand, felt alienated and rejected, kept in the dark about the divorce. Grandmother Bai said she did not mind the heavy housework load, but felt hurt by the way her adult daughter treated her:

She [daughter] often raises her voice at me, it makes me very upset inside. I am doing everything for her. If she had to engage a domestic helper, it would cost her one thousand yuan. I do everything free of charge for her. I care for the child, cook and work from morning to night, do laundry and house chores ... I told her I do not blame her. I understand she has her own struggles. I do all this out of love and I take pity on her. If I didn't love her, I could have led my own life after retirement.

There was a clear imbalance of power between these two women. In relation to the adult daughter, Grandmother Bai appeared low in all the three sources of power namely, relational, personal, and cultural. Grandmother wished to have a close bond with her daughter, but Madam Bai shut her mother out of her emotional life and preferred to keep her own struggles and grief over her broken marriage to herself. This left Grandmother Bai with little relational power of influence over her daughter, since she did not allow her mother to get close to her. In terms of personal resource, the adult daughter was a successful professional with a high income, whereas grandmother was deemed to be a simple-minded retired person who was out of touch with the working world. Culturally, Grandmother Bai did not occupy the prestigious, high position that grandparents once used to occupy in traditional China.

Madam Bai showed no inhibition when she vented to me her frustrations about her mother. She acknowledged that she was impatient by nature, but felt her mother aggravated her temper. From her perspective, her mother was too simplistic, absent-minded, and stubborn. She admitted that she sometimes lost her temper with her mother, especially when the older person did not follow her instructions regarding childcare practices. She felt bad about raising her voice at her mother in front of her daughter, but felt she could not help it:

> Initially I did try to pull my mother aside when we had disagreements. But now my daughter has grown older, she notices the tension between us [mother and grandmother] and tails behind us. My mother is easily irritated, when I want to talk to her nicely, she becomes impatient. So now, I will just tell her when I disagree. I know those [parenting] books say adults should settle their differences away from the children so that they will not manipulate us, but in reality it is very difficult.
>
> (BB-M 30/07/06)

Madam Bai seemed to think her ways and methods were superior to her mother's and therefore had little motivation to understand the grandmother's perspective. Of the five families participating in this study, this is the smallest parenting coalition but the one filled with the most open conflicts, contradictions, and ambivalence. As mentioned earlier, coalitions that involved mother-in-law and daughter-in-law (as in the cases of the Jiang and Wang families) were challenging, as it is probably one of the most difficult relationships in Chinese families. However, it seems the contradictions between mother-in-law and daughter-in-law tended to be hidden. Data from the Bai family shows that a daughter–mother coalition is not necessarily blissful. In fact, open conflicts were common occurrences in this coalition.

During casual chats with Grandmother Bai she often lamented that she was tied down and could not do things as she wished. Whenever I had a chance to chat individually with her, she would be sobbing quite intensely and vented continuously about her bitter life (Field notes 19/05/06, 2/06/06).[6] Grandmother Bai told me that given a choice, she would have liked to enjoy her retirement and lead a carefree life. She thought there was potential in her that had had no chance of being realized as she had been locked into marriage, work, childbearing, and childrearing all these years. She believed that now that she was retired, and was healthy and physically strong, she could participate in sports, and take up painting and music classes and other leisure activities. However, since she was caring for her grandchild, she was tied down.

The other factor that accentuated her sense of ambivalence was the lack of a support network. Like the Tian grandparents, she relocated to Xiamen after retirement from another county in Fujian province in order to care for her then newly born granddaughter. After her daughter's divorce, she felt an even greater sense of obligation to stay on and help. Although Grandmother Bai's husband had also relocated to Xiamen, she had limited contact with him as their marital relationship was chronically strained. She described her life in Xiamen as one of isolation:

Researcher: Do you have friends in Xiamen?
Grandmother Bai: Very few. One older lady staying in a nearby block called me on the phone and asked me to visit her in her apartment twice, and we went shopping once. I don't like to trouble people … In fact I would love to enjoy my own life. I like to go traveling, take pictures. But I can't, I need to be here.

(BB-MGM 7/08/06)

As noted above, the misery experienced by Grandmother Bai was not confined only to her own isolation and lack of personal time but also the tension-filled day-to-day interaction with her daughter. Grandmother expressed puzzlement over her daughter's bad temper. Her only comfort in this helping role came from the close bond with her five-year-old granddaughter. "It gives me some joy sometimes when I watch Bei Bei play. I taught her many nursery rhymes and she kept singing them" (BB-MGM 7/08/02). During the day when Bei Bei attended kindergarten class, Grandmother Bai would sometimes do little things to cheer herself up. As she did not have friends in Xiamen, she would visit the vegetable market or browse books in the public library or book stalls for a few hours before she picked up the child around noon (Field notes 27/08/06). Although the adult daughter acknowledged that her mother had been a great help to her since the child's birth, she rarely showed appreciation explicitly. That caused the grandmother to feel that she was doing a thankless job. But she continued the caregiving role despite her unhappiness because she believed her daughter was all alone after the divorce and considered the help she rendered as the "natural" duty of a grandmother.

One area of constant conflict in the mother–daughter coalition pertained to childrearing practices. Madam Bai felt she had developed her own parenting ideology, which was very different from her mother's. All the middle generation parents in this study, including Madam Bai, were born and raised in the 1960s or early 70s, which was right in the midst of the cultural revolution, an epoch of Chinese history marked by intense political upheaval and campaigns. In addition, China as a nation went through difficult times like the three years of natural disasters in the 1960s, where 30 million died of starvation (Pomfret 2006), and extremely low wages under the state-controlled planned economy. Parents were busy making ends meet. Madam Bai described the way she and her younger sister grew up:

> When I was growing up, it was a very different era. We were all poor. Also, she [mother] did not invest much effort in bringing us up. My sister and I were somehow *la che da de* 拉扯大的 (pulled and dragged along). My mother did not have experience as a parent. But I am different. If I am in doubt, I will read up. Perhaps I am going by the book ... but I feel my mother is not concerned about methods.
>
> (BB-M 30/7/06)

For these reasons, Madam Bai perceived the senior generation's way of handling children as inadequate and to some extent inferior. For instance, Madam Bai was often upset that her mother would not persevere in executing an instruction to the child until the child complied. She believed that giving in to the child would spawn undesirable behaviors.

Another area of ambivalence for Madam Bai concerned household chores. As discussed earlier, Madam Bai tended to leave the bulk of the housework to her mother. She also easily tired of listening to the grandmother's complaints about her exhaustion from housework. As noted earlier, she claimed that the grandmother threw tantrums to protest her heavy load of housework. She felt the grandmother's exhaustion was self-inflicted as she had offered to engage a part-time domestic helper to do the chores, but grandmother refused:

> I told her I will engage a part-time maid. But the *lao ren* (old person) felt it was a waste of money and preferred to do it herself. Of course it would mean incurring extra expense, but I pay for everything at home. She is really so *mao dun* 茅盾 (self-contradictory). She wants to save money for me by doing all the work, but then feels exhausted and vents her frustrations on me.
>
> (BB-F 30/07/06)

It was intriguing to hear from the two sides of the same coin. The conflicts and ambivalence persisted between the dyad as they could not arrive at a common understanding or an agreed way to resolve the differences.

Bird's eye view of the Bai family

Despite the frequent conflicts and mutual dissatisfaction between Grand-mother Bai and her adult daughter, neither had any intention of leaving the coalition. They were bound together by two cords: the lack of options and their love for the grandchild. For Grandmother Bai, residing under one roof with her adult daughter and grandchild was a way to escape from her strained marriage. Besides, her self-imposed obligation to her daughter made it almost impossible for her to consider other options. On the part of Madam Bai, although she had many complaints about her mother, she knew she needed her help with childcare as she had no other support network. The other important cord that bound them together was the love for the child, Bei Bei. The welfare of the child was always their highest concern. In fact, the child was a mediator between the two adults, as will be presented in the next chapter.

The Fu family

The last family in this study was included as an anomaly so as to allow us to compare and contrast with the other four families. This family was different in three aspects, namely socio-economic background, configuration of the parenting coalition, and the number of children cared for. The Fu family had migrated from rural Sichuan province to Xiamen more than a decade before as unskilled workers in search of employment. When he found that he needed to live away from home in order to secure a factory job, Mr Fu, the adult son, divorced three years ago, and unable to take care of his two sons, sought the help of his parents who gladly took in the two boys and assumed the role of surrogate parents. Hence, the parenting coalition was dominated by Grandparents Fu, with the middle generation playing only a peripheral role. The two boys resided under the same roof as their grand-parents in a small slum quarter for migrant workers.

In this family, the analysis of the sense of agency will not look at division of childcare tasks and housework, as the middle generation did not reside under the same roof, so there was no sharing of tasks. Instead, agency could be reflected in how the senior generation constructed meaning in taking on the role of surrogate parents and the middle generation's construct of receiving help from the senior generation. My interactions and relationship with this migrant family as a researcher challenged and shifted the assump-tions and subjective perceptions I had brought with me into the field. In my mind, since grandfather was a security guard with a meager income and the illiterate Grandmother Fu worked as a part-time cleaner, having to care for the two grandsons must be a burden to them. It was also my subjective assumption that this burden was unfair to the grandparents as they had to shoulder all the responsibilities in raising the two boys. The grandparents proved me wrong by their positive attitude about their caring role. They thought it was "no big deal" to raise their two grandsons alone with the middle generation only marginally involved.

The important driving force behind this commitment was what grandfather termed *qin qing* 亲情 (blood ties):

> Grandfather taking care of grandson is a duty given by heaven ... life is hard, but when they are grown up, things will be much better. Every year passes very quickly, one year after another, the children will be grown up in no time. By then, they will be independent and have no need to depend on us anymore ....
>
> (FS/FC-PGF, 8/08/06)

This pair of grandparents demonstrated a high sense of agency at all three levels: autonomy, construct, and action. They made a volitional decision to take over the grandsons without it being imposed on them. Their perception of the role as "heavenly duty" enabled them to take on the task willingly and without any bitterness or sense of unfairness. They did not just provide custodial care to the boys, but took proactive action by saving money for their education and nurturing high educational aspirations in their grandchildren. Grandparents Fu were like parents to the two boys.

The 32-year-old Mr Fu was the eldest of three adult children in the Fu family. The entire family, including his parents and both his sisters, had completed rural–urban migration to Xiamen. Mr Fu was a construction worker and lived at the construction site. When I asked him whether he thought his parents were obliged to help him with childcare or had made the choice freely, he replied:

Mr Fu: No, no, it was not an obligation, they chose to help me out. It is a matter of choice. My parents helped lighten my load. This is how I feel.

Researcher: What kind of load are you referring to?

Mr Fu: Both financial and practical burdens, they have helped me a lot. Sometimes I cannot raise enough funds for the boys' school fees,[7] and they will chip in. My parents are very understanding. My sisters also help me. Without all this help ... the pressure will be too great for me to bear. So I think I am rather lucky.

Researcher: Can the two boys stay with you?

Mr Fu: My living conditions at the work site are very poor. It is an underground room and they [the company] do not allow outsiders onto the site. Besides, I cannot leave my children in the living quarters without anyone attending to them, it is not safe.

(FS/FC-F 11/08/06)

This migrant family was closely knit and pulled its resources together to help Mr Fu through the crisis. The middle generation saw the grandparents as making a choice to care for the boys and did not think it was an obligation. Mr Fu felt very grateful for the assistance his parents extended to him and considered himself to be "lucky."

For the Fu family, the dynamics of power of influence can be accessed through the way the two generations agreed on disciplinary methods used on the boys. Grandfather Fu enjoyed the role of a traditional, powerful male figure. The adult son (middle generation) visited his sons and his parents once a fortnight and did not interfere with the way grandfather handled the boys. He readily agreed even with the occasional harsh disciplinary measures grandfather used on the boys. I asked Mr Fu if he felt heartache when his father spanked the boys rather severely. He replied:

> No, I never have such thoughts. In fact, I would tell the boys that grandfather *dadehao* 打的好 (did the right thing) by disciplining them because they deserved it. I feel it is necessary that my father disciplines the boys regarding their school work or daily matters.
>
> (FS/FC-F 11/08/06)

I posed the same question to Grandfather Fu and asked if his son ever disagreed with his choice of disciplinary measures. Grandfather's response was congruent with Mr Fu's position:

Grandfather Fu: He [adult son] has no opinion. You see, in every family, there must be at least someone the children obey. If not the family will be in chaos.

Researcher: Would their father feel heartache when you spank the boys?

Grandfather Fu: No, he would not. Because I do not spank them [grandsons] very often. Also, whenever I spank them, I do not overdo it and do not use too much force ... .

(FS/FC-PMF 10/08/06)

Hence, grandfather was accepted as *yi jia zhi zhu* 一家之主 (the head of the household) by the middle and junior generations, which was a form of cultural power ascribed to the oldest male in the traditional Chinese patrilineal family.

Grandmother Fu was the nurturer who showed her love to the children explicitly. She felt sorry for the two boys because they did not have a mother. Although she tried her best to compensate for their lack of mother's love, she thought a grandmother's love was not the same:

> I attended the children's day celebration in their [grandsons'] school last year. All the other children had their parents with them, I was the

only grandmother. I could not control myself, but tears kept welling up. I felt very bad for the boys, and very awkward for myself. The other mothers were 30 and over years old. I am nearly 60 years old. I would like to think I can compensate for [their lack of mother's love] but I know it is still different.

(FS/C-PGM 8/08/06)

Grandmother Fu thought it was a joy caring for the grandsons because they were *bu ben*不笨 (literally "not stupid" – a modest way to say that her grandsons were quite intelligent) and sensible as well. She proudly displayed the many awards and certificates Da Fu won in his school. The hardest part of caring for the two grandsons was washing their thick laundry during winter (they did not have the luxury of owning a washing machine, so the clothes had to be hand-washed). Because Grandmother Fu was suffering from arthritis in both wrists, wringing out the washcloth caused her a lot of pain. She insisted however, it was worth it. Although she developed headaches when her husband was too harsh in punishing the boys she would restrain herself from sheltering the boys:

I feel very painful seeing them suffer [when grandfather spanks them] but I cannot protect them. If one person spanks and the other person shelters, the children will have no fear [of the adults].

There was neither competition for power nor discrepancy among the adults in this family. Both grandparents treated the boys as if they were their own children. Being "parents" for the second time seemed to have given this pair of grandparents the opportunity to transfer their unfulfilled hopes onto their grandchildren. Grandfather regretted that his three adult children had not received a good education and attributed it to the difficult times of the Cultural Revolution. To ensure the same thing would not happen again, the grandparents wielded their power of influence by transferring their aspirations to their two grandsons.

What set this family apart from the other four I observed was the absence of ambivalence on the part of either the senior and middle generation. The marginal role played by the middle generation probably reduced the opportunity for conflicts among the members of the parenting coalition. Nevertheless, even though the coalition was only loosely knit it impressed me as being cohesive, and mutual understanding between the generations seemed to permeate their relationships.

Bird's eye view of the Fu family

In the Fu family, the grandfather played a strong leadership role. As with Mr Wang, the other adults in the coalition deferred to him for decisions and directions. However, unlike Mr Wang who relied largely on relational power of influence in the coalition, Grandfather Fu drew his power of influence from cultural as well as relational resources. To some extent he resembled the image of a traditional Chinese patriarch. In this family, the perspectives of both the senior and middle generations about grandparents caring for the two grandsons were complementary. The grandparents gladly cared for the two boys as a "heaven-given duty" while the middle generation felt grateful and appreciative of the help received. This scenario is rather different from that of Madam Bai and Grandmother Bai. Although both Mr Fu and Madam Bai were single parents who faced the crisis of marital breakdown and needed childcare help from grandparents, the latter was not at all as appreciative and grateful as the former.

The hidden intergenerational conflict

In examining the intergenerational parenting coalitions of the five participating families in this study, it is clear that grandparents make vital contributions to their adult children's households in urban Xiamen. The ethnographic data presented in this chapter reveals that the grandparents' motives for providing services to their adult children include a desire to: relieve the young families of economic burdens so that they do not have to engage domestic maids (Grandmother Jiang); lighten a daughter's load in balancing childcare, housework and paid work (Grandparents Tian and Grandmother Wang); and assist adult children who are divorced with much-needed childcare (Grandmother Bai and Grandparents Fu). Each of the grandparents explicitly stated that the calls for practical help from their adult children were valid and necessary, and hence, requests they could not refuse. Only the paternal grandmother of the Wang family hinted at the benefit of helping as paying in advance for her own elder care. In most cases, however, not only was there no conscious calculation of cost involved, but the grandparents were ready to provide unilateral contribution to their adult children on a long-term basis.

Yet, in nearly all the families, grandparents were expected to take the bad with the good. In a sense this confirms the results of the survey discussed in the preceding chapter where almost half of adult children do not think there is a need to reward grandparents for services rendered since "they are part of the family." The figure was confirmed in three of the five families where I observed in their natural settings over a sustained period of time. Grandparents of the Jiang, Tian, and Bai families felt their adult children (children-in-law) were stingy in their expression of gratitude (either in actions or words) which made them feel taken-for-granted. On the other hand, the adult children from the same families also had their fair share of grievances towards their older parents. Despite the difficulties and challenges faced by the middle generation in handling the seniors they seemed to be at the receiving end of the benefits of the relationship more often than the seniors.

The research effort to make sense of these intergenerational relation-ships is still in its early stages. A dearth of extant research on grandparents' involvement in their adult children's households tends to portray multigen-erational Chinese families as harmonious, with relationships shaped solely by the traditional Chinese ideal of filial piety and mutual obligations (Yang 1996, Guo *et al.* 2007). Virtually nothing is known about the challenges faced by older parents and their adult children jointly caring for grandchil-dren. The five families described above give us a first look at the inherent difficulties in raising children within an intergenerational parenting coali-tion. To give further shading to this issue, however, it is important to take a fuller view of the household dynamics by incorporating the views of the child.

5   The power of little suns as agentic beings

Parents and children interact within a system of culturally embedded social relationships. In most of the literature on childrearing in China, children have been treated as the recipients of their parents' attention and direction. There is much to be gained, however, in seeing both young and adult children as agents who have a hand in shaping their caregivers' behavior and who are active participants in all social behavior, just like adults. This requires conceptualizing children's agency in families by considering the children themselves as agents – that is, people with an ability to exercise agency – and to understand the extent to which they feel like agents (Cummings and Schermerhorn 2003).[1] In treating little suns as active agents I will refer to the three dimensions of agency: the universal motive of exercising autonomy and self protection; the cognitive aspect of agency, that is, the ability of the child to actively interpret information; and the capacity of the child to express agentic behavior irrespective of their social power (Kuczynski 2003). In this book, I consider little suns and their caregivers to be bidirectionally influencing each other. Parents, grandparents, and children all interpret and construct meanings from each other's behaviors and anticipate, resist, negotiate, and accommodate each other's perspectives during interactions. I also assume that contradictory processes such as conflict, ambiguity, and ambivalence are inherent in parent (grandparent)–child relationships and give rise to qualitative change as adults and children mutually and continuously adapt to each other over time. In viewing the family in this manner, the Chinese child is examined as an active agent embedded in an interdependent, three-generation relationship system.

Within this set of interdependent relationships the power relations among family members are often unequal. But while the dynamics of power between caregivers and children tend to favor one party more than another, their context – these interdependent relationships – means that each partner is both receptive and vulnerable to the other's influence. Members of these three-generational families draw on resources to enhance their ability to assert influence on each other. The three types of resources that constitute power are: individual resources, relational resources, and cultural resources (Kuczynski 2003).[2] This idea, that family members across the generations all have resources to influence each other from a culturally embedded, relational context is useful for research on family dynamics across the globe, and, in this case, in understanding families in contemporary mainland China. On a micro level it helps to explain how an adult can be both receptive and vulnerable to the influence of seemingly powerless young children who nevertheless are perceived to act as "little suns" and "little emperors." The consideration of culture as a source of constraint for human actions provides a way of linking changes in the macro-cultural context to the actions of family members as agents in their daily lives.

This chapter examines three families to show the dynamics of parent–child and grandparent–child relationships at a time when grandparents are significantly involved in supporting their children by providing care to the grandchildren. Close attention will be paid to how young children embody and understand their agency in interacting with their caregivers and to relate these to the cultural and relational resources afforded by their family contexts. Contrasting the cases of Jie Jie and Wei Wei with the migrant siblings – Da Fu and Xiao Fu – will demonstrate the varied sense of agency and the extent to which children are able to exercise agentic behaviors in different family settings. The chapter will close with some further reflections on how the agency of these children is both enabled and constrained by the intergenerational parenting coalitions.

Jie Jie and the Jiang intergenerational parenting coalition

Like every primary school boy in Xiamen, Jie Jie shaved his head. He looked tanned, sporty, and lean, and spoke with an occasional stutter. The boy seemed to express more through actions than words. He was physically very active and could hardly sit still. My rapport with him began with playing hopscotch and board games, which he invented during our first encounter.

Jie Jie had three adults who cared for him daily. He told me that his paternal grandmother could only exercise marginal influence over him and that he only "listened" to her two out of ten times. With regard to his mother, Jie Jie said he would comply with her five out of ten times. Although he claimed to love his mother most among the three adult caregivers, his compliance rate to her was half of that to his father. The child said: "Out of ten times I will *ting hua* 听话 (obey) my father at least nine times ... and the one time of *bu ting hua* 不听话 (disobedience) is on small matters." When probed further why this was the case, Jie Jie replied: "My father is so tall like a *ju ren* 巨人 (giant), if I disobey him and make him mad, it is really frightening!" (JJ 30/8/06). Sometimes Jie Jie's father, Mr Jiang, exercised rather harsh punishment on him as a means of discipline. From what I observed, these physical punishments were inflicted either owing to Jie Jie's behavioral problems in school which father deemed serious or as a result of grandmother's complaints of misbehavior.

Jie Jie's level of felt and exercised agency and emotional bonds with adults

Faced with such a seemingly powerful father, Jie Jie only had a limited range of avenues to resist instructions or to exhibit noncompliant behaviors. One way was to invoke his schoolteacher's name to defy his father. When his father demanded that Jie Jie do more exercises as part of his school work, the child would resist him by responding that his teacher did not require him to do extra work. Since father was the most powerful person at home, Jie Jie needed to "borrow" strength from an outside source to effectively resist him. In Xiamen, teachers were usually well respected by parents, hence it was probably the best source of outside strength the child could draw from. On the other hand, sometimes when his father was angry and he would start spanking Jie Jie and all Jie Jie could do was to wait and hope that his mother would rescue him:

Jie Jie: Mum would come to rescue me, but *nai nai* (paternal grand-mother) would stop her instead, *nai nai* would ask my father to hit harder.
Researcher: Hit harder? It must be painful?
Jie Jie: Of course! But once it was not very painful because dad did not pull down my pants [when he spanked].

This remark by Jie Jie implied a sense of a small victory on his part in that there was one time the spanking was not painful. In doing so, he appears to offer an agentic construct similar to Scott's (1986) model of everyday resistance, whereby victims of oppression do not passively submit to their victimization but try to lessen the physical or psychological impact.

Despite father's periodic harsh punishments, Jie Jie thought he was close to both parents. He felt especially close to his mother as she was the only one who liked his way of expressing love through kisses and hugs, whereas his father and grandmother both had an aversion to these outward expressions of affection. The child rated the most-loved adult as his mother, followed by his father. He described his relationship with grandmother as *bi jiao huai* 比较坏 (less good) as she was strict and fierce to him. He said sometimes in his heart he felt like punching her (*hen xiang zou nai nai* 很想揍奶奶). Probably this was an expression of his pent-up anger about the frequent beatings he suffered from his father as a result of *nai nai's* complaints.

However, Jie Jie's relationship with this grandmother was not entirely antagonistic. He told me that she was the one who took him to and from school every day. Jie Jie especially liked it when occasionally *nai nai* rewarded him with an ice-cream for good behavior. He was concerned about her impending major knee operation and wanted to be the first to visit her at the hospital. Jie Jie slept in the same room with his grandmother and agreed that she took care of him, did the cooking and spent more time with him than his parents did. Jie Jie also commented that he would take care of the seniors when they grow old since they treated him very nicely

Grandmother's relationship with Jie Jie

Conversations with the grandmother corroborated Jie Jie's description of their relationship. She said the child complied more with instructions from his parents, especially the father.

> Sometimes I tell them [son, daughter-in-law, and grandson] jokingly, "in this family I am the one with the *zui mei you di wei* 最没有地位 (lowest status) at home." In the eyes of the child, father and mother definitely come first.

> (JJ-PGM 13/08/06)

Jie Jie's grandmother claimed that although she would raise her voice and verbally reprimand the child, she refrained from using corporal punishment. "If the child misbehaves, I will let them [parents] know .... If I hit the child, the child may bear grudges against me. Besides, my daughter-in-law may not like it," his grandmother claimed. The grandmother frequently mentioned how exhausting it was for her to care for her grandchild, prepare all the meals, and do the housework. But she thought it was an obligation on her part. As discussed earlier, her health had recently begun to deteriorate rapidly and she was always feeling tired.

The sometimes antagonistic relationship between grandmother and grandson was worsened by the latter's hyperactive nature. Their interactions formed a vicious circle: the child's misbehaviors exacerbated the grandmother's sense of tiredness. Her exhaustion caused her to be short-tempered and harsh in her verbal reprimands. Because of all this, there was a lack of warmth in their relationship. Grandmother tolerated all the exhaustion of her caring role yet felt that the middle generation did not appreciate it. In the analysis of one transcript of a conversation with grandmother Jiang, the word *lei* 累 (tired/tiredness) came up 16 times. It is my suspicion, therefore, that lodging complaints against her grandson was probably a way for her to hint at, and in doing so draw the attention of the middle generation to, the fatigue brought about by her caring role. It went without saying that Jie Jie was unhappy with his grandmother for "telling tales" to his father and causing him trouble by encouraging the father to discipline him. This further aggravated the grandmother–grandson relationship. Hence Jie Jie would not comply with grandmother's demands or instructions, and grandmother had little influence over the child because there was no strong relational basis for her draw upon in order to exert her influence.

Parents' relationships with Jie Jie

Despite the seven-year-old boy's constant misbehavior in school and the challenges of handling the paternal grandmother's complaints on a daily basis, Mrs Jiang considered her child a gift from God:

> The happiness I derive [from raising a child] is much greater than the hard work … yes, I am very happy when I am spending time with him [child], I love to be with him, although I only have very little time with him, usually evenings and weekends ….
>
> (JJ-M 1/8/06)

How does Mrs Jiang's according such high emotional value to her child affect the child's bargaining power when negotiating with his parents? His mother reported that she would modify her demands on the child according to his physical condition, interest, and abilities. She considered herself more flexible concerning nonacademic issues, for instance, food and games. But there would be no compromise regarding school work. To Mrs Jiang, the bottom line was that he finished his school work promptly every day. She also said that she was the more "relaxed" adult among the three caregivers and would sometimes have fun by singing and dancing with Jie Jie. The more relaxed relationship with mother might explain why Jie Jie thought he would only comply with his mother's requests five out of ten times, despite ranking mother as the most loved. Unlike her husband and mother-in-law who tended to exercise strict control over the child, Mrs Jiang relied on the forging of a close personal relationship to exercise influence over him. However, Mrs Jiang was also conscious of the need to leave some room for compromise and negotiation, and thereby facilitating Jie Jie's ability to exercise successful expression of his will and agency with his mother. She described her relationship with Jie Jie as one of mother and playmate:

> My [son's] relationship with me … I feel he is always excited to see me, I feel he treats me as a friend yet relies on me as a mother. But when it comes to play, I feel he treats me as a playmate.
>
> (JJ-M 1/08/06)

As mentioned earlier, Mr Jiang would occasionally use physical punishment on his child. While he was a powerful father who could coerce his son by inflicting pain, Mr Jiang was always thinking about better ways of dealing with his son. Despite the disciplining, Jie Jie did not show a corresponding improvement in his behavior or results in school. This caused his father a great deal of uncertainty and left him at a loss:

> He [son] makes me feel *wu neng wei li* 无能为力 (helpless) or rather, I feel *wu suo shi cong* 无所适从 (bewildered). I don't know whether to

punish him severely or give him many more chances and let him change slowly. Also, I asked myself whether I am being too demanding. Sometimes I feel helpless and also *cuo zhe gan* 挫折感 (a sense of failure).

Jie Jie's father reported that fathering his child made him experience a sense of failure. Far from his ideal of children being "angels" with good qualities of intelligence, politeness, being sensible, and understanding toward their parents, Jie Jie shattered his fantasy of parenthood as a blissful experience. He often received complaints from schoolteachers and from his mother about Jie Jie's behavior. He admitted that this process of getting to know his child was time consuming, exhausting, and requiring of patience. He lamented that this was his first and probably only time to be a father, hence he lacked experience. Though he wished to be Jie Jie's playmate, he was too often compelled to be the disciplinarian.

> In fact I need to see the positive side of him [his son]; sometimes he really makes me so mad. The teacher complains about him through *nai nai* [paternal grandmother], about his mischievous behaviors in class. He often does not pay attention in class. He does completely different things from what the teachers are teaching. Sometimes he hits other children. The teacher has already made him change seats three times. I am really 郁闷 *yu men* (upset) ....
>
> (JT-F 25/7/06)

It seems that despite Mr Jiang being a rather powerful father, his seven-year-old son exerted a profound influence on him through his active nature and his tendency to cause trouble in school, although these behaviors were not necessarily intentional. By being who he was, Jie Jie forced his father to rethink his unrealistic image of an ideal child and slowly come to terms with the tough reality of being a father. Hence, in Mr Jiang's experience, feelings of power co-existed with helplessness and bewilderment. That was his experience of being a contemporary urban father.

Interplay between Jie Jie and his intergenerational parenting coalition

Figure 5.1 depicts the interplay of power of influence among the three generations in an ordinary stress-provoking scenario in the Jiang family. In the occurrences discussed here stress was precipitated by two possible sources: to appease the relentless complaints from the grandmother regarding Jie Jie's misbehavior or complaints from schoolteachers regarding Jie Jie's misbehavior in school. In these situations, his father would execute discipline on Jie Jie by beating. Usually his mother would attempt

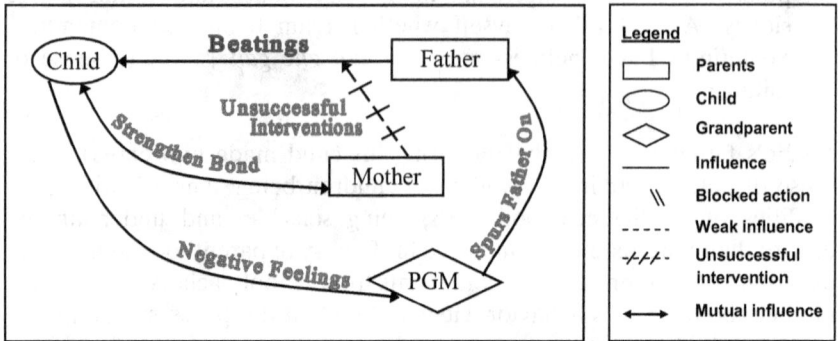

Figure 5.1 Left: Jie Jie – Interplay of three generations. (PGM = paternal grandmother.)
Right: Legend for figures in Chapter 5.

to intervene to relieve Jie Jie from further pain. The paternal grandmother,
however, usually thwarted her interventions as the grandmother thought
her son should be stricter in his parenting style. Jie Jie's grandmother would
in fact spur her son on in the beatings, and by "adding fuel to the flame" she
naturally spawned negative feelings in her grandson. Although his mother
was not very successful in stopping father from beating him, Jie Jie said
he loved his mother most. What is difficult to depict in the figure is that
Mr Jiang also felt guilty for using harsh measures on his son. This guilt
explains why Mrs Jiang lamented that the child is both the *run hua ji* 润滑剂
(lubricant) of the generations as well as the *shou hai zhe* 受害者 (victim).
"Lubricant" because the child enhanced the bonds between the three
generations, but also the victim, as he sometimes had to suffer unwarranted
punishment from his father as an act of "showing respect" to grandmother
or to "appease" the older lady.

Bird's eye view of dynamics between Jie Jie and the intergenerational parenting coalition

From the findings presented, it can be seen that Jie Jie could only exercise a
limited range of agentic behaviors in dealing with his intergenerational
parenting coalition. He could exercise more direct, relational power of
influence on his mother because she tended to be more lenient and
provided leeway for him to negotiate, particularly in comparison with his
father and grandmother. However, he could not usually escape the
combined forces of the grandmother's indirect power executed through the
powerful father's discipline. Residing under one roof, Jie Jie's lowered level
of agentic behavior can be better understood by closely examining the
three-generational dynamics. Although love for the child was the glue that
held the two senior generations together, the child might be "sacrificed" at

times in order to save face for the senior generation and maintain family harmony. It is interesting that in this situation the father often felt guilty about his own harsh measures. He frequently reflected on his interactions with his son and felt helpless and bewildered as he searched for a better way to handle him. He was also torn between hoping to be Jie Jie's playmate but usually felt compelled to be the disciplinarian instead. In addition, the boy's characteristics of being active and frequently getting into trouble in school brought about a profound shift in his father's experience as a parent, from being idealistic to realistic.

Wei Wei and the Wang intergenerational parenting coalition

Wei Wei, a seven-year-old boy, had bright eyes and two missing front teeth. He spoke with a husky voice. Because his father wished to train him to be well-rounded, his weekends were filled with extra-curricular lessons ranging from swimming, badminton, and painting to piano lessons. It was obvious from my initial encounter that Wei Wei was the center of attention for the adults in his family. As mentioned in the earlier chapter, Mr Wang was clearly devoted to Wei Wei. During my first visit, the father was keen to take up my offer of providing free English tuition to his son, but said that he would have to discuss it with Wei Wei as he did not want to impose on him. One could see the "consultative" parenting style employed by Mr Wang.

Wei Wei's levels of felt and exercised agency and emotional bonds with adult caregivers

Wei Wei said he would usually obey his father because his father always explained things nicely to him even though he could be fierce at times. When asked what he would do if he did not want to comply with father's instructions, Wei Wei replied that it was not possible for him not to *tinghua* (obey), because his father had warned him that he could be very fierce if he was upset. With regard to his mother, he thought he needed to comply when he observed that she was angry. Wei Wei admitted that he often fought with his paternal grandmother. However, he reported that he would usually comply with his maternal grandmother's requests, as he loved her most.

Wei Wei's exercised agency could be seen in the strategies he used to resist or defy his paternal grandmother. For instance, Wei Wei felt he was old enough to walk to and from school on his own without any adult super-vision. He told me:

> I hate it [his paternal grandmother walking him to school daily]. I want to be independent. My horoscope belongs to tiger[3] (he made a fierce-looking face at me); do I need anyone to take me? I am already in primary two!

(WW 29/08/06)

Wei Wei had a clear goal, to be independent. However, this goal was blocked by the intergenerational parenting coalition. Mr Wang did not want the child to walk alone the ten minutes' distance to and from school for fear of bad influences along the way, and the paternal grandmother volunteered to take him (this information was gathered from a personal communication with the paternal grandmother). In Wei Wei's mind *nai nai* (paternal grandmother) was the one who frustrated his goal. I once witnessed how he made *nai nai*'s job very difficult when I accompanied her as she walked the child to school (Field notes 27/04/06). He pulled a long face at *nai nai*, and ran way ahead, leaving her to pant along trying to catch up with him. With the intention of shaking her off, he deliberately took short cuts that were not accessible to her, climbing over walls and ducking through a broken gate. Apparently *nai nai* was used to all these and was not upset. On the other hand, if Wei Wei wanted toys and snacks from the little stalls on the way home, he would whine persistently. Grandmother told me that she frequently had a "tug-of-war" with Wei Wei and would often lose the battles.

In addition, according to Mr Wang, he was well aware that the child often used his name to defy the other caregivers. Knowing that his father was the leader among the four adults, he could "borrow power" from his father if he did not want to comply with a particular adult's instruction by saying that father did not require him to do it (WW-F 24/07/06).

The boy claimed that he loved his maternal grandmother most as "she often cooked his favorite food and gave him some freedom'; he also slept in the same room as this grandmother. Father was ranked second as he would take the child swimming and to play ball games every weekend. Wei Wei placed paternal grandmother as the third-most-liked person as she sometimes cooked him noodles. He ranked mother as the least liked, as she always forced him to practise the piano against his will. According to Wei Wei he was very afraid when his mother was upset:

> When she is angry, she will pinch my buttock and scream at me "what are you doing, how dare you …" (Stuck his tongue out to show that he was really scared) I do not dare to answer back and quickly apologize to her. What can I do?
>
> (WW 29/8/06)

It seemed Wei Wei's mother had to assert physical power in order to control him. On occasions when he observed that his mother was "mad," he would quickly comply in order to avoid being hurt. From the child's viewpoint, he liked his maternal grandmother most as she satisfied his desires for freedom and choice of food. Therefore he would comply with her instructions, and subjected himself to her influence. When asked whether he would take care of his parents and grandparents when they grow old, Wei Wei mentioned:

Wei Wei:	I will give them money, buy food for them, cook for them, take care of them and help them with chores.
Researcher:	Why do you want to care for them?
Wei Wei:	They treated me so nice since [I was] young, so I will look after them. *Jing lao ai you* 敬老爱幼 (respect the elder and love the young), don't we say *"jing lao ai you"*? I will buy a three-storey house, my father would stay on the top floor, my grandparents on the second floor and I stay on the ground floor.

What was noteworthy was that the remark *"Jing lao ai you"* was repeated twice in Wei Wei's response. His tone of voice was as if to "respect the elder and love the young" was an accepted fact of life. He even seemed puzzled why I asked him the question.

Grandmothers' relationships with Wei Wei

Wei Wei's paternal Grandmother Wang smiled when she related to me how her grandson tended to bully her, and the constant battle between the pair. Her narratives corresponded with Wei Wei's description of how he would not "listen" to *nai nai*. The smile on her face could be interpreted as meaning that she actually did not mind his mischievous defiance. The child would pester her to buy snacks and toys on the way home from school, but grandmother was a frugal woman who only spent money on basic necessities.

Paternal grandmother:	He bullies me because of all the adults at home I am the nicest and most soft-hearted.
Researcher:	Oh, so he bullies you.
Paternal grandmother:	Whenever he wants to buy little things, he comes to me. I told him I don't have money . . . he would retort and say, "but you have a pension back in the home town." I asked him to get money from his father to buy these small things but he dared not approach his father. So he resorts to bullying me into buying them for him. He bullies me every day, he thinks this *nai nai* is so naïve and easily tricked.

(WW-PGM 24/7/06)

As mentioned earlier, grandmother felt she did not have enough strength to win the daily tug-of-war with her grandson. She therefore resorted to channeling all these grievances to her adult son, hoping that he would discipline the boy instead. This, however, accentuated Wei Wei's dislike for her, as he perceived her as telling tales. As in Grandmother Jiang's case, this constant lodging of complaints soured Grandmother Wang's relationship with her grandson and further weakened the influence she could have on the child.

Differing from Wei Wei's self-assessment that he usually complied with instructions given by *a-ma* 阿嬤 (maternal grandmother in *Minnan* dialect) this 80-year-old lady said that in fact he only "listened" to his father. However, she did acknowledge that there was a very strong bond between her and her grandson: "[laughed] He dares not bully me, I have taken care of him for a longer time, so he has some *ganqing* 感情 (emotional bonds). In the night he sleeps with me, so there is *ganqing*."

With this strong bond, Wei Wei's maternal grandmother was able to execute some mild discipline without provoking resentment from the child. Besides, she commented that her son-in-law and daughter would always back her up in front of the child:

Researcher: When the child misbehaves, do you discipline him?
Grandmother: Sometimes I will verbally threaten him, or the moment I lift up the bamboo stick, he [child] will quickly appease me by apologizing.
Researcher: Do you really beat him?
Grandmother: Yes, one or two strokes on the buttocks occasionally, but usually I only need to lift up the bamboo ... [to make him comply].
Researcher: After you have punished him, will he be angry with you?
Grandmother: No. Sometimes he says, "I don't like you any more, I don't like you." But the next moment he would come to sweet-talk me, "*a-ma* this, *a-ma* that," he would do that.

(WW-MGM 4/08/06)

In contrast to the paternal grandmother, *a-ma* seemed to have a strong bond with the child. She claimed that the boy would sometimes notice she was suffering from backache and volunteer to rub her back. This close bond enabled her to exercise a considerable amount of influence on him. Maternal grandmother considered Wei Wei to be generally *guai* 乖 (good and obedient).

One surprise finding was the existence of some subtle competition for loyalty and affection between the two grandmothers. On one occasion, the maternal grandmother told me that the grandson, Wei Wei, felt closer to her than to the paternal grandmother, and asked me to keep it confidential because the latter felt jealous (WW-MGM 4/8/06, p. 8). She also claimed that, in addition to his parents, Wei Wei would "listen" to her most of the time. On a separate occasion, the paternal grandmother told me that she was more capable as a caregiver because she was younger and more respon-sible (WW-PGM 24/7/06 p. 3). It is interesting to see how these subtle competitions among members of the intergenerational parenting coalition actually boosted the power of influence of the child.

Parents' relationships with Wei Wei

Mr Wang felt he had given up many opportunities to advance his career in order to spend time with his child. Being actively involved with the boy was physically exhausting, though Wei Wei's father thought it was worth it:

> Yes, I feel sometimes, as I said just now, very tired. Because I need to *yong xin* 用心 (use my heart to) observe every detail. If I do not *yong xin*, I would not have noticed he [son] was feeling upset yesterday and I might have hurt him further, being too harsh with my words . . . .
>
> (WW-F 24/7/06)

Mr Wang was also quick to make amends or apologize if he perceived he had been unduly harsh to the child. Father's attentiveness to Wei Wei's situation could be the reason for him "always complying" with father's instructions and requests. However, father pointed out that the "giving" was not one-way. It is interesting to see a mirroring effect between the father–son dyad in terms of being attentive to each other's needs. He claimed that the child was sensitive and quick to notice his parents' moods. There were times when the father had had a bad day at work, so Wei Wei would take the initiative to ask, "Daddy, are you not in a good mood? Have I done anything wrong?"

Wei Wei's father was also attentive to how the child interacted with the other members of the intergenerational parenting coalition. He was very aware that Wei Wei was not as compliant with the other adult caregivers. Even though all the other caregivers would confer with the father when making decisions about childcare, he lamented that his plans would not usually be executed thoroughly and there would be many loopholes. It was especially problematic with the paternal grandmother, as Wei Wei would strategically use his father's instructions to sabotage the plans. Mr Wang then found himself dealing with complaints from his own mother about the child. He would act as a buffer and filter out content he assessed as unfair or unnecessary, and find ways to communicate with the child on issues that he thought warranted attention.

Mr Wang saw himself as neither an authoritarian nor a democratic parent. He described his style as "setting a boundary for the child," and within the boundary he allowed his son to make choices. Like many parents in this book, he was uncompromising where school assignments were concerned. He insisted that the child complete every assignment and turn them in the next day. In a way, he was consciously shedding the traditional "all-powerful father image." This can be demonstrated by his deliberate choice of words during one conversation to describe his power/control relations with his son:

Researcher: You seem to be the important decision-maker at home, other adults will align themselves with you, is my observation correct?

(I tried to verify my observation with the participant.)

Mr Wang: Yes, you can say so.

Researcher: So Wei Wei [son] is also aware of this?

Mr Wang: Yes.

Researcher: So in your family, no one actually challenges your *quan wei* 权威 (authority)?

Mr Wang: What you said is not very accurate, it is not *quan wei*. I can only say I guide my child in his learning and his living arrangements.

Researcher: Yes, but there must be some sense of *quan wei* that comes with this role.

Mr Wang: I don't call it *quan wei*, I should say I want my son to have *wei xin* 威信 (respect and trust) for me.

Researcher: Yes, to build respect and trust with your son.[4]

(WW-F 24/07/06)

Mr Wang clearly did not like the term *quan wei* and made it a point to correct me twice. Instead, he preferred *wei xin*. In using the term *wei xin* Mr Wang hinted at his preference for a slightly more egalitarian relationship with his son as well as with other members of the parenting coalition.

What about Mrs Wang? I once asked her why she had a child. She looked puzzled that I would even ask her a question like that. "It is only natural," was her response. Mrs Wang told me that if one does not want children, one should not get married (WW-M 21/07/06 p. 9). She said although she was not sure of the long-term reward of raising children, at least for the moment her child brought the family a great deal of joy:

Right now, I should say he [Wei Wei] brings us a lot of happiness. Of course there are moments of annoyance, but in general, it is only normal for every family to have some squabbles. It will not feel like a family if it is all peace and quietness!

This high emotional value accorded to the child by the parent invariably elevated his standing with the adults and his ability to assert influence in the family. Although in Wei Wei's view his mother could be very powerful when she was angry, from the mother's perspective she consciously refrained from asserting the power of influence and control on the child and instead, allowed him room for negotiation. On the other hand, his mother acknowledged that at this young age she would demand the child obey her in certain non-negotiables, but would take into consideration that as he grew older her expectations of compliance would diminish accordingly:

Mother: I tell the child, "when you are able to make judgments, we will leave it to you to make decisions. But now you are still young, you are not able to make judgments yet." So we expect him to *ting hua* (obey instructions). If he does not *ting* (obey), we will use slightly harsh methods like beatings. Yes, we will do it.

Researcher: Would you say he is usually *ting hua* (obedient)?

Mother: Not necessarily. Sometimes my son will obey me, but other times he may not. Since he was little, I have taught him how to behave when he goes out, he was able to do it then. But now that he is older, sometimes he refuses to obey.

Researcher: The child is changing as he grows…

Mother: He is developing his own mind and may not *ting* (obey) us.

Researcher: So it seems you need to adjust accordingly.

Mother: For sure I need to adjust myself, only after adjusting can I guide him.

In addition to making provision for developmental changes in her child that constrain her power of influence, Wei Wei's mother confessed that she actually made leeway for him to negotiate and influence her in return:

Mother: Sometimes he [Wei Wei] will say to me, "mum, sometimes you are not a good mother, when you beat me, you are not a good mother." I told him, "I know it is bad to beat you. But the problem is you don't *ting hua* (obey instructions). If you *ting hua*, mum will not beat you." When I heard him say that, I felt actually I was somewhat wrong to do that, it was not right to spank him.

Researcher: You mentioned to me before that after the second semester of primary one, you have reduced the amount of corporal punishment.

Mother: Yes, I have refrained from beating him.

Researcher: You feel you are consciously making adjustments?

Mother: Yes, I am making adjustments.

Researcher: Why do you want to adjust?

Mother: Because of what the child told me. Honestly, I feel the child is right in some ways. Sometimes when we adults are mad, we lose control of our anger … I must admit that I can be unreasonable sometimes.

This mother wondered whether it was appropriate for her to continue corporal punishment on her child. Her reflection was evoked by her child's comments that "you are not a good mother because you beat me." It is rather obvious that there was room for bidirectional influence in this mother–child relationship. Also, Wei Wei's mother knew that as the child grew older he would increasingly develop a mind of his own. She was mentally prepared for these changes and was cognitively making room for the child to exercise his own agency in making judgments for himself in the future. But for now, she believed he was still too young to decide for himself and hence it was reasonable for adults to expect compliance from him; she did, however, question her own method of inflicting physical pain as a way to ensure compliance.

Interplay between Wei Wei and intergenerational parenting coalition

The parenting coalition in Wei Wei's family formed what is known as a *wan luo jia ting* (networked family). Both paternal and maternal grandmothers were involved in the coalition but in different settings, hence, the interplay of the generations needs to be presented in two figures. I will first examine the dynamics between the child and the adults living under the same roof, namely father, mother, maternal grandmother. Figure 5.2 depicts the interplay of the generations.

According to Mr and Mrs Wang all the adults under the same roof would "put up a united front" to minimize opportunities for the child to play them against each other. However, Wei Wei seems to demonstrate a relatively high sense of agency and exercised considerable level of agentic behaviors. It can be seen that Wei Wei strengthened his position by the relational resources he forged with maternal grandmother as illustrated in the same diagram.

The maternal grandmother related this incident to me. She said that her son-in-law would sometimes discipline the child by beating him with a thin wooden stick. She felt sorry for the child and would intervene. Once, Wei Wei used foul language at home. Both his parents were very upset and his father started beating him with a thin stick. But his maternal grandmother tried to reduce the beating by "putting in a few good words" for the child.

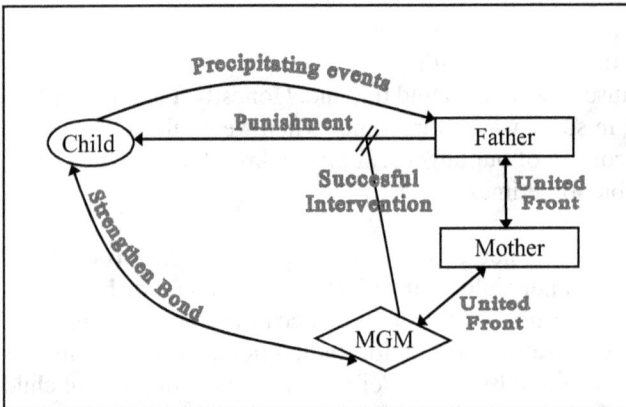

Figure 5.2 Wei Wei – Interplay of three generations (A). (MGM = maternal grandmother.)

She reported to the father that the child had behaved very well that day and had finished all his school work on time, hence, requesting that they spare him from more beating. The intervention was successful. Interventions like these enhanced the bonds and positive feelings Wei Wei had toward his maternal grandmother.

The interplay of three-generational dynamics between Wei Wei, his paternal grandmother, and his father was a very different scenario. The paternal grandmother did not live under the same roof as Wei Wei's family, but resided with her elder son's family within the same estate. Her role as a carer was to take Wei Wei to and from school on foot every day. The child yearned to be independent and to walk by himself, but this clashed with the judgment of his father as carried out by his paternal grandmother: that he was too young to walk to and from school by himself.

In the child's view, his grandmother had thwarted his goal. Wei Wei did not hide his negative feelings toward this grandmother and often openly defied her. Although she was frustrated with these noncompliant behaviors, she refrained from disciplining him fearing that her daughter-in-law would not like it, and instead lodged daily complaints with his father. Unlike in Jie Jie's family, the tension-building interactions between the senior and junior generations were buffered by the middle generation. Mr Wang would listen patiently to his mother's complaints and calibrate his actions toward his son. Mrs Wang, on the other hand, usually removed herself from the picture where her mother-in-law was concerned. Hence, the interplay of the three generations between grandmother, father, and grandson is as shown in Figure 5.3.

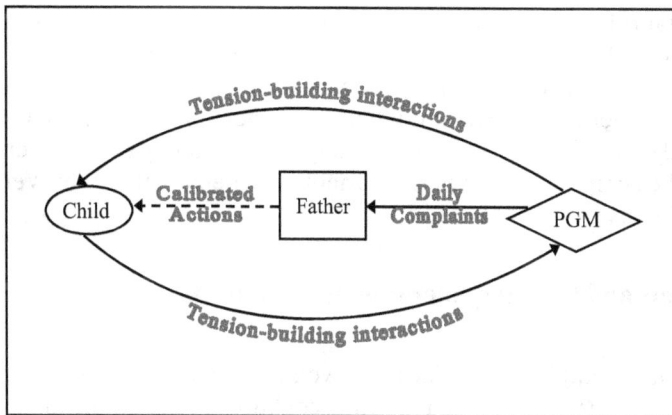

Figure 5.3 Wei Wei – Interplay of three generations (B). (PGM = paternal grandmother.)

Bird's eye view of dynamics between Wei Wei and his intergenerational parenting coalition

The parenting coalition of the Wang family was relatively close knit. This could be largely attributed to Mr Wang's proactive leadership in communicating his childcare plans to the members of the parenting coalition. For instance, the united front put up by the intergenerational parenting coalition under the same roof empowered the maternal grandmother during the father's absence. However, even with this close coordination and united front, Mr Wang admitted that the child could still defy the other adults behind his back. The child perceptively knew that his father was the most powerful person among the caregivers. He could see that other adults in the coalition "borrowed" power from the father. Hence, Wei Wei perceptively understood that his sense of agency and ability to exercise agentic behaviors could be enhanced by using his father's words against the other adults.

Two other factors that facilitated Wei Wei's ability to exercise a fair amount of interdependence and influence on the adults were his parents' receptiveness to his use of negotiation, and the function of distance. Although Mr Wang was the most powerful adult, he was far removed from the "all-powerful traditional father." He was keen to forge a strong bond with his son and preferred to use a more egalitarian approach with him. Of course there were non-negotiables. Always reflective in the way he dealt with the boy, Mr Wang often made corresponding adjustments. If he did assert power or control over the child, it was mainly based on the relational resources that he had with him. The same applied to Mrs Wang. Wei Wei's comments made her seriously consider withdrawing the use of corporal punishment.

It was noted that Wei Wei was least compliant with his paternal grandmother's instructions. This grandmother did not reside under the same roof, but lived a stone's throw away. This short physical distance seemed to play a small yet pivotal role in the dynamic as shown in Figure 5.3. It served as a double-edged sword that worked both ways for the child. On the one hand, he could play on the communication loopholes between his father and paternal grandmother owing to their not living together. On the other hand, he did not need to face the consequences of defying her directly as his father would buffer the complaints from her. Invariably, the penalty that Wei Wei faced was less intense.

The Fu brothers and the intergenerational parenting coalition

The two boys Da Fu and Xiao Fu, nine and seven years old respectively, did not have a typical intergenerational parenting coalition as seen in the other four families. They were mainly cared for by their grandparents with only marginal involvement by their father, who lived in construction site housing some distance from home. Their parents were divorced three years earlier. Their mother had since returned to her village and was hardly in touch with the boys. Of the two boys, freckle-faced Da Fu was more articulate and sociable. He was often smiling. Xiao Fu was more reserved but his eyes were often observing quietly. Both boys were tanned and slim. Their clothes were always clean though wrinkled, as if they had not been pressed. Whenever I visited the family, either to have lunch and chat with them or to give English tuition at their quarters, the brothers had to wait for me at the bus stop to lead me into the slum where they lived. Although I overcame my fear of walking in the slum after the first few visits, I could never navigate my way through the heaps of gravel and trash and those winding sandy paths without any signposts. The two boys would be waiting for me at the bus stop and call out *"wu lao shi"* (teacher Wu – my surname in Putonghua) to me as I got off the bus.

Boys' levels of felt and exercised agency and bonds with caregivers

Although Da Fu thought that his grandparents loved him, he said that on rare occasions his grandfather could be very fierce and harsh in his punishments. Sometimes he would hit them with his belt when they disobeyed. Da Fu therefore reported that he would comply with his grandfather's instructions nine out of ten times. The boy used the traditional term *yi jia zhi zhu* 一家之主 (the head of the household) to describe his grandfather. With regard to his grandmother, he thought there was leeway as to whether or not to comply, as she would only verbally reprimand him but would not hit him physically:

Researcher: So you are saying you will almost always *ting* (obey) when *ye ye* 爷爷 (paternal grandfather) instructs you to do something. How about *nai nai* (paternal grandmother), what are some of the instructions from *nai nai* that you sometimes don't like to obey?

Da Fu: Like when I have already finished my summer assignments yet she wants me to repeatedly check my work to make sure there are no mistakes. I have checked and found no mistakes but she thinks that I have not checked carefully. I just refuse to listen or hear.

Researcher: What would you do when you do not want to *ting* instructions from *nai nai*?

Da Fu: I will sleep or slip outside to play.

I was initially surprised when the younger brother Xiao Fu told me he would comply with instructions given by his grandfather only six or nine times out of ten, since *ye ye* was seen as the head of the household and was rather strict. Upon further probing, the child explained that he felt very uneasy if grandfather asked him to do something he did not want to do. In his mind he would refuse to do it but behaviorally would still comply every time:

Xiao Fu:	I will feel very uncomfortable inside.
Researcher:	What do you mean?
Xiao Fu:	I will think about how I can take revenge when I grow up.
Researcher:	So then, what would happen?
Xiao Fu:	But I will still do it, because if I don't do it, *ye ye* (paternal grandfather) will beat me. Since I cannot not do, so I do it.
Researcher:	Out of ten times, how many times do you do what *ye ye* instructs you?
Xiao Fu:	Sometimes nine, other times six.
Researcher:	What do you do during the four times you refused to do it?
Xiao Fu:	I don't know, I have not done it before.
Researcher:	Do you mean you only refused in your mind but actually you will do it?
Xiao Fu:	Yes.

(FC 28/8/06)

It can be seen therefore, that even though the grandfather was perceived by the children to be an authoritarian *yi jia zhi zhu* (head of household), there was room for the children to exercise their agency. For instance, Da Fu said he would comply with grandfather's instructions nine out of ten times. As for the younger boy, although behaviorally he would comply most of the time his sense of agency could be seen through the way he cognitively resisted grandfather in his mind.

Boys' bonds with caregivers

Da Fu, the older boy, said he preferred to stay with his grandparents rather than with his father, as the hostel in the father's factory was too small to accommodate all of them. Da Fu felt closest to his grandmother and described how he cared for her when she was unwell:

> Once *nai nai* had a bad headache, she wanted to go to buy the medicine on her own. I helped her search the house but could not find any. So I ran to the hospital and bought the medicine for her. After she took the medicine she needed to rest, so I went out to play so as not to disturb her sleep.

(FS 28/08/06)

Grandfather was second closest, followed by his father. Da Fu said he felt rather distant from his biological mother. The older boy reported that although his family was poor, they were happy. According to Da Fu, his grandparents were like parents to him. Da Fu treated *nai nai* (paternal grandmother) as his confidante:

Researcher: When you encounter some problems, whom would you confide in?
Da Fu: I will talk to *nai nai*.
Researcher: How would your *nai nai* treat you?
Da Fu: If it is something bad, she may be upset. Otherwise she will be very gentle with me.
Researcher: Could you give me an example?
Da Fu: Once my brother did not finish his school assignment and was reprimanded by the teacher. Later, the teacher sought me out in school and complained to me about him [Xiao Fu]. I felt very frustrated because I always remind him to do his work, and he had got me into trouble. *Nai nai* comforted me and told me I only need to remind him [brother] to do his work, and not to worry too much.

Unlike his older brother, Xiao Fu was ambivalent about staying with his grandparents. Although he would have preferred to stay with his father, he disliked the idea of having to stay with his stepmother. He ranked father as closest to him followed by grandmother, grandfather, and brother. With regard to caring for the grandparents when they grow old, the two boys commented they would send part of their salary back to support their folks if the latter were still healthy and mobile. When they grew older, the children said they would be there to assist them and keep them company.

Grandparents' relationships with boys

Unlike the other families discussed thus far, these grandparents seemed to have full say over how to raise the two grandsons. Although their grandfather was more traditional in his outlook and left little room for negotiation, he was very demonstrative in his love and care for the boys. The following field note illustrates this point. I was invited for lunch at the migrant quarters and arrived earlier than the boys who were coming back from school. Reflecting on the visit I wrote:

It was quite a sight to observe the interactions between the two boys and the grandparents. Grandfather heard their [boys'] footsteps and walked to open the door. Entering the small room, the boys did not acknowledge anyone. I smiled at the older boy and he smiled back. Grandfather was quite obvious in favoring the older boy. He stroked the head of the older boy and wanted to give him a hug, but the child gently pushed him away. I smiled at the younger boy. Grandfather saw a lump on his back and asked what had happened to his clothes. He

checked and found a towel inside the boy's shirt and pulled it out . . . .
The older boy commented that his brother had been feeling unwell
since last night and was sweating this morning. Grandmother added
that they had only had a bowl of plain rice porridge for breakfast this
morning as she was very tired and did not wake up early to fry them an
egg each . . . .

(Field notes 17/05/06)

Whenever I went to give English tuition to the boys both the grandparents would sit beside the children throughout the lesson, even though they
did not know a word of English. They showed their care and love in action.
These illiterate grandparents would serve drinks to the boys and me,
sharpen their pencils, and make sure that the faulty fan was blowing in the
right direction. Although raising the two boys was tough on him, their
grandfather thought it was an honor to have the chance to bring them up
and be a parent again. He wanted to do his best to provide for them, saving
on his own food so as to set aside money for a tertiary education fund for
the boys, as discussed in the preceding chapter. Their grandmother, on the
other hand, was nurturing, and often praised the two boys in front of me.
She proudly displayed all the awards and certificates won by her elder
grandson on the wall of their dilapidated migrant quarters. The grandmother did not consider the boys a burden and seemed happy to cook and
do all the chores for them. According to her, her greatest reward in caring
for them was that both of them were *bu ben* 不笨 (literally "not stupid," it is
a polite way to mean they are relatively intelligent) and that they were *ting
hua* (obedient). Grandmother claimed that the boys would not demand
pocket money as they knew that the family's financial situation did not
permit it. She said that the two grandsons did not get much adult supervision as both grandparents had to work. However, she praised them for
being self-disciplined. For instance, the boys were allowed to play with
other children after completing their school work but they were not to loiter
in the slum beyond 8 pm. They would go to bed on their own accord by
9 pm. Although Grandfather Fu portrayed himself as a traditional grandfather and exerted his cultural power as a grandfather, part of his power
and influence on the boys was also based on the loving bond he forged
with them. It was impossible for anyone to fail to notice the love and care
transmitted through the grandparents' interactions with the boys.

Parent's relationships with boys

Mr Fu lamented that his relationships with his two sons were not as close as
he wished. However, he thought he was fortunate to have parents to help
take care of them and relieve him of the pressure. He said that he would not
interfere with how their grandparents dealt with the boys, and supported
grandfather's use of physical punishment. Mr Fu also accepted the fact that

his father played a more important role in the children's life than he, and that his own role was only peripheral: "I am almost like a stranger to them, whether I come to visit them or not does not make a big difference. They don't have much impression of me ..." (FS/C-F 11/8/06).

Interplay among boys and intergenerational parenting coalition

Figure 5.4 demonstrates the nature of the loosely knit parenting coalition of the Fu family. The two main caregivers were from the senior generation. Influences from grandparents to children are represented by a solid line, whereas influences from children to grandparents are shown by dotted lines to reflect an indirect and perhaps weak influence. Father stands at the periphery of the figure with the dotted line indicating an indirect influence from father to sons.

Bird's eye view of dynamics between the siblings and their intergenerational parenting coalition

Although the Fu family did not fit into the strict definition of intergenerational parenting coalition (refer to Chapter 1 for definition), it served as a very helpful sample to contrast with other families studied earlier. From the presentation it can be seen that the main caregivers were the grandparents. Although the father was only marginally involved, there was a high level of agreement among the three adults. The grandfather was accorded the position of head of the family. There were few if any loopholes among the adults that the children could manipulate. Relationships between the senior and middle generations were cohesive. Mr Fu's infrequent interactions with his parents and his children could have helped them to avoid conflict. Mr Fu

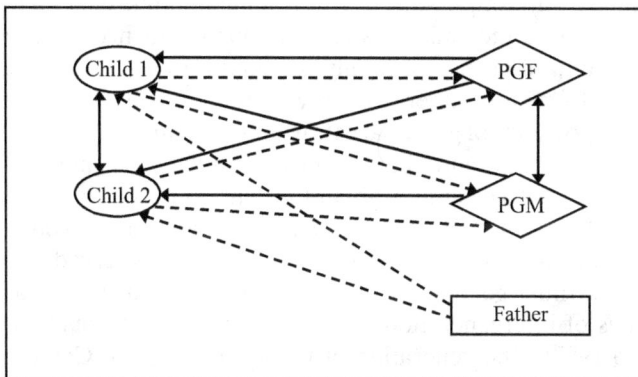

Figure 5.4 The Fu brothers and surrogate parents. (PGF = paternal grandfather; PGM = paternal grandmother.)

was grateful for the help his parents extended to him and the senior generation was glad to help.

Although there were few instances of agentic behaviors in the form of overt resistance compared with children from the other families, Da Fu and Xiao Fu's sense of agency can be seen in ways they chose to comply without monitoring from adults.[5] For instance, while both grandparents worked, the boys would return home after playing with other migrant children in the slum by the stated time for dinner and go to bed by nine o'clock on their own accord. Only-children like Jie Jie and Wei Wei seemed to suffer from "overattention" from their multiple caregivers. These two boys had fewer material things and enjoyed fewer privileges (e.g., no pocket money, no choice of food). However, they were no less happy than the only-children.

Agency and power in the changing Chinese family

According to popular culture – which often laments the unintended consequences of the one child policy – Chinese children have changed from being filial, dutiful and obedient to spoiled little emperors. My research on only-children growing up in three generational families in Xiamen has found that the little suns are agentic children – children that have a kinship with assertive Western children despite distinctive cultural particularities in their expression of agency. What the stories in this chapter show us, however, is that while today's only-children may be getting a lot more attention from their multiple caregivers, we also have to bear in mind that the "overattention" they are receiving happens within intergenerational family settings where the distribution of power remains asymmetric.

Agency and power in shifting cultural norms

How children manifest their agency depends on the cultural norms of specific parent–child relationships. Analysis of my ethnographic data highlights three domains where the children's agency shows evidence of such ongoing changes in cultural norms for family relationships. These include the changing image of Chinese fathers, the caregivers' receptivity to children, and the shifting positions of grandparents within the family.

Through the past two thousand years, Chinese scholars and political authorities have maintained a clear idea about the concept of the child, the meaning of childhood, and the function of family education for the young (Ho 1996a). The Confucian concept of filial piety (*xiao* 孝) has served as a guiding principle governing general Chinese patterns of socialization, as well as specific rules of intergenerational conduct, applicable throughout one's life span (Ho 1987). The veneration of the aged for which Chinese society has long been renowned also owes its ethical basis to filial piety (Ho 1996b). In feudal China, the family was an economic unit in which interdependence between members was crucial for survival. Parents were obligated to raise children and children, in turn, to be filial to their parents. Fathers, especially the patriarch (oldest male), enjoyed supreme power. Also, since property and wealth were transferred from father to son, the father–son relationship was absolutely binding (Tu 1985). Fathers had total control over their sons, and sons unconditionally obeyed and submitted to their fathers' will (Wang 2004). Hence, filial piety justified absolute parental authority over children. The classic family precepts *yan shi jia xun* 颜氏家训 (admonitions for the Yan Clan) instruct parents to be strict with children so that they will be deferential and dutiful toward parents. Inability to be strict with one's children was considered a weakness for a parent. Doting and indulgent parenting styles were thought to breed arrogance and defiance toward parental authority. The precepts also state that "a father should be awe-inspiring and not too familiar with his children, for familiarity breeds contempt" (Yang *et al.* 2004). It was said that Confucius himself maintained a distant reserve toward his son and avoided tutoring his son personally. Hence, psychological distance rather than closeness between father and son was idealized by Confucians (Ho 1996b).

The findings presented in this chapter show that contemporary fathers in urban China have departed from the image of the distant authority figure that is so prevalent in traditional Chinese conceptions of fatherhood. This can be seen in the cases of both Mr Jiang and Mr Wang. Although the children showed high levels of compliance with their fathers' requests or instructions, these fathers did not command absolute paternal authority as their traditional counterparts have been said to do. Instead, the high compliance shown by children can be attributed to the bidirectionality of mutual responsiveness between father and child. The fathers of Jie Jie and Wei Wei often struggled within themselves about their performance as responsive parents. They questioned whether they were too harsh and how they could be better attuned to their children's characteristics. Wei Wei's father, Mr Wang, for instance, claimed that caring for his son was exhausting because he had to *yongxin* (use his heart) to observe every detail in his interactions with his son. This style of fathering is congruent with the dynamic concept of "meta-parenting" proposed by Holden and Hawk (2003) as a replacement for unilateral models of parenting which portray parents as rigid, unthinking or relating to children in a programmed manner. Here the fathers show evidence of anticipation, assessment, problem solving, and reflection in relating to their children. They actively sought feedback from their children and modified their style accordingly.

Although the fathers in this study could be stern and harsh in their punishments, these measures were employed mainly as means to get their children to perform well in school. This is because the success of the child's academic performance would bring about joy and "face"[3] (Hwang 2004) to their parents and probably ensure a better economic future for the whole family (Fong 2004). Even in the case of the surrogate father in the Fu family, where the grandfather was regarded as the "head of the household," there was no lack of explicit display of affection and love toward the children. This is confirmed by Zhang's observation (1997) that urban fathers in China are more maternal yet also more demanding because they have higher expectations for their children. Similarly, Abbot *et al.* (1992) found in a sample of southern Chinese fathers an increase in active involvement with child rearing coexisting with traditional functions of the father as an authority figure and teacher.

The mothers of Wei Wei and Jie Jie, acknowledged how the children had influenced them as parents. Wei Wei's mother consciously provided avenues for her son to sway her. Of course, although parents were receptive to children's influence, there were limits to children's ability to influence (Goodnow 1994); neither mother would compromise where school work was concerned.

The role of the father is not all that is changing in contemporary Chinese families. The position of elders in the family today is very different from the "high" and "venerated" position they once had. Almost all the children assessed their emotional bonds with grandparents, especially grandmothers, as "close." This is not surprising because grandparents were the ones taking care of their daily needs and spending the most time with them – and most of the children slept with grandmother in the same room or in the same bed. Therefore the grandmothers had some relational power over the children although their influence was limited.

The low compliance accorded to grandparents in the cases of Jie Jie and Wei Wei reflects the changed status of the grandparents in the family and the ambiguous guidance afforded by persisting traditional norms regarding filial piety. Parents in the study's five families were keen to teach their children to respect their elders: "*zhang you you xu*" 长幼有序 (respect and observe the hierarchy of order from old to young). However, because most grandparents refrained from taking concrete disciplinary actions (except Grandparents Fu and occasionally for paternal Grandmother Wang), the children learned that the expressed principles of this traditional precept did not always coincide with the reality of everyday practices. Children's rude behaviors, bullying, ignoring, and undermining the grandparents were common occurrences. This lack of grandparents' power over the grandchildren was a known fact to the parents, but they failed to successfully mediate the situation. Some were even resigned to the fact that the position of the grandparents has declined, compared with the only-children, recognizing this as an inevitable consequence of the one-child policy. Jie Jie's father likened grandparents to a *zhi lao hu* 纸老虎 (paper tiger) to the children – one that looks fierce on paper but will never bite.

The findings here support Ho's (1989) prediction that Chinese society is becoming less age-centered and more child-centered; the child is the center of attention whose needs and interests are to be met above all else. There is evidence that traditional norms regarding filial piety persist though in a dynamic, changing form, one that means that the older persons in the family are experiencing a decline in their power, influence and positions. It is now the only-children who enjoy an elevated position at home with enhanced leeway regarding their expression of agency in interactions with the multiple caregivers who revolve around them.

Agency and power within the context of interdependent relationships

The young children in this study were remarkably candid about the strategic nature of their influence and resistance to the various adults in their lives, and, indeed, their agentic behaviors and influence were recognized by caregivers. One form of agency was to resist an adult's instructions or requests through subtle and creative ways, but it was also done through behavioral compliance accompanied by private rejection of parental messages, and sometimes by strategically using relationships with some adults to offset the influence of others.

Instead of being passive recipients of socialization by parents and grandparents as portrayed in traditional family precepts, the little suns today have much more leeway for negotiation in their interactions with adults at home. Children are not isolated agents but embedded in a relationship system that constrains and enables their agency. In that regard the three-generation one-child family form affords several routes for children's expression of agency and influence. That there are fewer children in the typical household – in contrast to larger families of previous generations – allows each child to have stronger, one-on-one personal relationships with his or her caregivers. Each adult caregiver has a greater emotional stake in the child. This means that the child's relationships with multiple caregivers increase the child's relational resources to be exploited in order to meet the child's goals (Kuczynski, 2003). The children in this study reported that they viewed each of their relationships as distinctive, both in terms of the needs they fulfill and the possibilities for affording leeway to achieve their own goals. Wei Wei explained one example of how he capitalized on the loopholes created within the intergeneration parenting coalition when he described how even after his father attempted to communicate his plans and desires to his various caregivers, it was not uncommon for Wei Wei to resist instructions from his paternal grandmother in the "name of his father." This would send his grandmother back to her adult son for clarification and the execution of discipline. The lapses of time in transferring information and implementing discipline inevitably reduced the intensity of the problem. The child therefore, would escape heavy punishment.

Careful observations show that a sense of agency is not absent even in the children's compliance. For instance, Wei Wei's agency was shown through voluntary compliance. The child claimed that he would usually obey his father because the latter always explained things nicely to him. In this case, Wei Wei willingly chose to comply because he deemed his father's requests as reasonable. On the other hand, Jie Jie remarked that he had to comply out of fear of punishment. However, Jie Jie did not acknowledge full compliance. He noted a small victory where once he did not feel pain because his father hit his buttocks without pulling down his pants. That was a hint of his sense of agency despite being punished.

In contrast, the two boys from the migrant family seemingly had no loopholes to exploit or maneuver. The grandparents were the main caregivers and grandfather was the authoritative but caring figure at home. Hence, there were few opportunities to exercise agency in terms of overt resistance. However, the two boys were not devoid of agency. The younger boy, Xiao Fu, for instance, resisted grandfather's instruction cognitively although outwardly he knew he had to comply. On the other hand, the two boys' sense of agency can be seen in the way they do not defy their grandparents' instructions in not loitering around the slum beyond the allowed time stated by their grandparents. Their willing compliance, without adult supervision (as both grandparents had to work night shifts sometimes) is in itself agentic behavior. The close emotional bond which Da Fu reported, especially with his grandmother, made it easy for him to want to please her and comply with her instructions. On the other hand, the explicit demonstration of affection by the two grandparents toward the boys reinforced the virtuous cycle of bidirectional influence between the generations.

6 The plight of little suns as lone tacticians

... although I feel like the precious child, I am always the first victim ....
(Tian Tian, 10-year-old girl)

Parents shape the behavior of their children with their actions. This is a universal truth across cultures. Scholars are increasingly noticing, however, that the less powerful party in this dyad, usually the child, can influence the more powerful party (usually a parent) as well. The extent of this influence depends on the cultural context of the relationship (Kuczynski and Lollis 2004, Trommsdorff and Kornadt 2003). Some cultures permit children to find and assert power, and hence have a higher degree of influence, while other cultures are less hospitable to this behavior, leading to different types of bidirectional relationships between parents and their children across cultures, depending on the role children's actions play in shaping their parents' lives. In this study, it is taken as a given that there exists a bidirectional, that is to say mutual, influence between children and their caregivers that is embedded in the intergenerational family system in contemporary urban China. Seeing families this way enables us to understand the ways that only-children act strategically in order to get their parents and grandparents to fulfill their needs. These young strategists, most of whom find themselves having to navigate parents and grandparents on their own, have turned into lone tacticians.

Throughout this chapter the term "lone tactician" will be used to name the position and actions of the child in the intergenerational family system. "Tactician" encapsulates how the intergenerational family relationships system enables and provides leeway for the child's expression of agency and power, and affords many relational resources so that the child is rich in means for getting things done. On the other hand, the word "lone" reflects how only-children born into the situation of a multigenerational one-child system (through no choice of their own) are constrained by the system. As only-children, they have to handle not only the multiple caregivers individually but also the parenting coalition as a whole. It is in this light that I will proceed to discuss the two dimensions of the dynamic bidirectionality between the lone tacticians and their parenting coalitions and the "power" and "plight" of the lone tacticians.

The sentiments expressed by 10-year-old Tian Tian at the beginning of the chapter reveal the essence of the pleasure and plight of only-children, the lone tacticians. In what follows, readers will see what this role means, particularly for Tian Tian and Bei Bei as they interact with their adult care-givers. Tian Tian demonstrated the widest range of tactics. She displayed her ability to act agentically even in the face of a fierce father. On the other hand, the youngest of the six children studied, five-year-old Bei Bei, utilized passive noncompliance or even covert defiance[1] to achieve her goals. Scenarios from the lived experience of the other four children, Jie Jie, Wei Wei, Da Fu, and Xiao Fu, from the preceding chapter will also be drawn upon to further illustrate this underexplored dimension of the lives of only-children in China.

Tian Tian the lone tactician

Tian Tian wore two French plaits slightly above her ears. She was a flam-boyant character who used many gestures and facial expressions. Whenever she talked, her plaited hair swayed to the movements of her head. She was lean and very athletic. In our first meeting, I recognized it might be profit-able for me to play "one-down" in order to build rapport with her, so I asked if she minded being my badminton coach. She quickly and gladly agreed, and our friendship started there. Tian Tian's maternal grand-parents, who shuttled between Xiamen and Nan Pin, happened to be in Xiamen during the first three months of my fieldwork, which allowed me plenty of opportunities to interact with them.

The younger couple often had heated verbal arguments. Tian Tian told me that she was especially fearful when her parents fought. She described her father as "very strong physically." Tian Tian also said, however, that her father's temper "comes and goes" quickly. When either she or her mother gave in to him, his temper dissipated quickly (and she knew that her father loved them). Tian Tian mentioned that she preferred to have her grandpar-ents around, since they buffered her from these parental fights.[2] Being an only-child, Tian Tian had to develop a repertoire of tactics in order to handle individual members of the intergenerational parenting coalition as well as to survive the four adult caregivers as a collective.

Tian Tian's tactics for interacting with her father

Tian Tian's father was the disciplinarian at home. He used harsh, physical punishment on the child at times. Tian Tian said she had to obey her father because his punishments could be severe. When asked the reasons for her punishments, Tian Tian answered with some hesitation: "I am not sure … well … sometimes because I lied or cheated, other times because I did not do my homework or did not do well in my exams." However, her compliance was never wholesale. She developed many ingenious tactics to resist her father's impositions. These included strategic delay, evasion, and putting up obstacles to her father's monitoring:

> I will sleep, take a long time to finish [assignments given by her father, and it will be] so late that he has to let me go to bed. But when he leaves the room, I will bring out my story books and start reading. Or I will take the assignments he gave me to school so that he cannot find them, or even throw them away, tear them up or sometimes burn them.
>
> (TT 25/8/06)

Another tactic observed by Mrs Tian, the mother, was the child's shrewd use of the power balance between grandparents and father for her benefit. When father threatened to spank her for some misbehavior, she would solicit *wai gong*'s (grandfather) support. She knew that if the matter was not too serious, she could overcome her father's threat by stating that *wai gong* did not think it deserved such punishment. In order to grant "face" to *wai gong*, Mr Tian would sometimes give in. This was corroborated with my conversation with Tian Tian one day:

Researcher: If your father punishes you, would your mother or grandparents come to your rescue?
Tian Tian: Yes, sometimes. Probably five out of ten times. My mother cannot rescue me, she is too weak. Sometimes when my father hits me too hard, my grandparents will come to stop him. My father usually spanked me in my room. If they [grandparents] heard that it is too harsh, they may come [into the room] and stop my father. They will think of a way to get me out of it. They are very nice to me.

She engaged in both overt and covert tactics in her dealings with her rather harsh father. She also knew how to invoke sympathy from other adult members so that they aligned themselves with her against the relatively powerful father, and the father sometimes responded to the grandparents' interventions by reducing the intensity of his beatings. However, their interventions were not always successful.

The father's perception of Tian Tian's tactics

Compared with the fathers of the Jiang and Wang families, Mr Tian paid less attention to the intricate dynamics between himself and his 10-year-old daughter Tian Tian. His main means of controlling the girl was physical punishment, that is, by coercion. According to reports from the other adults in the Tian family, as well as from the girl, occasionally the punishments inflicted on the child could be quite severe. Mr Tian admitted that he had to play the *hei lian* 黑脸 (bad guy) as he was the only one who could get Tian Tian to do her school work. He believed these measures would gradually decrease in frequency as she matured and became more self-disciplined. But at least for now, he believed this to be an effective way of managing her:

> Yes, I am stricter with her [child], perhaps because I don't have time to reason with her. If I sit down and spend half a day reasoning with her, she may still not get things done, still be as lazy. I would rather use the rod. I told her, "if you *bu tinghua* (do not listen) I will use the rod to teach you". So, she has this conditioned response with me. She knows if she does not obey, I will use the rod....
>
> The moment I stepped into the house she quickly switched off the TV, ran to her desk and pretended to read ... I told her there was no need to pretend because I could feel the TV set was still warm. If she finishes the assigned work quickly I will allow her to watch TV or surf the internet.
>
> (TT-F 31/7/06)

Tian Tian's father reported that he knew the child disliked him "from the bottom of her heart" as he was the one who applied pressure. Nevertheless, he believed being strict was for her own good. He also trusted that when she grew up, she would thank him for doing this for her. Contrary to Mr Tian's perception, Tian Tian was rather clear that her father loved her. She elaborated to me,

> although he [father] would spank me, make my life difficult, but he actually loves me. For example, in the previous summer camp, I did not have enough pocket money. My father, mother, *wai gong* and *wai po* they all gave me some money, but I felt it was not enough. On the way taking me to the camp, he [father] gave another ten yuan.

Tian Tian's tactics toward her mother

The array of tactics Tian Tian reported using on her mother included quarreling, crying, and engaging in shouting matches. She admitted that she would quarrel with her grandparents too, but more frequently with her mother. Tian Tian thought that her mother tended to take the initiative to make up after they quarreled, although sometimes she would be the one who tried to reconcile. Depending on the extent of disagreement, if quarreling with her mother was not helping her get her way, she would escalate the situation by crying or shouting.

Tian Tian: Hmm ... to my mother sometimes I will cry.

Researcher:	Why cry? She is afraid when you cry?
Tian Tian:	[When I cry] she will comfort me. And she will soften down. If she does not get soften, I would have to yell or shout real loud.
Researcher:	When would you start shouting?
Tian Tian:	When crying does not work. If crying and shouting do not work, I will give up. For small matters she will give in when I start to cry. If it is big a matter, I need to scream at the top of my voice. Sometimes I scream so loud the roof may collapse [smiled as she made this remark].

One such incident occurred during one of my home visits. It was a rainy Wednesday evening and I was scheduled to be at their apartment to tutor Tian Tian in English at 7 pm. Both grandparents had returned to their hometown for a couple of weeks. I arrived 15 minutes early, and the rain turned heavier minutes after I arrived, as was common in Xiamen during the summers. There was no sight of the girl. Mrs Tian told me that she and her husband were worried sick because Tian Tian had not come home after school. School usually ended at 3 pm and their home was only 10 minutes on foot away from school. I witnessed the mother frantically calling Tian Tian's friends to find out her whereabouts but to no avail. Mrs Tian told me the girl often did this kind of "disappearing act." Despite being told countless times that she needed to ask for permission from her mother to go out with friends so that her parents were aware of whom she was with, Tian Tian had not heeded these instructions. Mrs Tian was visibly angry as she related her frustrations to me. She promised herself that she would punish Tian Tian when she came back. About half an hour later, the child knocked at the door. Both parents rushed to open the door. The anger I saw on Mrs Tian's face disappeared instantly and was replaced by a sense of relief. Apparently the child had decided to go to a classmate's house after school. Without a word, Mr Tian quickly went to the kitchen and fixed Tian Tian some dinner. In a gentle tone of voice, Mrs Tian asked why the child did not inform her of her whereabouts. The child replied without looking at her mother and kept eating her dinner: "I called your mobile but it was busy." It sounded, at least to me, as if the child was blaming her mother for not picking up the phone. Mr Tian, on the other hand, remarked, as if to silence the wife from further questioning the child, "as long as she is back, it is fine." Turning to the child Mr Tian said "Eat your dinner quickly. Teacher Wu is waiting for you for English tutoring."

Despite her seemingly bullying tactics toward mother, Tian Tian considered her mother to be her confidante:

Researcher:	When you are down, whom would you talk to?
Tian Tian:	Mum. When I feel bullied by my friends in school, I will throw myself into her bosom and cry. She will comfort me. If anything

bad happen in school, I will look for mother the first thing when I come home.

Researcher: She would comfort you.

Tian Tian: Although she appears cold at times, she loves me a lot. If I keep those bad feelings inside me, I will suffer. So I need to find a chance to tell her.

The mother's perception of Tian Tian's tactics

Mrs Tian appeared to be relatively powerless in her relations with her daughter. She vented her frustrations and powerlessness to me:

> Sometimes I feel I am powerless, for instance, I want to drag her into the room, but I don't have the strength, I hope my husband will give me a helping hand. Yes, if it does not concern school work, but something about daily habits [about which she wanted to talk to the child] he [husband] says, "You settle it, don't bother me."

(TT-M 31/07/06)

Having her parents come to Xiamen periodically to help with childcare and housework made it easier for Mrs Tian to balance work and family. Ironically, however, the presence of the maternal grandparents, who were highly educated and had strong opinions on the younger couple's performance as parents, accentuated Mrs Tian's sense of powerlessness. Mrs Tian's reliance on her parents to "lend her power" helped to relieve the frequent mother–daughter tension that came from not being able to get her child to comply. In the long run, this reliance on the power of the grandparents actually increased Tian Tian's sense of her mother's lack of ability to deal with her. This enabled her to further play on her mother's lack of power over her. It must be added, however, that the mother–child relationship was not always tense. Despite the child's strong-willed character, Mrs Tian did have warm moments with her.

Tian Tian's tactics toward wai gong and wai po

Tian Tian exercised her power of influence over her grandparents by the intimate relationships they mutually forged with each other. She claimed that if she wanted something from *wai po* (grandmother), she would behave like a pest "sticking" herself to the older lady to a point where *wai po* had to give in to her. With *wai gong* (grandfather), she would behave like a spoiled brat by whining. For instance she would persist in whining if she wanted some money from *wai gong* to buy a can of soda. She was rather confident that these tactics would get her what she wanted.

Besides these little tactics to get her whims and fancies, Tian Tian reported that her grandparents were her emotional buffers. As mentioned earlier in the chapter, Tian Tian felt miserable when her parents fought. She found it especially tormenting if those fights between her parents happened when her grandparents were not in Xiamen. Only her grandparents could intervene into her parents' fights and prevent the situation from escalating. Tian Tian thought that she should not intervene, lest she became the victim. In other situations, she ended up being the unwilling messenger. Her father ordered her to "tell your mother this and this" and mother would do likewise, which she truly hated. To prevent herself from becoming the unintended target of her parents' fight, she would climb into the upper deck of the clothes cabinets where blankets were stored and would hide there until she heard that the fighting had stopped. Although she admitted that her grandparents spent more time in Xiamen than in their hometown, she wished that they could stay in Xiamen all the time. According to Tian Tian, she could have peace and quiet only when her grandparents were around. Moreover, her grandparents were the ones who were able to rescue her when Tian Tian's father punished her. It was no surprise that Tian Tian ranked her grandmother, followed by grandfather, as her most-liked persons at home as they provided her with both material goods and with some protection, thanks, in part, to her acting as a strategic agent.

Grandparents' perception of Tian Tian's tactics

Both *wai po* and *wai gong* enjoyed close, strong bonds with Tian Tian. They tried to turn a blind eye to tension-provoking issues in their interactions with her, and would not try to keep her from watching TV or make sure she had completed her school work. Instead, the grandparents tended to focus their attention on taking care of the child's practical needs, such as providing meals, forging close bonds with her, and lending a sympathetic ear. Also, as a subtle way of expressing their displeasure toward their son-in-law, the older couple overtly aligned themselves with the child against her father. On many occasions I observed, they offered excuses for her misbehaviors and instead blamed the father for setting a bad example or using the wrong parenting methods with her. For instance, the grandparents blamed Tian Tian's poor eating habits on their son-in-law's bad habit of snacking on junk food (Field notes 5/05/06). *Wai po* excused Tian Tian's procrastination in completing assignments because she felt her son-in-law handled the child inappropriately.

> That girl has no self-discipline and does not take initiative to finish her homework. She procrastinates until her father comes home to check on her. Why? Because her father will *jia ma* 加码 (literally means add a bigger size, here it means give her more assignments). So she would rather not finish her work in case her father gives her more work to do. This is the way the father handles her, we have nothing to say!
>
> (TT-MGM 1/08/06)

The relationship between grandparents and grandchild was not always blissful. Grandmother recalled instances where when she was strict with the child; Tian Tian was unhappy and remarked that "perhaps you should go back to Nan Ping and don't bother with me." Grandmother knew that being a disciplinarian would leave a bad impression on the child. Hence, she refrained from disciplining her and left it to the father to play that role. This does not mean that the grandparents condoned Tian Tian's misbehaviors. But they tried to influence her using gentle methods of persuasion. For instance, grandmother Tian would seize teachable moments she observed in the child to do *si xiang gong zuo* 思相工作 (attempts to change the child's thinking through reasoning). According to her, this was most effective at night when her granddaughter was lying in bed with her. She would take the opportunity to talk gently and reason with the child. Nevertheless, the grandparents were well aware that their influence on the child was extremely limited, as explained by the grandfather:

> To the girl, *wai gong wai po* cannot command any muscle. We cannot handle her. She often screams, yells and whines to get her own way. She is not even afraid of her mother. The only person she has some fear of is her father. He has muscle because he pressures the girl and even spanks her. Recently, he spanked her and left a mark on her leg. The child was not ashamed. Instead she went to school to show her friends [and complain to them] how "bad" a father she has.
>
> (TT-MGF 2/08/06)

Grandmother knew the child considered her the "most-liked" person in the family. However, she was aware of the "subtle competition" among the adults to be "liked" by Tian Tian. That was why she coached the child not to express her love for her grandmother openly, but encouraged her to instead be explicit about appreciating her father so as to gain his favor:

> Once, my son-in-law brought the girl for an outing and asked her who she liked best at home. He was upset and complained to me [grandmother] afterwards that despite his buying so many nice things for the child, Tian Tian told him "grandmother is the best." So I told Tian Tian she must always say daddy is the best.
>
> (TT-MGM, 1/8/06)

Tian Tian – the lone tactician and her parenting coalition

In comparing across the cases, Tian Tian's family was probably the most complex in the interplay of the three-generational dynamics (Figure 6.1). It was the only family with two grandparents in the parenting coalition who coresided under the same roof. In the case of the Fu family, although both grandparents were present, the middle generation was absent. In the Wang

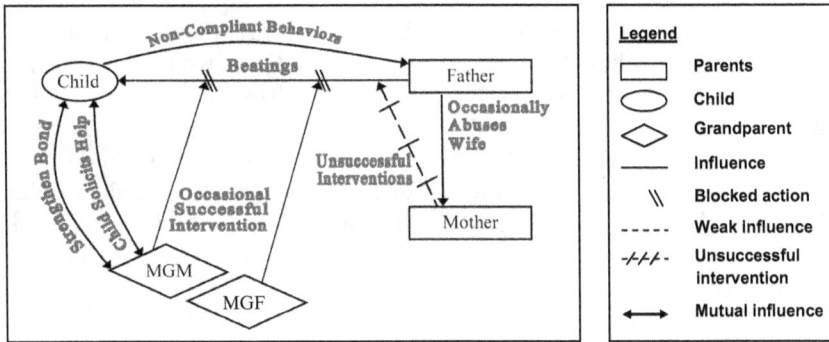

Figure 6.1 *Left:* Interplay of Tian Tian's tactics and the forces of three generations. (MGM = maternal grandmother; MGF = maternal grandfather.)
Right: Legend for figures in Chapter 6.

family, there were two grandmothers helping with childcare, but they lived in separate locations.

As discussed earlier in this chapter, Tian Tian had developed a wide range of tactics in relating to the host of adult caregivers around her. The harsh disciplinary measures taken by Mr Tian were largely precipitated by Tian Tian's persistent noncompliance with her father's instructions. One way Mr Tian exercised power and control over his child was by inflicting physical pain.[3] According to Tian Tian, her mother could not rescue her during these incidents because her father disregarded her mother's protests. Instead the grandparents would intervene and these interventions were occasionally successful. In this sense, the grandparents commanded more power than their daughter. Besides, Tian Tian's father would have to "give face" to his parents-in-law when they intervened, as they were his seniors. However, in situations where her father was very upset, and when he deemed her misbehavior very serious, even the grandparents' interventions would not succeed.

Despite difficult circumstances Tian Tian was able to exercise a high level of agency. She managed to gain a rather high level of autonomy through the strategies and tactics she developed in dealing with the parenting coalition. She could construct goals in her mind and execute actions to achieve them. Although she was not always successful, she could frequently influence her mother and get her way. Even with a powerful father who used harsh disciplinary measures to assert power and control over her, Tian Tian could occasionally escape punishment through inviting the sympathetic intervention of her grandparents. The competing forces of grandparents and father within the parenting coalition provided an avenue for the child to maneuver. This analysis may give the readers an impression of Tian Tian as shrewd or even manipulative. But one should also frame her actions as grounded in a need for survival. As quoted at the beginning of this chapter,

Tian Tian disclosed to me during an interview how she felt, saying, "... although I feel like the precious child, I am always the first victim ...." Tears rolled down her cheeks when she shared with me what it was like for her to be the only child having to face all the adults at home. She revealed that she felt very lonely being the only child at home and noted that she would be blamed for things that she did not do. As the only child in the family of all adults, Tian Tian had to formulate her tactics alone. Her survival and ability to achieve her goals hinged on her ability to calibrate her tactics appropriately according to circumstances and depending on who she was dealing with.

Bei Bei the five-year-old lone tactician

Bei Bei (which literally means the "precious one') was a fair-skinned five-year-old who was said by her mother to be a shy girl who needed a long time to warm to people. She wore her hair bobbed, with a fringe hanging down her forehead and covering her brows. When I first came to visit her family, Bei Bei hid behind her mother and observed me. After a while, she came to sit by me, but was still shy and did not speak. Instead, she communicated by gestures and drawings. At the end of the visit, with encouragement from her mother, Bei Bei gave me a goodbye hug at the door. I responded with a big hug, and we both smiled.

When I was first introduced to this family, Bei Bei's parents had been divorced for a year. Madam Bai was a successful accountant with a *wai qi* 外企 (foreign investment company). She was still raw with grief and hurt from the marital breakdown. Her mother, Bei Bei's *wai po* (maternal grandmother), had lived with them since the birth of Bei Bei, having taken early retirement at age 50 from her lower-management job in a state-run factory. The grandmother assisted her adult daughter and granddaughter by providing childcare and assistance with housework. She felt obliged to continue her caring role after the divorce, primarily out of pity for her adult daughter. The relationship within the grandmother–mother dyad was however, characterized by tension and strain. Madam Bai wanted to maintain her privacy and keep the reasons for the marital breakdown to herself, and this left the grandmother feeling excluded and unappreciated despite all the help she provided. This observation was borne out by data collected separately from the grandmother and adult daughter converged as they both assessed their relationship as strained. Let us turn now to see how Bei Bei, a five-year-old tactician, handled her relationships with the two adult women.

Bei Bei's tactics with the two adult women

Bei Bei was the youngest among all the child participants in this study and hence one may question the reliability of her answers during research conversations. However, experiments by Frye and Zelazo (2003) show that although three-year-old children have difficulties with causal sequence, by five years, children demonstrate marked developmental progress. This improvement allows five-year-olds to perform suitable, intentional actions in more complex situations. These age-related changes in children's awareness of the constituents of action expand the range of actions that children can perform intentionally. This finding supports my definition of agency: the capacity to interpret and evaluate messages coupled with the ability to engage in strategic action (including resistance) in order to meet one's goals. It is worth noting, however, that I corroborated the information from Bei Bei with data from observations and through interviews with her mother.

Bei Bei said she tended to comply with her mother's instructions as she felt her mother loved her more than grandmother. Her strategy for not complying was to "pretend to listen" but actually ignore the instructions.

Researcher: You said you sometimes do not *ting* 听 (obey) instructions from your mother. What exactly do you do?
Bei Bei: Pretend I am listening [without intention to obey].
Researcher: Would your mother or *wai po* try to persuade you or punish you or do something to make you do it?
Bei Bei: No, they would believe I am really listening.
Researcher: If they do not allow you to do something, like going to the playground, what would you do?
Bei Bei: I will sneak downstairs when they are not looking and I will stay for a long long time in the playground.

(BB 27/08/06)

In Bei Bei's view, when she did not want to comply, there was almost nothing the two adults could do to make her comply. A typical scenario of noncompliance was during meal times. Both adults would coax her into finishing her bowl of rice but Bei Bei merely sat there quietly refusing to compromise (Field notes 14/5/06). This five-year-old child did not actively protest, rather, she employed the tactic of passive resistance to achieve her goals. Bei Bei also utilized persistent whining to get her way. I had an opportunity to witness her grandmother giving in to her insistent demands. One late morning, I visited Grandmother Bai and Bei Bei close to lunch time. After a brief chat with the older lady I offered to buy a simple lunch for the three of us in a nearby noodle shop, as I knew the grandmother liked the food there. On our way there, Bei Bei threw a tantrum on the street and insisted that she wanted to eat Kentucky Fried Chicken. Even after much persuasion she would not relent, so we had to give in to her demands. I had a taste of helplessness in the face of Bei Bei's forceful insistence. Neither *wai po* nor I could change her mind and in order not to create a scene on the street, we gave in to a five-year-old.

Gan qing 感情 *(emotional bonds) – the ammunition of Bei Bei's tactics*

When asked to describe her relationship with her mother and grandmother, Bei Bei drew a full circle in the air with her outstretched arm to indicate her perception of her mother's love for her. With regard to her grandmother, she held her arms slightly apart in front of her, showing approximately a 30-degree slice of a full circle. She said her mother loved being kissed by her and her grandmother refused such physical expressions. Also, she thought her grandmother could be loud and fierce at times, whereas her mother had never raised her voice with her. She thought that her mother loved her more than her grandmother and that was why she complied with mother's requests more often.

Bei Bei talked about the friendly fights the two women usually had over whom she should sleep with. According to the child she felt good about being "fought over."

Bei Bei:	But sometimes mum wants me to sleep with her, but she is too late [coming home], I would ask her to come over to *wai po*'s room to "steal me."
Researcher:	Why did your mother steal you over to her room?
Bei Bei:	Because I like her to steal me over.
Researcher:	If *wai po* wants you to sleep with her and mum also wants you to sleep with her, what do you do?
Bei Bei:	Well, I will sleep with *wai po* first and ask mum to come steal me in the middle of the night.
Researcher:	How do you feel about both of them fighting to have you sleep with them?
Bei Bei:	What? [She seemed to have difficult understanding my question, so I modified it into a closed-ended question.]
Researcher:	Do you feel happy that both of them want you to sleep with them?
Bei Bei:	Yes.

Bei Bei was the source of emotional comfort and joy for the two adult care-givers in the family. The subtle competition between the two women for a more intimate bond with the child granted the five-year-old child considerable amount of power of influence over the adults. This can be further juxtaposed by Madam Bai's claims.

Mother's perception of Bei Bei's tactics

Madam Bai claimed that Bei Bei was her pillar of strength following the divorce. If not for the child, she said, she would have ended her life (BB-M, 30/7/06). Her daughter was a very important source of emotional support as

Madam Bai kept the divorce all to herself and was not willing to talk about it to anyone, even her mother. When asked how the child resisted following adults' instructions, mother corroborated Bei Bei's claim that "pretending to listen but actually ignoring the adult" was the method she used. Madam Bai deemed her mother incapable of commanding respect from the child and easily giving in to her resistance. By contrast, she claimed that she herself was gentle but firm with her daughter. The mother also confirmed the "friendly competition" between herself and her mother over whom Bei Bei should sleep with, and agreed that the child would always come up with solutions to appease both parties. For instance, she would say "Mummy, I slept in your room last night, so tonight I will sleep with *wai po*, and, tomorrow night I will come to your room, is that all right?" (BB-M 30/7/06). Between herself and grandmother, Madam Bai claimed that she was the decision-maker regarding childcare issues. She said she was always open to negotiating with her daughter, while maintaining some matters as non-negotiable. Hence, she felt she had greater power of influence over her child. The way she influenced Bei Bei was through persuasion and reasoning. She never raised her voice or was harsh with her child. And this strategy worked. In essence, Madam Bai's reliance on her child as her emotional pillar provided her child ammunition with which to exercise tactics on adults. The power of influence from mother to child did not arise from hierarchical authority. Instead, gentle persuasion, negotiation, and emotional coaxing were used – a more egalitarian form of influencing power.

Grandmother the dethroned lao zu zong 老祖宗

The grandmother felt very close to Bei Bei because she had done a good deal of the caregiving. She noted that she had carried the child in her arms from the day the child was born. When the infant opened her eyes the first person she saw was her grandmother. She also said that the child had slept in the same bed with her since she was a baby, and could only fall asleep when wrapped around by grandmother's big arms. Grandmother claimed Bei Bei asked her once: "'*Wai po*, why don't you be my mother?' I told her, 'No, I am your *wai po* 外婆 (maternal grandmother).' 'What is *wai po*?' the child asked. "*Wai po* is your mother's mother" (Field notes 2/6/06 p. 4).

This account shows the extent of intimacy in the grandmother–child dyad. However, the grandmother said she encouraged the child to be closer to her mother after the divorce, as she perceived her adult daughter to be lonely and depressed. She sometimes complained about the child being spoiled by her mother and nicknamed Bei Bei as "*lao zu zong*" (patriarch/matriarch), meaning that caring for Bei Bei required mindfulness, patience, and energy, like serving the oldest patriarch or matriarch in the traditional Chinese family. There is a role reversal here. Traditionally, grandmothers were revered as the *lao zu zong*. Now, the only-child has taken the throne in the family.

Despite the intimate bond between grandmother and granddaughter as discussed in the preceding segment, *wai po* lamented that Bei Bei would usually comply more with her mother's instructions.

Researcher:	Between *wai po* and mother, who does Bei Bei *ting hua* (obey) more?
Grandmother:	She obeys her mother.
Researcher:	Why so?
Grandmother:	I guess it is my problem, because I do not insist on my instructions. For instance, I tell her only one candy is allowed, but when she comes to ask me again, I will give her another one. I treat this girl as my own child. We are very close. Sometimes I really take pity on her [because child's parents are divorced].

Hence, in general, Bei Bei and her grandmother had a very close relationship. But grandmother commanded very limited power of influence on the child. Grandmother told me that she found Bei Bei's persistent whining and passive non-compliance very difficult to handle; she tended either to give in or leave it to her daughter to handle the situation.

Bei Bei – the lone tactician and her parenting coalition

Figure 6.2 depicts the interplay of three-generational interaction between Bei Bei, her mother, and her maternal grandmother. Bei Bei's family seems much simpler in its interactions when compared with the other four families in this study. The child did not need to navigate her way through a host of

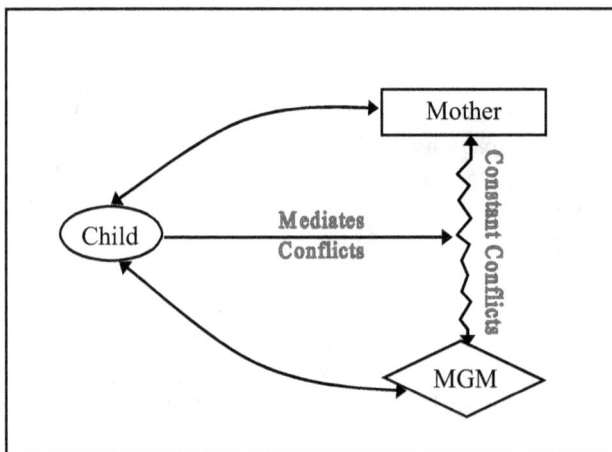

Figure 6.2 Bei Bei – Interplay of three generations. (MGM = maternal grandmother.)

caregivers. Although there were frequent conflicts between Madam Bai and Grandmother Bai, these conflicts did not affect their collaborations in caring for the child. Grandmother Bai readily gave in to her daughter where childcare issues were concerned, and hence there was no competition for power. Neither Madam Bai nor Grandmother Bai would leave the coalition owing to their lack of options; this dyad is therefore very stable. Bei Bei did not feel she needed to play the adults against each other to obtain her goals.

She was very secure in the love of both adults, although she thought her mother loved her more than her grandmother. Instead, Bei Bei was the mediating force between the two adults. Madam Bai related this incident to me:

> Sometimes I feel quite ashamed of myself. This afternoon she [Bei Bei] came up to me to tell me that I was impatient when talking to my mother. She said, "Mum, mum you don't get angry. Talk slowly with *wai po*." She will say things like this to me. Sometimes when we fight, she will remind us. I told my daughter that if I lose my temper, she should remind me.
>
> (BB-M 7/08/06)

From the presentation it can be seen that Bei Bei, despite her young age, is quite an effective lone tactician. She employed strategies like passive resistance or active whining to get her way. Although she complied with mother's requests because she felt mother loved her most, she also commanded significant power and influence on her mother. The influence between mother and child was obviously bidirectional. Despite the conflictual relationship between Madam Bai and her mother, Bei Bei was not the victim of their conflicts but rather the source of emotional comfort for both women, and often played the mediator's role when the two adults fought. We can see and understand Bei Bei's ability to get her caregivers to work together primarily because we are using a lens of investigation that sees that children are agents. This perspective reveals only-children's contributions to the dynamics of influence and power in the context of multigenerational families in contemporary China. Viewing children as agentic beings, however, is not the perspective taken by most scholars of childrearing research conducted in China.

The power of the lone tacticians

This lens of bidirectional influence, where children are considered to be active agents, contrasts with the unidirectional viewpoint of parent–child relationships, which assumes a deterministic, one-way influence or control from parent to child. The unidirectional perspective has led to a body of research that is primarily concerned with the dimensions and characteristics of parents and parenting in which children are viewed as outcomes of their parents' socialization. In this model, immediate compliance was considered a form of child competence, whereas noncompliance was considered incompetent behavior (Kuczynski and Hildebrant 1997). While the lone tacticians who were my informants also showed high levels of compliance, particularly with their fathers' requests or instructions (several of the children assessed their compliance with fathers' demands at nine out of ten times), a bidirectional view makes clear that this does not reflect a lack of agency on the part of the children. Rather, I would argue that these lone tacticians were exercising their agency in the context of their overt compliance. Indeed, many of their tactics matched the categories of children's agentic responses to parental demands developed by Kuczynski and Lollis (2004, p. 219). For instance, Tian Tian's delay in completing her assignments as a way to avoid getting additional homework from her father would fall within the "uncooperative negotiation" category of the coding schema. Although generally complying, the lone tacticians resisted influences by exercising agentic strategies, as when Wei Wei got his mother to wonder if she should do away with corporal punishment after he told her "you are not a good mother because you beat me." It is rather obvious that there was room for bidirectional influence in this mother–child relationship.

Much easier to see than the child's agency in their high level of compliance with fathers' instructions, is the clear set of tactical actions taken by the lone tacticians with those with whom they showed much lower levels of compliance: the mothers and grandparents. All the children exercised their relational power of influence on their mothers (including surrogate mother) to a greater extent, based on their strong bonds. They recognized that their effectiveness as "tacticians" was derived from their mothers' sensitivity and responsiveness to their needs and requests (Kuczynski and Parkin 2006). This could be seen in the relationship between Bei Bei and her mother. Sometimes Bei Bei even played "mother" to her mother by coaching her to "talk nicely to grandmother" and not to raise her voice. Several of the mothers in this study explicitly told me how they derive emotional value, for instance joy, happiness, comfort, and sense of satisfaction, from their only-children. There is a strong interdependence when mothers rely on their only-children to meet their needs for a sense of worth and value, while children depend on their mothers for love, security, and care. This mutual dependence, as in all intimate relationships, both enables and constrains the assertion of power and influence. Although mothers had more personal resources, hence, were more powerful, they usually did not use their power and deliberately left room for their children to negotiate. Interestingly however, most mothers had their bottom line which the children understood as non-negotiable.

The amount of influence each mother was able to wield varied from family to family. Mrs Wang would sometimes use physical punishment as a way of asserting her influence on Wei Wei. Correspondingly, Wei Wei thought that when mother was angry, he had to comply with her demands.

On the other hand, Mrs Tian's influence on her daughter Tian Tian was least of all the mothers.

Grandparents had even less influence on the lone tacticians than mothers. Most grandparents (with the exception of Grandfather Fu) restrained themselves from disciplinary action, perceiving it as inappropriate. Although their adult children had, for the most part, granted them permission to execute discipline, grandparents thought it was not within their jurisdiction to use it. They believed inflicting pain on grandchildren would cause tension in their relationships with their children or children-in-law. Besides, avoiding disciplinary action was a tactic grandparents employed to forge close bonds with their grandchildren. Grandparents Tian for instance, did not want to be the "bad guys" as they knew they would be deemed more likeable by their grandchildren. The children knew that they would not be punished if they resisted or even defied their grandparents' requests. Hence, they were able to utilize an even wider range of strategies with their grandparents for achieving their goals. The grandparents influenced their grandchildren by "talking nicely to them," by persuasion, and through their close, intimate relationships. Using the bidirectional approach here allows us to see that generally children seemed to have a stronger influence over their grandparents than their parents, and that they were forever defying their grandparents' dictums.

It is important here to avoid the impression that the lone tacticians are willing to assert their influence at the expense of straining their relationships with their caregivers. In fact, the children seemed to value their close bonds with these adults and look forward to having a long-term relationship with them. Indeed, the empirical data discussed thus far seems to point to the relevance of conceptualizing relationships between children and their adult caregivers in a long-term context with time as an important component influencing their dynamics. There is a distinction between understanding parent (in this case including grandparent)-child relationships as moment-to-moment interactions and as relationships that are formed and endure over time (Hinde 1979, Lollis and Kuczynski 1997). Lollis (2003) aptly points out that time is what allows us to speak of a caregiver–child relationship as having a "past" based on a history of interaction, a "present" based on immediate interactions and a "future" based on an anticipation of interactions to come (ibid.). These six Chinese children showed a strong commitment to filial piety to both their parents and grandparents, which can be understood as recognizing the importance of the ongoing time dimension. When asked why they would want to take care of their seniors when they grew up, they referred to the past experiences of how their parents and grandparents had taken good care of them and raised them. An ongoing time perspective on parent–child relationships is emphasized in Confucian values. The Chinese saying *yin shui si yuan* 饮水思源 (while drinking water ponder the source of the river) is often used to encourage children to have an attitude of gratitude toward those who have contributed to their lives, especially parents. This saying poignantly denotes the Chinese way of perceiving relationships between caregivers and children as ongoing and unfolding from past to present. Because parent (grandparent)–child relationships are involuntary, stable and permanent, the anticipated future becomes very important in these relationships. Not only did the children keep in their minds the goal of fulfilling their filial responsibilities, the Chinese parents considered filial piety an integral quality of an ideal child. Even 10-year-old Tian Tian, who complained to me of how her father often punished her severely, was able to symbolically reconstruct (Blumer 1969, Mead 1929) these unpleasant experiences and give them a positive frame and thought she would definitely be filial to her father in the future. I asked Tian Tian whether she would she take care of her parents and grandparents when they grow old. Her answer was definite: "Yes, I will. I have promised them. I told them I will earn good money to support them. If I don't take care of them I will be an unfilial child."

Chinese parents defined being filial to one's parents as meaning to reciprocate when one's parents are old the kind of care one received while growing up. Filial piety is one of the core values of Confucius's teaching, which is a deeply ingrained value in much of Chinese society (Goh 2006). One should be clear that this is an idealized future, co-constructed by both the children and their caregivers. But the constructed future inevitably influences how the children and adults interact in the present. So, the Chinese parents and grandparents in this study have invested much of their time, energy, and resources on this one child, also see that child as perhaps their only hope (Fong 2004).

The plight of the lone tacticians

The agency of the child that is revealed when the relationship between lone tacticians and their adult caregivers is viewed as bidirectional may suggest an image of children casually enjoying advantages at the expense of the adults in their family. The agentic tactics children develop to negotiate and resist adult requests may also project an unintended impression of them as self-centered and self-serving. It is not my goal to echo the dominant view of children in urban China as "little emperors," who are spoiled and self-centered. While it is undeniable that these labels reflect a real phenomenon of only-children who inevitably receive the best resources from their families – they also reflect a deterministic view of children as passively molded by their indulgent caregivers into "little emperors." But seeing these urban only-children this way leads one to overlook another equally important, but little explored dimension of the phenomenon: the ways lone tacticians suffer in their position.[4]

As noted above, only-children in China often bear the full weight of both their parents' and grandparents' sacrifices and hopes. They are the vessels of their expectations for academic and financial success, and partially responsible for maintaining the family's reputation, all the while serving as one pole of the complex relationships of the multigenerational households. It is this that underlies Fong's observation (2004) of the enormous amount of pressure to excel academically that adolescent only-children in Dalian city faced, as this is seen as the way of upward social mobility not only for themselves but also for the whole family. Here the focus is more on the plight and pressure that only-children face in their day-to-day interactions with their multiple caregivers: the daily monitoring from their multiple caregivers, which can be suffocating, and service as a kind of sacrifice to maintain peace within the parenting coalition.

Lubricant, victim, and fighter

In the preceding chapter, Mrs Jiang appropriately described her seven-year-old son Jie Jie as both lubricant and victim of the intergenerational parenting coalition. She admitted that love for the child was the force that enabled the three adults (father, mother, and paternal grandmother) to work together even though they might not see eye to eye on many issues. When conflicts arose in the collaboration process, their love for the child acted as a lubricant to oil the rough edges. However, at other times the child was left to suffer, a victim whose existence facilitated a momentary peace or a state of power equilibrium between the grandmother and the middle generation. Mrs Jiang felt that her husband sometimes punished Jie Jie unnecessarily to appease the grandmother. As can be recalled, Jie Jie thought he had to comply with father's instructions because his father was "as tall as a *juren* 巨人 (giant)"; the mere fact of the stronger physique of the parent legitimated his authority (Damon, 1977). It is easy to see how a tall, strong, and strict father spurred on by the grandmother to be more severe while executing discipline on the child could lead to one act of misbehavior by Jie Jie being magnified by having two adults focusing on him, and with no way for him to escape. This must have been very stressful for Jie Jie and made him feel helpless, since his mother could not rescue him from the beatings.

The other child who played the lubricant role was the five-year-old Bei Bei who was discussed earlier in this chapter. Both her grandmother and mother admitted that there were many open conflicts between them. Unlike Jie Jie, Bei Bei did not have to be sacrificed to bring about peace between the two women, because she provided a pillar of emotional support to both adult women. She lubricated the coalition by mediating the conflict in a number of ways, including reminding her mother not to raise her voice to Grandmother Bai.

Tian Tian, the 10-year-old girl, had similar yet different experiences. She was the child with a four-member intergenerational parenting coalition living under the same roof. I sometimes wonder if the beatings Mr Tian inflicted on Tian Tian were his way of asserting his authority as the "leader" of the coalition, since grandparents Tian often challenged his ways of handling the child and blamed him for setting her a bad example. However, I must qualify that this remains only my suspicion as I did not verify it with any of the Tian family members. In addition to having to navigate (as well as utilize) the micro-politics of the parenting coalition, Tian Tian expressed her ambivalence about being the only child. She felt that she was both the precious only child and the first one to get blamed if anything went wrong as the adults would treat her as the most likely culprit, for instance, when things at home get misplaced or go missing. She voiced her dilemma of wanting to remain as a child but wishing to grow up quickly:

Researcher: I have never been an only-child. Can you tell me how it is like to be one?

Tian Tian: To be an only-child is good and bad at the same time. Good because I am treated like the precious one and always the one to get all the rewards. Bad because if anything went missing they would accuse me. So I sometimes wish to grow up quickly. But other times I don't want to grow up.

Researcher: Hope to grow up fast?

Tian Tian: *Hen mao dun* 很毛盾 (very conflicting).

Researcher: Why do you want to grow up fast?

Tian Tian: So that I can be independent and don't have to endure such unfair treatment [accusation from her caregivers].

Only-children may also be a victim of the dynamics within the parenting coalition, much as Tian Tian claimed.[5] It is no wonder she developed such a wide range of tactics to cope with the "undercurrents" between the members of the parenting coalition. It is not fair, however, to see Tian Tian as a total victim. She perceptively seized opportunities from the conflicts within the coalition to turn to her own benefit too. She was a fighter as well as a victim.

The role of lone tacticians as lubricant in the parenting coalition "machinery" must be understood from the Chinese cultural context. The traditional notion of *chuan zong jie dai* 传宗接代 (extending the ancestral line) is still very much alive in contemporary urban Chinese families (Zheng *et al.* 2005).[6] The vital mission of the parenting coalition machinery is to ensure the growth and well-being of these only-children. It is interesting to observe that only-children are not just at the receiving end of nurturing and attention from the parenting coalition, I would like to take it one step further to argue that they also contribute to the maintenance and smooth running of this machinery. As members of the closely knit multigenerational systems, these only-children inadvertently had to play the role of lubricant to distract, diffuse, or soften the covert and overt conflicts arising from the daily intimate collaborations between the two senior generations. Sometimes children have to be temporarily sacrificed so that they can act as safety valves for the release of pent-up tensions within the machinery.

Surveillance and freedom

Urban Chinese only-children raised by parenting coalitions are under constant surveillance by different adult caregivers taking "shifts" to ensure that they are monitored at all times. According to the survey conducted in Xiamen, an average of 1.7 grandparents care for one child. Including two parents, this will make almost four adults caring for one child. This 4:1 ratio of caregivers to child naturally ensures that children are well cared for, but it also means that children have little time to be alone or with other children without adult supervision. The frustrations of being so closely watched can be seen clearly in Wei Wei and Jie Jie, both seven-year-old boys. Wei Wei wanted to be independent and believed he was old enough and tough enough to walk the 10-minute trip to and from school on his own. But his desire was frustrated by his paternal grandmother who always accompanied him. It was not uncommon for Wei Wei to take out his frustration on his grandmother by throwing tantrums. There was a clash between Wei Wei's desire to exercise autonomy and the parenting coalition's concern about bad influences and safety. Jie Jie's situation was that he could not escape his father's discipline, as grandmother reported daily happenings at school back to father. That could be the reason for Jie Jie saying hat he sometimes felt like "punching *nai nai*," as he considered her behavior to be telling tales. There is no doubt that this monitoring by the adult carers is done out of love and good intention. Nevertheless, it can be rather suffocating for the children, as they are not given their own breathing space.

Another aspect of the tight daily surveillance was to monitor and ensure that children complete their school work. It has been well documented that only-children carry their parents' high education aspirations since they are their "only hope" (Fong 2004). In my six-month interactions with the Jiang, Wang, and Tian families[7] I observed the day-to-day pressure parents exerted on the only-children to perform well in school. Academic work, unlike other aspect of parent–child relationships, was always considered non-negotiable with little room for compromise. Much of the tactics devised by Tian Tian was used to resist her father's incessant demands for extra-academic exercises so as to ensure she perform better in the next test.

The relative freedom enjoyed by Da Fu and Xiao Fu – the pair of siblings from the migrant family – can be understood as contrasting with the experience of the only-children. They did not receive close monitoring from their grandparents and having another sibling seemed to lighten the load of being the "only hope," at least for Xiao Fu, the younger boy. Owing to their low skill, their grandparents (who were their surrogate parents) had to do jobs with irregular hours and shift work to make ends meet. For this practical reason, the grandparents could not provide constant surveillance for the boys. It was common for the boys to be left by themselves while grandfather worked overnight in his security guard job and grandmother did part-time cleaning in a public sports stadium. Grandmother Fu usually worked from

3 to10 pm. She would prepare dinner for the boys in the rice cooker, usually just rice and a simple dish all in one pot, before leaving for work. The boys were free to go out to play with other children in the slum after completing their homework, as long as they came home for dinner between 7 and 8 pm. They would heat up the food for themselves, and go to bed by 9 pm. As the wooden door of their little quarters could only be padlocked from inside, the boys usually placed a chair behind the door before going to bed, and the grandparents would lock it after they returned from work. Although grandfather periodically checked on them by calling home, Grandparents Fu seemed to think the boys were *hen guai* 很乖 (very obedient and well behaved) on their own. Unlike their only-child counterparts, whose parents and grandparents often played cat-and-mouse games with them, these two siblings were trusted by their grandparents. Also, because the attention the boys received from their surrogate parents was divided between them, this helped to alleviate some of the academic pressure that comes with being the only target. It was grandparents Fu's hope that Da Fu, the older boy, could fulfill their dreams of becoming the first to enter university in their family, since he was academically inclined. However, they did not put unrealistic pressure on Xiao Fu as they knew he was rather weak in his school work.

Conclusion

Lack of time on their own, the need to make peace between adult caregivers within the parenting coalition, and pressure from these multiple caregivers all play into *the plight of the lone tacticians*. Before moving on, it is worth noting that this understudied phenomenon is in need of further exploration. Since this project is not outcome-driven research, it is not appropriate to comment on whether these seeming downsides of being a lone tactician have negative effects on only-children in multigenerational families. Researchers may want to consider reframing their perspective of these only-children not only as "little emperors" but also look at the situation bidirectionally in order to see these children as lone tacticians who engage with their parents and grandparents not only to bend them to their will, but also to try and navigate what are clearly challenging pressures they face as the youngest member of the multi-generation households.

7   Conclusion

This book has addressed the prevalent but often overlooked phenomenon of only-children raised by multiple caregivers within three-generational families in contemporary urban China. These three-generation families in urban China have arisen and become an important household unit as a result of the dramatic social changes that have been occurring over the past few decades including economic liberalization, an increase in women's employment, and the one-child policy. These changes have altered family structures and the way they function and, as a consequence, childrearing practices. One result of these societal changes is the increased importance of grandparents as coresidents of three-generation households.[1]

There has been a vacuum in the academic literature regarding the challenges faced by grandparents and parents in their new-found role as joint caregivers to only-children. Few researchers have studied the ways that the impact of macro-level changes in society have resulted in distinctive new dynamics in the family including new patterns of influence, tensions, and conflicts or the potential consequences for children raised in these three-generation families. The findings from the large-scale survey and ethnographic data reported in the preceding chapters have made clear the need to move beyond the longstanding socialization frameworks that researchers borrowed from western models, models that emphasize nuclear families and unidirectional patterns of intergenerational influence. What I am proposing here is a different framework: *kua dai yu er zu he* 跨代育儿组合 (the intergenerational parenting coalition, IGPC), which can serve as a unit of analysis for future research in childrearing and child development in urban China. In what follows I will first draw out the essential characteristics of the IGPC and the justification for the use of this framework, discuss how it can and should be used as the unit of analysis in studying childrearing in urban China. By examining a few of the key aspects of the micro-dynamics within the IGPC I hope to illustrate the potential usefulness of treating IGPC as a unit of analysis, not least because of the previously undocumented insights it yielded. My attention will then turn to the focus on the IGPC, the only-child and the value of reconceptualizing only-children as lone tacticians interacting with members of the IGPC.

Only-children should be treated as active agents embedded within the intergenerational family relationships system, a system which both enables and constrains the child's ability to exercise agency and power. To conclude, I will present new directions for future researchers studying childrearing in urban China.

Reconceptualizing parenting

One important lesson I have learned while conducting this study in China is the problem of applying the concept of "parenting" as a "given" in the Western research community. According to Trommsdorff and Kornadt (2003), parent–child relations have been studied mostly in Western cultures and by researchers who were socialized in the West. The situation in China is rather different. As early as 2004, during my first field visit to Xiamen, I was told that grandparents played an imperative role in childrearing. After subsequent visits and a prolonged immersion of six months in the field, I can now propose this new concept of the intergeneration parenting coalition to capture the characteristics of parenting in Xiamen. An overarching framework which I termed the "contemporary Chinese intergenerational family relationships system" (CCIFRS) can be used to integrate the key findings I've discussed and provide a sketch of the dynamics of children and their multiple caregivers in urban Xiamen (Goh and Kuczynski 2010). This overarching framework consists of two components, namely the IGPC and the "lone tactician." These two integral parts relate to each other in a dynamic way. Figure 7.1 depicts a generalized structure of the CCIFRS.[2] Consistent with the bidirectional model of parent–child relationships' principle of holism, the three-generation framework is embedded in the cultural context of contemporary China. This enables recognition that Chinese culture is undergoing modification because of the abrupt changes in Chinese demographics and intergenerational norms. The macro context shapes the dynamics and gives cultural meaning to interactions among the relational subsystems of the CCIFRS. Also depicted are three classes of social dynamics which are relevant to this parenting system: interactions between grandparents and parents; interactions between the child and each of the adults of the IGPC; and interaction between child and the IGPC as a whole.

The term "coalition" has been chosen deliberately. According to the *Oxford Advanced Dictionary*, "coalition" refers to a group of people from several different groups who agree to work together for a particular purpose. In this case, the term "coalition" allows me to describe the workings of two groups of caregivers (grandparents and parents) who are collaborating together for the common interest of caring for the child. It carries neither positive nor negative connotations about the nature of their relationship. The IGPC, therefore, is defined as two groups of childcare-givers from two consanguineous generation cohorts (in the case of this study it refers to the grandparent and parent cohorts) collaborating on a regular

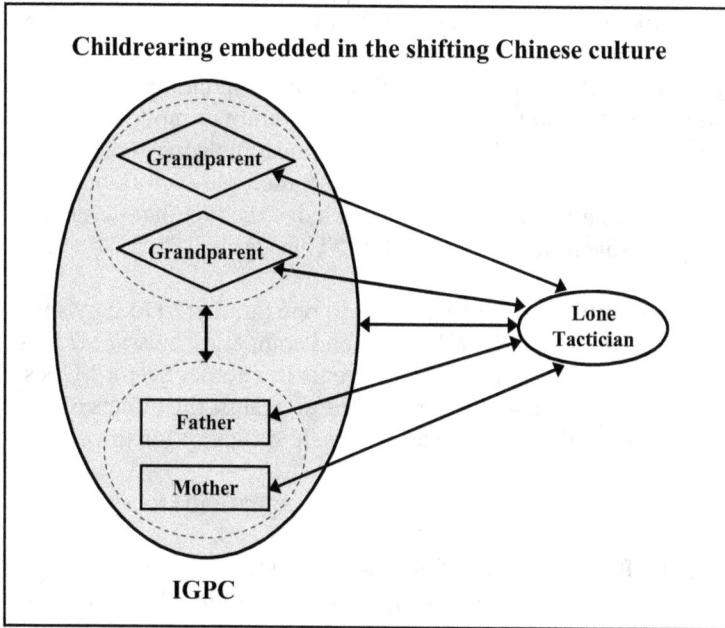

Figure 7.1 Contemporary Chinese intergenerational family relationships system.

basis in caring for children. Other forms of possible parenting coalitions comprising two generations of caregivers, for example, older relatives and biological parents, are valid components of the IGPC, although it is not the focus of this study.

IGPC as a unit of analysis

Utilizing the IGPC as a unit of analysis has a three-fold benefit. First, analyzing the dynamics between grandparents and parents is important as it allows one to determine how effectively the coalition acts in the service of caregiving. Second, it reveals how the specific nature of the coalition enables and constrains individual caregiver's experience and the practice of agency within this system. Third, it explicates how the target of care, that is, the only-child, practises agency with regard to the coalition and its members. This conceptual frame is especially useful for illuminating the bidirectional influence between only-children and their multiple caregivers. As much as these children are influenced by grandparents and parents, they also influence dynamics within the IGPC.

No known study on childrearing in China has framed the collaborations between grandparents and parents as the unit of analysis. I have applied the key assumptions of the bidirectional model of parent–child relationships

(Kuczynski 2003), namely, agency, interdependent power, and contradictions and resolutions, as sensitizing tools to examine the dynamic interactions between the two groups within the IGPC.

By treating the IGPC as a unit of analysis I am responding to Bugental and Goodnow's (1998) call to the research community to move away from the single-source, one-way effect method of conceptualizing socialization. They encouraged researchers to attend to the multiple-sectors nature of social context for socialization and to acknowledge the fact that parents are far from being the sole influence on children. They wrote:

> How are these multiple sectors related to one another? Do they speak with one voice to the child, or do they send competing messages? Does experience with one sector facilitate events in another sector? Does a good experience in one sector act as a buffer against the effects of poor experiences in another? Does variety create difficulty for the child or increase the options available?
>
> (Bugental and Goodnow 1998)

Bracketing the IGPC as a unit of analysis, this book attempts to offer an initial conceptualization of childrearing in urban China which may spur future researchers on to attend to this unexplored dimension, one that has the potential to generate a new arena of lively, creative, and fruitful research. To further demonstrate the relevance of the IGPC I will illustrate how bidirectional dynamics between the two older generations, including dialectic, conflict, and unity, can be brought to the surface by treating the IGPC as a unit of analysis.

Dialects and conflicts within IGPC concerning childrearing methods

Two sources of conflicts between the senior and middle generation were differences in childrearing philosophies and methods, and difficulties in coordinating disciplinary measures among adult caregivers. Viewing the interactions within the coalition as dialectical is especially relevant in contemporary China as the traditional norms governing intergenerational relationships are in transition. The once clear and accepted way of the Confucian teaching known as *wu lun* 五伦 (five cardinal relations), which stipulated the hierarchical relationships in traditional Chinese families, has largely been abolished by the Chinese Communist Party's effort to reform the "old China." For instance, according to tradition older persons occupied powerful positions in the family. Today, the weakened position of the grandparents can be seen by their unwillingness to execute discipline for fear of displeasing their adult children or grandchildren. Instead, they resort to giving in to grandchildren or lodging complaints to their adult children with the hope that the latter would discipline the children instead. The unintended consequences of these actions, however, fueled tension and conflicts within the IGPC as well as between the IGPC and the children. Nevertheless, despite conflicts and tensions, many grandparents still seemed very willing to be part of the IGPC. These findings support the underlying principle of the bidirectional model of parent–child relationships that conflicting parts of the system – in this case grandparents and parents – should be treated as integral parts of the whole system.[3]

The common goal shared by the different members of the IGPC is to jointly raise the precious only-child. This coalition, however, is far from a harmonious unit. In nearly every case, members of the coalition rarely acted with a united front when dealing with the child. Across-case analysis of the five participating families shows that cause of this was, to some degree, due to differences in childrearing philosophy and methods between the senior and middle generations in all families. Some families experienced it more acutely than others. Analysis of the coded ethnographic data shows 103 references made by parents and 34 by grandparents to differences in the methods of disciplining children. And there was no predictable way that the differences would manifest themselves. Contrary to the image portrayed in the popular media, that grandparents are the ones "spoiling" the grandchildren, the Jiang family reflected the reverse. The paternal grandmother was the strictest and most demanding person among the three adults in the IGPC. According to the adult son, his mother lacked patience with the child. The middle generation felt that the grandmother was always finding fault with the grandson's sense of cleanliness, respect for the elders, manners, etc. But the daughter-in-law deemed her mother-in-law's demands on the child unrealistic. And the daughter-in-law often felt frustrated by the strict demands and could only keep the tension at bay by suppressing her own annoyance.

The Tian family, on the other hand, revealed a pattern of strict parents and lenient grandparents. In this family, both the maternal grandparents were involved in the IGPC and both were highly educated. They disagreed with their son-in-law's use of physical punishment on their grandchild. Field notes from participant observations of this family dynamics showed that the maternal grandparents often sabotaged their son-in-law's method of discipline by criticizing him in front of their grandchild. The elders did not hide their displeasure and disagreements with their son-in-law's childrearing methods. When the son-in-law was asked if he thought his parenting efforts were being undermined by the maternal grandparents, he did not think there was a problem. He was confident that the child's improved school results would ultimately prove him right. The adult daughter, like her parents, did not see eye to eye with her husband about the way he dealt with the child, but she felt powerless to change his style. In an attempt to remedy the situation, she often formed an alliance with her parents against her husband. In this case, then, the difference in childrearing philosophies was not only intergenerational but also intragenerational in nature.

The middle generations of the Wang and Bai families claimed that their childrearing philosophies and methods were radically different from the way their parents brought them up. It is worth repeating that all the middle generation parents in this study were born in the 1960s or early 70s – in the midst of the Cultural Revolution when wages were extremely low under the state-controlled planned economy. When the Wangs' adult son was growing up, his parents were busy making ends meet; so his father told him that he had to "depend on himself and be self disciplined." In the absence of much to observe from his parents generation, he and his wife have invested a good deal of time and energy learning from books and taking the advice of experts on how to be good parents. They both perceived the grandparents' way of handling children as inadequate and to some extent inferior. These discrepancies within the IGPC in childrearing methods created a context where the child is aware of multiple standards for behavior (Goh 2006). Hence, there are more opportunities for these children to test boundaries, compared with children raised in two-parent families.

The difficulties of coordinating a unified approach to raising children by IGPC: an example of the dialectic nature of the family across generations

A second challenge within the IGPC is the lack of coordination in managing children's behavior. As discussed in the earlier chapters, children are not parented in a coordinated, top-down fashion. Rather, there exists a set of dialectic processes that shape the relationship between the IGPC and the child and within the IGPC. To see this more clearly, we take a look at the ways that parenting choices are made in the IGPC. In examining the inter-actions between family members it is easy to see how the dialectical relationships between adults of different opinions create difficulties for childraising.

Perceived obstacles in communication between the middle and senior generations were the main reasons for this lack of coordination. For instance, when asked if she attempted to communicate with her mother-in-law, the daughter-in-law of the Jiang family said that "talking" was a dead-end. She believed that honest communication between daughter-in-law and mother-in-law is to be considered culturally impolite and inappropriate. In a similar, but more extreme vein, the daughter-in-law of the Wang family would avoid communicating with her mother-in-law as far as she could. She said,

> Having my mother here to help me with childcare and housework, it is very convenient. It is very different when my mother-in-law was staying with us.[4] There were many occasions I bit my tongue and said nothing. To some mothers-in-law [who are sensible] it is possible to talk, but other mothers-in-law you cannot say anything because it may lead to

conflict. With my mother, I can speak my mind. We quarrel sometimes, but we get over it quickly.

(WW-M 21/07/06)

As mentioned previously, the relationship between mother-in-law and daughter-in-law is well documented as probably one of the most difficult relationships in Chinese families (Logan *et al.* 1998, Hu 1995). Hence, it is no surprise to see that these IGPCs experienced struggles and discomfort even before we take differences in parenting style into account. But parents and grandparents of the IGPC do have different childrearing philosophies and parenting styles; yet, raising children together requires them to confront these differences on a daily basis.

Poor communication and coordination occurred not only between the mother and daughter-in-law, but also between mothers and adult daughters. Madam Bai vented to the researcher her frustrations when talking to her mother. She acknowledged that she was impatient by nature, but felt her mother really pushed her buttons. From her perspective, her mother was too simple-minded, absent-minded, and stubborn. She admitted that she sometimes lost her temper with her mother, especially when she did not follow her instructions regarding childcare. It did not help that instead of negotiating, she issued directives to her mother on how she wanted her to care for the child. Her negative communication style generally elicited resistance from the mother, who might not agree with, or follow, the instructions. For instance, the adult daughter was often upset that her mother would not work to enforce compliance from the child, and worried that giving in to the child would breed undesirable behaviors.

When asked how he ensured coordinated execution of his childrearing plans as well as discipline in a family system with four adult caregivers for one child, the adult son of the Wang family lamented that it was very tough and that he had invested much energy and effort to communicate with each of the adult caregivers with the aim of achieving coherence in their approach. Nevertheless, Mr. Wang confessed that there are bound to be loopholes.

In the Tian family no active effort was made to coordinate the four adult caregivers within the IGPC. The grandparents did not agree with their son-in-law about disciplinary methods or the supreme priority he accorded to academic results. The adult daughter of this family wished that her husband would spend more time communicating and be willing to coordinate parenting strategies with her, but he was not interested. As a result, each caregiver interacted with the child without coordinating with the others. The son-in-law acknowledged that this created many differences among the four adults that the child could manipulate to her benefit (Goh and Kuczynski 2009).

Table 7.1 provides an overview of the dialectical nature of the five IGPCs observed in this study. It illustrates how the five IGPCs in this study managed their differences in childcare practice, values, and internal relationships.

Table 7.1 Characteristics of dynamics within five IGPCs

Family	Child age/sex	Configurations of IGPC/age		Living arrangements	Dialectics within IGPC	Status of coalitions
Jiang	7/M	Father	(34)	Coresidence	*Overt differences:* PGM: strict Mother: lenient Father: felt pressured by PGM to execute discipline against his will	PGM quit coalition in the name of poor health
		Mother	(32)			
		PGM	(70)			
Wang	7/M	Father	(32)	MGM = Coresidence; PGM = nearby	*Attempts to put up a united front:* Father: assumed leadership among caregivers. All 3 caregivers conferred with father for instructions pertaining to childcare	Relative cohesive among members
		Mother	(33)			
		MGM	(80)			
		PGM	(59)			
Tian	10/F	Father	(43)	Periodically coresidence	*Overt differences:* Father: Harsh MGM and MGF: lenient and often sheltered child from harsh punishments Mother: lacked power of influence over child	Mutual tolerance
		Mother	(42)			
		MGM	(71)			
		MGF	(76)			
Bai	5/F	Mother	(36)[a]	Coresidence	*Differences compromised:* Mother: permissive MGM: believed in stricter discipline but compromised	Mutual tolerance
		MGM	(55)			
Fu	7/M 10/M	PGF	(55)	Grandsons reside with grandparents	*Minimal differences:* PGF: regarded as head of household by all family members PGM: nurturing and protective over grandsons Father: agrees readily to PGF's ways of handling boys	Relative cohesion as adult son does not reside under the same roof
		PGM	(57)			
		Father	(33)[a]			

Note
a Divorced.

The nature of the dynamics within coalitions varied from relative harmony to covert tension and overt conflict.

Bidirectionality between lone tacticians and IGPC

The other part of the intergenerational family relationships system, along with the IGPC, is the only-child, or lone tactician. These contemporary little suns, raised in multigenerational families, experience a context-enhanced sense of agency in their interaction with adult caregivers within the intergenerational family relationships system.

In Chapter 5, I discussed the three main factors contributing to only-children's sense of agency. The first is a shifting image of contemporary fatherhood in China, one in which the traditional, authoritarian father is no longer an acceptable norm. Mr. Jiang and Mr. Wang, for instance, were constantly wondering whether they were too harsh with their sons. Each actively sought feedback from his son and modified his style accordingly. The second factor is the emotional pull these only-children command, which increases their mothers' receptiveness to their (bidirectional) influence. The children in this study were less likely to comply with instructions from their mothers, because of the close bonds within the mother-child dyad. Mothers dependent on their children to fulfill their emotional needs helped create children with higher relational resources, and in doing so made themselves vulnerable to bargaining, negotiation, and influence from their children. Finally, the declining power of grandparents in contemporary urban Chinese families also heightens the children's sense of agency. Let us now look in greater detail at some of the ways the interlocking web of relationships within the intergenerational family relationships system afforded agency to the lone tacticians. It is important to keep in mind, though, that the same interconnected web also constrains and limits the power of influence of these only-children.

Incongruence among caregivers affords leeway for child's agency

The more adults who are involved in providing care and the wider the extent of their incongruence in childrearing values and attitudes, the greater the number of opportunities for lone tacticians to exercise agency. This incongruence is particularly prominent within the IGPC because of the rapid changes in Chinese society, and it bears repeating that the parents and grandparents within the IGPC represent different generations with vastly different childrearing values and attitudes.

Tian Tian was the child who exercised the greatest sense of agency and developed the most sophisticated repertoire for handling different adults. As shown in the preceding chapter, her grandparents openly disagreed with her father's harsh methods of disciplining Tian Tian. These discrepancies provided opportunities for Tian Tian to play the adults against one another for her own benefit. For instance, the child knew very well that when her father punished her, her mother could not come to her rescue, as her mother had no power to influence her father. However, if the grandparents intervened, she had a better chance of "escaping" the severe beating. Upon close examination, one can see that this lone tactician was exploiting the delicate relationship between her father and grandparents. Traditionally, elderly parents' elevated position in the family cannot be challenged (Wen and Xiao 2005). Although in reality older persons today no longer occupy such a position (Yan 2003), as the son-in-law, Tian Tian's father was obliged to "save face" and show respect for the grandparents by giving in to them when they interfered with his disciplinary measures.

Wei Wei demonstrated another scenario: the child capitalizing on loopholes between adults. However much his father attempted to communicate with his various caregivers, in executing plans regarding childcare there were bound to be some loopholes. It was not uncommon for Wei Wei to resist the paternal grandmother's instructions in the "name of his father." When he did so, his grandmother had to refer back to her adult son for clarification and guidelines for the execution of discipline. These lapses of time in transferring information and implementing discipline inevitably reduced the intensity of the problem, meaning that the child would escape heavy punishment.

Contrast these scenarios with the two boys from the migrant family, in that case the grandparents were the main caregivers and the paternal grandfather was the authoritative figure at home. There were hardly any loopholes for the boys to seize or manipulate. However, the two boys were not devoid of agency. The younger boy, Xiao Fu, for instance, resisted grandfather's instructions cognitively, although outwardly he knew he had to comply. It is interesting to note that when I shared my key findings with the participating families in order to get their feedback, Grandparents Fu specially mentioned that there were no loopholes in their family for the boys to manipulate.[5]

Caregivers' competition for loyalty and affection boosts child's relational power

In Chapter 5, the findings indicated that there was some subtle competition among caregivers taking place in three families. Wei Wei's paternal and maternal grandmothers were secretly competing to be the "most liked" or "more capable" grandmother. Tian Tian's obvious preference for her maternal grandmother seemed to bring out some sense of jealousy in her father, which led her grandmother to teach the child to display "appropriate affection" for her father so as not to upset him. The almost game-like, yet friendly competition between Bei Bei's maternal grandmother and mother is especially interesting. It seems there were no hard feelings between the two women, playfully competing in front of the child so that the child had to decide whose room to sleep in each night. The competition provided a platform for the two caregivers to unreservedly display their affection for the child. Bei Bei's mother commented that the child knows she is the *qing gan xu yao* 情感需要 (emotional comfort) of the family.

This corresponds to the findings by Ye (1996) and Zheng and Tang (2005) that the value of children in China has shifted from an economic to an emotional one. Since there is usually only one child in each family to satisfy the emotional needs of the host of caregivers, each puts a greater weight on the interactions with that child. Translating this to the bidirectional caregivers–child relationship, children in these families would invariably enjoy a relatively high relational power.

Lone tacticians – a complementary image to the spoilt "little suns"

In the minds of most Chinese, the terms spoilt "little emperors" or "little suns" are synonymous with only-children in Chinese families. These terms were popularized in the early years of the implementation of the one-child policy by the media through popular publications of the 1980s (Wu 1996). Indeed, television serials were made using this as their theme. The underlying message of this popular image was to warn parents and relatives that a little emperor will be born into every Chinese family. This notion quickly caught the attention of the research community. It was no surprise that research in the early eighties tended to focused on the differences between only-children and those with siblings. These studies typically examined the cognitive, personality-related, and intellectual outcome of these little emperors in comparison with their counterparts with siblings. The Chinese literature, by local Chinese authors, tended to hint that only-children may be pampered and spoilt by virtue of their status. Some investigators suggested that more-negative social behavior patterns are found in Chinese only-children, arguing that these children: are being spoilt by their parents; show disrespect to elders and resistance to discipline; and are more egocentric (Tseng and Wu 1985, Jiao and Jing 1986). Writings by indigenous Chinese writers (Sun 1998, Wan 1993) echoed these observations and suggested that only-children were lacking in social skills and were less happy. These local authors alluded to the fact that in urban China today, newlyweds know even before their first child is conceived that this child will probably be their only one. Such knowledge may lead some parents to overindulge or overprotect an only-child, thereby harming his or her normal personality and academic development.[6]

Studies by foreign researchers, however, found otherwise. Poston and Falbo (1990) did a quantitative survey of 1,456 school children in the urban and rural areas of Changchun, an industrial city in Jilin Province in northeastern China. The results of the study report the only-child advantage in academic achievement, although found to be true in urban areas, was not found among rural children. When background variables are controlled, only-children do not appear to differ from children with siblings, both in personality and childhood adjustment as assessed by their teachers and mothers. The results therefore refuted the local Chinese researchers' presumption about the possible negative personality traits of the only-child. The lack of siblings is neither a help nor hindrance in developing a socially acceptable personality.[7]

Not only are the findings of these studies inconclusive, assuming only-children to be "spoilt little suns" limits the clear conceptualization of research questions. It will likely lead researchers to perceive only-children as passive recipients of "spoiling" from their parents and brings with it a negative connotation. In this vein parents are treated as agents of socialization who have goals and strategies with more power to fuel the relationship. In these chapters I call for an alternative conceptualization of only-children in China. Researchers need to understand them as active agents much as their adult caregivers are. They are bidirectionally influenced and being influenced by each other in the multigenerational family system. In this light, power does not rest solely with parents or grandparents but rather in the child–IGPC relationship. Lone tacticians and their multiple caregivers are bound by specific, enduring, close relationships in which all participants have an investment (Lollis and Kuczynski 1997). These relationships have a past history and all participants anticipate the relationships existing well into the future. Recognizing these relationship dynamics provides a basis for understanding the motivational issues underlying mutual receptivity to influence, conflict and negotiation. The relationship context is also crucial for understanding bidirectional influence (Kuczynski 2001) and has implications for how agency and power between lone tacticians and their multiple caregivers will be perceived.

Future research

The use of a bidirectional approach proved fruitful in capturing the richly dynamic interactions and influences in the family, both from adult care-givers to children and vice versa, which would not have been possible if a one-way, deterministic model had been employed to study childrearing in urban Xiamen. The model offers a good deal of potential for future research, and it should prove useful both quantitatively and qualitatively. For quantitative researchers, the findings of bidirectional dynamics between children and their multiple caregivers from this current study can be formulated into multiple hypotheses for further testing. As for qualitative methods, using the initial sketch of bidirectional relationships found by this current study as a launch pad will provide quite a bit of material for further, in-depth exploratory research into caregiver–child bidirectional relationships in China. Much remains to be explored, and in the following paragraphs I offer a few possible ideas for future research.

Surveys similar to the one conducted by the current study in Xiamen can be replicated in other cities to ascertain the prevalence, configurations, and living arrangements of intergenerational parenting coalitions there. Quantitative researchers may want to examine the notion of "context-enhanced agency" experienced by only-children put forth by the current study through the development of hypotheses for testing with large samples. These quantitative, generalizable findings will increase our understanding of the extent to which the context of contemporary one-child families in urban China brings about children's heightened sense of agency and ability to exercise agency with their caregivers. Another recommendation for quantitative method is to survey younger and recently retired grandparents in other Chinese cities to ascertain among other things: their willingness to take part in the intergenerational parenting coalition; their sense of obligation to conform to the traditional role of grandparenting; whether they are more assertive in meeting their own needs, compared with previous generations of grandparents; their aspirations and plans after retirement apart from caring for grandchildren. It will be useful to delineate the samples of these suggested surveys by educational background and the health of grandparents, so as to possibly predict the future trends based on the motivation of different groups of grandparents to participate in IGPCs.

Owing to resource and time constraints, the current study did not manage to include ethnographic data on two other forms of living arrangements in intergenerational parenting coalitions found in the survey conducted in Xiamen. It would be useful for future qualitative research to include IGPCs where parents take their children to the grandparents before going to work and picking them up daily, and other families where children stay with grandparents during weekdays and only return to their parents at weekends. The dynamics of these IGPCs could be quite different from those observed in this current study. A second project, which would help us understand how children's developmental stages may influence their ability to assert agentic behaviors in relation to their adult caregivers, would be to observe children from a range of developmental ages and with a balanced sample between the genders. It would also be worthwhile undertaking longitudinal, in-depth observations of a small number of children from preschool to middle childhood, late childhood, and adolescence, in order to ascertain how their agentic behaviors and dynamics with adult caregivers change over time. Another angle for qualitative inquiry is to compare and contrast the bidirectionality between children and their IGPCs with that of those raised only by biological parents without the involvement of grandparents. These comparisons may shed new light and enrich our understanding and theorizing of bidirectionality in Chinese families.

Finally, it is worth noting that the migrant family sampled (grandparents as surrogate parents with minimal involvement of adult children) in the current study is an anomalous case which enriched the findings by helping to generate new insights to the study when compared and contrasted with the other four families (only-children raised by IGPCs). Qualitative research into the childrearing practices and caregiver–child relationships in migrant families may have similar potential to generate new research findings.

The importance of understanding what grandparents do in the IGPC

The integral role played by urban grandparents as joint caregivers to children has not received the attention it deserves. It is my contention that childrearing research in China should move beyond examining biological parents and consider the IGPC as the unit of analysis. In addition, the analysis of the parenting coalition should be embedded in the overarching framework of the intergenerational family relationships system. This way of conceptualizing grandparents (or other nonparent caregivers) serves to provide a clearer view of older persons in China. Research into the aging population in China is permeated with negative, agist stereotypes (refer to Goh 2009 for details). Older persons are considered to be burdens, dependent, and "problems to be solved." This viewpoint gives grandparents a voice to make clear the sacrifices they make in contributing to long-term childcare in young families. This re-conceptualization of "parenting" is a wide-open door waiting to be further investigated. A concerted research effort is needed to understand how the dynamics within IGPC, between parents and grandparents, influence the effectiveness of caregiving by the parenting coalitions.

In conceiving of the only-children raised within the intergenerational family relationships system as "lone tacticians," this study is probably the first to systematically observe the agentic behaviors exhibited by Chinese children and the influence they assert on their adult caregivers. Conceptualizing these children as active agents who have their own intentions, are able to set goals, and take necessary actions to achieve their goals, is a fresh perspective not examined by previous studies in China. This study has also delineated the varying extent of the agency that children exercise on different adult caregivers. Their relationships with their caregivers both facilitate and constrain their ability to exercise agency. Instead of conceptualizing how "little suns" are spoilt by their parents and grandparents, future research could ask new questions that further explore children's agency in relation to their multiple caregivers. More information is needed to help us understand how children and their caregivers mutually shape each other and to get a better sense of the contributing factors that enhance children's agency. It should be asked how the forces within the multigenerational family systems interplay to enhance the bargaining power of children. Also, how does the phenomenon of context-enhanced agency in China differ from the shape of bidirectionality in other cultural contexts? All these wait to be discovered.

Conclusion

The present work brings to researchers' attention several new directions for research on childrearing in China. It proposes a culturally embedded intergenerational parenting coalition as an indigenous unit of analysis for Chinese research and documents the prevalence of this form in contemporary China. In so doing, it is one of the few existing studies that highlights the role of grandparents in the care and socialization of children in Chinese families. It advocates a shift in research orientation to complement the dominant focus on products or outcomes of socialization in China with an equal interest in the dynamic processes by which they come about. The bidirectional and dialectical framework that I have proposed for interpreting interactional and relational dynamics in Chinese families has proven fruitful for asking new questions and uncovering new insights. Although the bidirectional framework is challenging to implement, methodologically, it opens the door for exploring uncharted territory in cultural research and theory. Researchers may be tempted by the allure of an easy-to-manage research model that assumes a one-way influence from nuclear parents to children (Holden 2010). Yet I would urge them to avoid that siren call.

To better understand the new forms of childrearing in the context of the rapidly changing culture of China will require a shift to one that recognizes the bidirectional nature of family relationships and the complexity of the relationships within the family. As China continues to experience economic growth and as globalization progresses, transformation at the macro level will inevitably be transmitted to the micro milieu. While some aspects of the dynamics among children and their caregivers, childrearing practices and intergenerational relationships within the family environment may persist, and many may evolve and change. My hope is that others will build on this project and that future research will examine how the transitioning Chinese culture provides an array of cultural tools for grandparents, parents, and children to utilize in their interactions with each other.

Appendix A
Details of survey questionnaire

The items were all closed questions with a nominal scale. The questions addressed:

- demographic profiles including age, income, and gender of the various generations (9 items);
- living arrangements and childcare provided by grandparents (5 items);
- role division between grandparents and parents (4 items);
- past and the anticipated future duration of care by grandparents (1 item);
- advantages and disadvantages of the collaborations (6 items);
- the relationships between the only-children and their caregivers (3 items);
- parents' perception of grandparents' help as voluntary or obligatory, and the types of rewards they gave to grandparents for helping with childcare (2 items).

Teachers from the 39 participating primary schools distributed the questionnaires to their students, who took them home for their parents to complete. After the teachers collected the forms back from the students, a research assistant went to the 39 schools to check and collect the forms. All the valid questionnaires were coded, and two paid persons helped to key in the data. Cross-auditing was performed to check for possible errors in data entry.

Appendix B
Recruitment via key liaison persons

Tapping into the networks of the three key liaison persons, I spelled out the criteria for my samples and requested their help to cast their nets to recruit potential research participants. It was my intention to follow a few families in Xiamen with grandparents involved in different ways in providing child-care and raising the grandchildren jointly with their adult children. Yang (1995) claims that both the traditional and contemporary Chinese are well known for their strong reliance on interpersonal relations as the basis for social behavior. Having trusted and respected people acting as a key liaison in the field will probably lend some trustworthiness to the research project. Over the first month there was a gradual process of recruitment. A key liaison would make the initial contact by phone and explain briefly to the family my intention to recruit them as research participants. When the family indicated a tentatively positive answer, a home visit would be made for a formal introduction. Consent was granted mainly by the adult children with the exception of the Fu family where the grandfather was the one who gave the permission. Of the seven families approached, two were deemed inappropriate. One felt it was too sensitive a topic to discuss and declined to be included. The other was a single-parent family, mother and daughter residing with the maternal grandmother. At that point of time the separation had just occurred and there were many unresolved conflicts between the single mother and her ex-spouse, hence we decided to exclude this family from the sample.

Appendix C
Contact schedule sheet

Family	Date/Time	Date/Time	Date/Time	Date/Time	Date/Time	Date/Time	Date/Time	Date/Time	Date/Time	Date/Time	Date/Time	Date/Time	Date/Time	Date/Time	Date/Time
Wang	20/4/06 Visit PGM/ 9:30 am Initial contact with XL and FIL	20/4/06 Visit family 8:10 pm Consent with XL	27/4/06 Fetched child with PGM (lunch break) 11:10 am–1:30 pm	27/4/06 Fetched child with PGM (after sch) 4:30–6 pm	12/5/06 English tuition 8–9 pm	19/5/06 English tuition 8:30–10 pm	24/5/06 English tuition 8:30–10 pm	29/5/06 Met PGM for a chat 1:45–3 pm	30/5/06 English tuition 9–9:30 pm	7/6/06 English lesson 8:30–9:30 pm	18/7/06 English tuition 8:30–9 pm	21/7/06 Chat with Mrs Wang 8–9:30 pm	24/7/06 Conversation with Mr Wang 9–11 pm	4/8/06 Chat with MGM Wang 11–12 pm	29/8/06 Chat with WW
Jiang	20/4/06 Visit PGM 10:15 am–12 pm Reconnection with PGM	23/4/06 Invited for lunch with family 10 am–1:45 pm	25/4 Mtg with tchrs 4:45 pm	28/4/06 Mtg father to discuss 8–9:30 pm	30/4/06 Observe JJ did hm wk, Dinner, discuss with both parents 4:45–9:30 pm	12/5/06 Follow-up 9–10 pm	24/5/06 Dropped by to hand the SID brochure to JJ's mum	28/5/06 Home visit 8:30–10 pm	4/6/06 Invited JJ to my aprt to watch movie. I went over to discuss the SID assessment 8:30–9:30 pm	25/7/06 Chat with Mr Jiang 8–9:30 pm	1/8/06 Chat with Mrs Jiang 7–9 pm	13/8/06 Chat with PGM Jiang 10–12 pm	13/8/06 Chat with PGF Jiang 5–7 pm	30/8/06 Chat With JJ 4–5 pm	

Tian	5/5/06 Home visit 3–5 pm	9/5/06 English tuition and chat with GPs 12:30–3:30 pm	11/5/06 Badminton 6–6:35 pm	19/5/06 English tuition 1–2 pm	23/5/06 English lesson 7:25–9:30 pm	30/5/06 English tuition and chat with mother 8–10:10 pm	9/6/06 English tuition 8–10 pm	19/7/06 English tuition 10:10 am—11:30 am	31/7/06 Chat with Mr Tian 3–4.20 pm	31/7/06 Chat with Mrs Tian & lunch 10–1 pm	1/8/06 Chat with MGM Tian 3–5 pm	2/8/06 Chat with MGF 10 am–12 pm	25/8/06 Chat with Tian Tian 11–12 pm
Bai	7/5/06 Home visit 1–5 pm	14/5/06 Home visit from 2–4:45 pm	19/5/06 Chat with MGM 2:45–4:30 pm	21/5/06 Drop by to visit BB as she was sick	28/5/06 Dinosaur divorced 4–6 pm	2/6/06 Chat with MGM 9:30–11:30 am	4/6/06 Lunch with Mdm Bai	23/7/06 Chat with Mdm Bai	30/7/06 Chat with Mdm Bai	7/8/06 Chat with MGM Bai 9–11 am	7/8/06 Chat with MGM Bai 4–6 pm	27/8/06 Chat with BB 3–4 pm	
Fu	14/5/06 Visited the family 5–7 pm	17/5/06 Made home visit and had lunch in their home 11 am–1:30 pm	26/5/06 English tuition 8:15–9:35 pm	29/5/06 English tuition 8:45–10 pm	5/6/06 English tuition 8:05–9:20 pm	7/6/06 Lunch with PGM and two kids 12:15–1:35 pm	12/7/06 English tuition 9:30–1 pm	14/7/06 English tuition 9:30–1 pm	18/7/06 English tuition 9:30–11:30 am	20/7/06 English tuition 9:30–11:30 am	8/8/06 Chat with PGM and lunch 10–1 pm	11/8/06 Chat with Mr Fu and dinner 7–9 pm	28/8/06 Chat with Da Fu and Xiao Fu

Appendix D
Analytical strategies for ethnographic data

The field notes and memos collected over the six months, together with all the transcripts of conversations with all the members of the five participating families, were analyzed carefully by first reading them through thoroughly several times. The data regarding complex bilateral interactions across all three generation was categorized with the aid of the qualitative software Nvivo 7 (Richards 2005) into six layers:

- C⇔P; C⇔GP
- P⇔C; P⇔GP
- GP⇔C; GP⇔P

where C = child; P = parent; GP = grandparent; MG = middle generation. The symbol ⇔ denotes bilateral influence. The bilateral perspective of parent–child relationships guided the coding process.

Open and axial coding

The purpose at the open coding phase was to "break down, examine, compare, and conceptualize and categorize data" (Strauss and Corbin 1990). As many open codes as required were created to prevent losing the subtle differences in meaning as they emerged from the data: 52 open codes were created for the layers of interactions between P⇔C and P⇔GP (Table D.1); 43 open codes for those between GP⇔C and GP⇔P (Table D.2); 32 open codes for those between C⇔P and C⇔GP (Table D.3).

The second phase of coding is axial coding. The analyses at this level involved a process of relating codes (categories and properties) to each other, via a recursive process of inductive and deductive inference known as constant comparison. Open codes relating to similar concepts/themes were merged together under axial codes (Strauss and Corbin 1990):

- Four open codes related to the middle generation's perceived difficulties in the IGPC collaborations were merged under an axial code of "Differences in childrearing methods – MG."

- Another four open codes of difficulties in executing coordinated discipline expressed by the middle generation were merged under an axial code of "Difficulties in executing coordinated discipline – MG."
- Six open codes concerning children's influence on the dynamics within the IGPC were merged together under an axial code of "Child's influence on IGPC as perceived by MG."
- Five open codes of differences in childrearing methods expressed by grandparents were merged under the axial code of "Differences in childrearing methods – GP."
- Three open codes on the difficulties in disciplining grandchildren were merged under the axial code of "Difficulties in executing coordinated discipline – GP."
- Four open codes on children's influence on grandparents were merged under the axial code of "Child's influence on IGPG as perceived by GP."

Selective coding

Selective coding was the final phase of the analytic process used to integrate and refine central themes (Peters *et al.* 2006). The dialectic assumption of bilaterality of the social relational theory guided the emergence of the central themes. After categorizing the open and axial coding discussed above, the data were categorized into higher-order patterns of meaning (Table D.4). The two axial codes of "differences in childrearing methods" by both MG and GP and "difficulties in executing coordinated discipline" expressed by MG and GP were subsumed under the selective code of "dialectics and conflicts," while the two axial codes of "child's influence on IGPC" expressed by both the MG and GP were subsumed under the select code of "bilaterality." Analysis was conducted to compare and contrast the themes that surfaced across the layers. Attention was paid to contradictory data to avoid a common pitfall of qualitative research termed as "cherry picking" by Scott (2002), that is, the selective analysis and presentation of data so that one finds what one wishes to find. In addition, paying attention to contradictory data served to illuminate the different viewpoints from different participants and unpack the dialectical nature of intergenerational interactions. Data sets collected from the different generational cohorts (namely grandparents, parents, and grandchildren) were used to juxtapose and illuminate the different dimensions of the same issues being examined. Triangulating these data sets also helped to enhance the validity of the findings.

Open and axial codes

Table D.1 Axial and open codes: P⇔C; P⇔GP data set

Axial codes		Open codes
Nature of joint project	1	Why coresidence
	2	How does it happen
	3	Network family type
	4	Maternal *vs.* paternal joint project
Division of labor within joint projects	5	GPs' role
	6	Fathers' role
	7	Mothers' role
MG's perception of own and GPs' childrearing values and practices	8	Perception of similarities and differences
MG's perception of GPs' help	9	GPs' negative influence on child
	10	GPs' positive influence on child
MG's perception of GPs' power and position	11	GPs' power and position in relation to child
	12	GPs' relational styles
MG's concept of an ideal child	13	Manners
	14	Smart
	15	Good in academics
	16	Love parents/filial piety
	17	Good social skills
	18	Good character
	19	Good communication skills
	20	Independence
	21	Healthy and happy
	22	Confident
	23	Positive about life
Parent–child bilateral relationships	24	Expressions of mutual influences
	25	Child manipulates adults
	26	Child expression of agency/resistance
	27	Child sense of power
	28	Parents' power and influence on child
	29	Parents' attempts to repair relationships
IGR tension and conflicts	30	Problems between adult children and elders
	31	Middle-generation couple's differences in handling IGR
	32	Blaming
	33	Differences in childrearing methods
	34	GPs interfere in childrearing matters
	35	Impact of IGR tension on child
IGR harmony	36	Conflict avoidance tactics
	37	Art of handling complaints from GPs
	38	MG showing appreciation to SG
	39	MG mediating between 1st and 3rd generations
	40	Similar childrearing methods between 1st and 2nd generations

Table D.1 Continued

Axial codes		Open codes
Parenting issues	41	Parent–child relationships
	42	Greatest challenge in childrearing
	43	Greatest joy in childrearing
	44	Parenting style
	45	Supremacy of academic results
	46	Use of corporal punishment
	47	Aspiration for child
	48	Intensive fathering
MG's experience as parents	49	Life of a working woman in China
	50	MG's own growing up experience influenced his/her parenting style
	51	MG's VOC
	52	MG's projection of whether they will provide grandchild care in the future

Note
GPs = grandparents; MG = middle generation; SG = senior generation; IGR = intergenerational relationship; VOC = value of children.

Table D.2 Axial and open codes: GP⇔C; GP⇔P data set

Axial codes		Open codes
Toughest aspects of joint project	1	Child bullies grandmother
	2	Child does not respect GPs
	3	House chores are a heavy load
	4	Deteriorating health of GPs
	5	GPs' fatigue in caring
Positive aspects of joint projects	6	Joy of caring for GC
	7	Enable MG to concentrate on their work
	8	GPs' sense of esteem
	9	Consensus between 1st and 2nd generations on childrearing issues
	10	GPs' value of children
IGR between GPs and GC	11	Bonds between GPs and GC
	12	GC is more compliant to MG
	13	Conflicts between GC and GPs
	14	Generation gap between GC and GPs
	15	GPs tactics with GC
	16	GPs as surrogate parents
Positive IGR between GPs and MG	17	GPs' positive relationship with MGs
	18	GPs felt appreciated
Negative IGR between GPs and MG	19	Conflicts
	20	Differences in disciplinary methods
	21	Differences in childrearing methods
	22	GPs felt taken for granted
	23	GPs affected by MG's divorce

Table D.2 Continued

Axial codes		Open codes
GPs' perception of child's agency	24	Child manipulates loopholes between 1st and 2nd generations
	25	Child developed unique relationships with different adult caregivers
	26	Competitions among adults for child's loyalty
	27	Child's non-compliance
GPs' needs	28	Elders' health
	29	Need for leisure
	30	Need for social network
	31	Plans for elder care
	32	GPs' retirement plans
	33	Medical expense
	34	Pension
Division of labor in joint project	35	Coordination between GPs
	36	Division between MG and GPs
Nature of involvement in joint project	37	Duration of care
	38	Chinese GPs' perception of obligation
GPs' lived experience in joint project	39	GPs' perception of ideal living arrangement
	40	GPs' lack of power and position
	41	GPs' own marriage compromised
	42	Sacrifices made by GPs to provide care
	43	GPs' desire for independence

Note
GPs = grandparents; GC = grandchildren; MG = middle generation; IGR= intergenerational relationship.

Table D.3 Axial and open codes: C⇔P; C⇔GP data set

Axial codes		Open codes
Bilateral relationships with parents	1	Bilateral relationship with father
	2	Bilateral relationship with mother
	3	Child's perception of parents' control and influence over him/her
	4	How child showed love to parents
Child's perception of own agentic behaviors/cognitions	5	Resist parents' instructions
	6	Resist grandparents' instructions
	7	Compliance to parents' instructions
	8	Selective compliance to grandparents' instructions
	9	Tactics used to achieve goals
	10	Child's perception of own aspiration *vs.* parents/grandparents' aspiration for him/her

Table D.3 Continued

Axial codes		Open codes
Bilateral relationships with grandparents	11	Child's perception of advantages of having grandparents care for him/her
	12	Child's perception of disadvantages of having grandparents care for him/her
	13	How child showed care and love to grandparents
	14	Child's perception of instruction from grandparents
	15	Who spend more time with him/her
	16	Closest to which adult
Being a single child	17	Pros and cons of being a single child
	18	Having a sibling
Child's perception of family cohesion	19	Perception of long-term relationships with adults
	20	Relationship between 1st and 2nd generations
	21	Child's sense of filial piety
	22	Emotional bonds
	23	What is fun about my family
Child's perception of role division	24	Role played by each adult
	25	Child's role at home
	26	Who takes care of him/her
Child felt loved	27	How does child feel loved?
	28	Child's contentment
	29	Touch as a language of love
	30	Rating of bonding with adults
	32	Love and time spent with child

Selective coding

Table D.4 Selective coding

Selective codes	Axial codes
Bilateral influence	Parent–child bilateral relationships Parent–grandparent IGR Grandparent–child relationships Grandparent–parent IGR Child–parent relationships Child–grandparent relationships
Child's agency	Parents' perception of child's expression of agency Grandparents' perception of child's expression of agency Child's perception of his/her own agency in relation to adult caregivers

Table D.4 Continued

Selective codes	Axial codes
Interdependent power of influence	Middle generation's perception of grandparents' power and position Middle generation's perception of division of labor between parents and grandparents Grandparents' perception of lived experience of joint project Grandparents' perception of sharing of childcare and house chore roles
Dialectics: conflict, tension, and resolutions	Middle generation's perception of IGR conflicts Middle generation's perception of IGR harmony Middle generation's perception of the positives and negatives of the joint project Middle generation's perception of own and grandparents' childrearing values and practices
	Grandparents' perception of positive aspects of IGR Grandparents' perception of negative aspects of IGR Grandparents' perception of neutral aspects of IGR
Ambivalence	Grandparents' perception of positive aspects of IGR Grandparents' perception of negative aspects of IGR Grandparents' perception of neutral aspects of IGR
Nature of joint project	Living arrangements across generations Grandparents' perception of the toughest aspect of joint project Grandparents' perception of positive aspects of joint project Nature of involvement by grandparents

Note
IGR = intergenerational relationship.

Appendix E

Influence of unilateral model on childrearing research in China

Year	Authors	Antecedent factor(s)	Dependent factor(s)	Methods	Remarks
1997	Zeng, Q., Lu, Y. L., Zhou, H., Dong, Q., and Chen, X.	Parenting styles	Child's school adjustment	Self-reported survey ($N = 304$) Instrument: CRPR	
2003	Chen, H., Li, D., Hou, J., and Chen, X.	Parental strategies	Children's noncompliance	Observation in natural settings ($N =$ 42 pairs of mother–child dyad)	Some hints of children's agency was considered
2003	Chen, H., Zhang, Y., and Chen, X.	Parenting practice	Inhibition behavior in 2-year-old	Laboratory observation	
2003	Hou, J., Chen, H., and Chen, X.	This study set out with the assumption that children are not passive recipients of influence from parents. It did not embrace a unidirectional model. It aimed to observe the interaction patterns between mothers and children during games		Observation in home environment Videotaping of games played by mother and child ($N = 61$ Semi-structured interview with mothers	Findings show mother and children influence each other in their interactional processes
2003	Chen, H., Zhang, Y., and Chen, X.	Parenting practice	Behavior inhibition in children	Lab observation ($N = 122$) Parenting practice – CRPR self-reported questionnaire	
2004	Niu, Z., Chen, H., Wang, L., and Zhang, H.	Parenting practice	Prosocial behavior in children	Laboratory observation and parents self-reported CRPR Q sort	
2005	Hou, J., Chen, H., and Chen, X.	Parents' controlling/ warmth	Children's inhibition behavior	Home observation and video recording on parent–child free play session	

Continued overleaf

Appendix E continued

Year	Authors	Antecedent factor(s)	Dependent factor(s)	Methods	Remarks
2006	Ye, Y., Zou, H., and Li, C.	1. Family communication dimensions; 2. Parental control; 3. Family harmony	Adolescents' mental health	Self-reported survey (N = 928) Instruments: SCL, Chinese family assessment instrument	
2006	Wang, S., Zhang, W., and Chen, H.	Parenting styles	Youth's ego identity	Parents self-assessment (N = 639) Instruments: Steinberg parenting style questionnaire	
2006	Li, C. N., Ma, C. R., and Zou, H.	Parent–offspring perceptual differences in family functioning	Adolescents' self-esteem	Self-reported assessment (N = 1317) Instruments: Chinese family assessment instrument; Rosenberg self-esteem scale	Only parents were involved in the survey
2006	Li, Y., and Sang, B.	Maternal style	Children's theory of mind development	Lab experiment (N = 53) Self-report parenting style survey – EMBU	
2006	Li, Y., and Sang, B.	Maternal interaction styles during play and child's interaction styles during play	Children's theory of mind development	Lab experiment (N = 60) child–mother dyads Structured play tasks	
2007	Liang, Z. B., Zhang, G. Z., Chen, H. C., and Zhou, B. F.	Early maternal parenting styles	Child's school adjustment	Parent and teacher self-assessment (N = 208) Instruments: CRPR Q Sort; Teachers' report (T-CRS)	Two-wave survey at age 2 and age 11
2008	Guo, H., Ding, W., Ma, X., Wang, L., and Lin, C.	Interventions on parenting styles	Children's personality	Parents and children of intervention group (N = 125) and control group (N = 124) were assessed on EMBU and EPQ pre- and post-intervention	

Year	Authors	Antecedent factor(s)	Dependent factor(s)	Methods	Remarks
2009	Yin, X., Hu, T., and Chen, X.	Parenting styles	Children's academic achievements	Self-assessed EMBU (parenting styles) and SDQII (Self-concept of children) administered to achievers ($N = 76$) and underachievers ($N = 82$)	
2009	Liu, Q., Zhou, S., Yang, H., Chu, Y., and Liu, L.	Parenting styles of Chinese college students	Correlations between parenting styles with college students' gender, single or nonsingle child status, amount of care received	PBI (Parental Bonding Instrument) was administered to students between ages of 17 and 23 ($N = 849$) from three colleges in Hunan province to ascertain their parents' styles	
2009	Du, D., and Su, Y.	Maternal childrearing styles	7–11-year-old children's multiple levels of theory of mind abilities development	Two *faux pas* stories and EMBU revised questionnaire were used to test 150 primary school students aged from 7 to 11 years and their mothers	
2009	Liu, B., Chen, X., and Wang, X.	Parental childrearing patterns	College students' mental health	Self-assessed parenting styles (EMBU) and mental health state (SCL-90 factors) were administered to ($N = 464$) college students	
2009	Yang, C., and Hou, D.	Parental childrearing patterns	Adolescents' trait anxiety	Undergraduate and graduate students ($N = 306$) assessed their own parents' style (EMBU) and anxiety traits (T-AI)	
2009	Zhou, X., and Yang, D.	Parental traits include: marital status, styles, education attainment	Adolescents' mental status	Two self-assessed instruments (SCL-90) and EMBU were administered to adolescents ($N = 269$) in Liaoning city	

Continued overleaf

Appendix E continued

Year	Authors	Antecedent factor(s)	Dependent factor(s)	Methods	Remarks
2009	Shen, Y., and Chen, J.	Family environment; Peer relationships	Theory of mind (ToM) development of 3–5-year-old children	1. FES-CV instrument was administered to random sampled ($N = 242$) parents of 3-year-olds in three preschools in Harbin city. 2. Peer nomination social status conducted by using class photo based on Dodge's (1983) method. 3. Assessment of ToM development – although authors did not state how the assessments were conducted, it is possible that they were carried out as laboratory tests	
2010	Chen, M. L., and Zhang, M. L.	Parents' self-assessed unhealthy habits (alcohol, smoking, gambling, etc.)	Children's mental health state (six emotional pathological symptoms; six behavior problems; seven interpersonal problems)	Self-assessment questionnaires administered to parents of preschool children ($N = 1280$) in Lanzhou city	

Note
These research items only include empirical research conducted within mainland China, not including any conducted in Hong Kong, Macau, or Taiwan. The list is not meant to be exhaustive as some publications may not be included in the China National Knowledge Infrastructure. Instead, it serves to demonstrate the influence of the unilateral model in empirical studies on childrearing in China. All these papers are published in academic journals within mainland China and in the Chinese language. Literature reviews are not included in the list.

Notes

Preface

1 At the end of the fieldwork, two sets of parents were overjoyed when reporting to me their children's improved English results. I told the parents that equal credit should go to the children for working hard. Nevertheless, I was delighted to be deemed useful by them.

1 Introduction

1 Owing to the lack of published statistics on the extent to which grandparents are actively involved in providing childcare, I can only gauge by indirect evidence the prevalence of three-generation coresidence. Logan and Bian (1998, Logan *et al.* 1999) conducted two large-scale surveys in Shanghai and Tianjin with sample sizes of 1,042 and 1,054 respectively and found that 43 percent of parents aged 60 and older lived with a married child. A survey of urban families in seven cities (Beijing, Shanghai, Chengdu, Nanjing, Guangzhou, Lanzhou, and Haerbin) by Shen and Yang (1995) found that the modified stem family constituted one quarter of all family types, second only to the nuclear family.

2 It is reported by *Beijing Morning Press* (2007, Oct 12) that of the younger cohort of middle-generation couples who are both only-children themselves, 70 percent "push" childcare responsibility to their aging parents.

3 Kuczynski (2003) observed that research questions and analyses continue to resemble correlational efforts of the past: parental antecedents on the left of the equation and child antecedents on the right. Holden and Edwards (Holden, 1997; Holden and Edwards, 1989) criticized the continuing use of "quick and dirty" parent attitude questionnaires. They asserted that these surveys portray children as generic, parents as trait-like and unthinking, and parent–child interactions as unidirectional and acontextual.

4 Research on grandparenthood in China is limited. One study conducted by a foreign researcher, Toni Falbo, was published in 1991. Falbo surveyed parents of 1,460 only-children of school age from Changchun city who were first and fifth grades in 1987. Contrary to common belief that grandparents tended to overindulge their grandchildren and hence, caused negative effects on them, Falbo found more contacts with educated grandparents was positively academic for outcome of children. Parents who grew up between 1960s and mid-1970s were referred to as the "lost generation" in China's history because schools were closed and many families were fragmented during the Cultural Revolution. Hence, many grandparents were better educated than parents.

   A dearth of more recent studies on grandparents could be found. Their findings were less positive about grandparents' care than Falbo's. Yan (1997) highlighted that the research community has neglected the role of grandparents since the 1980s. To establish the role of grandparents in the lives of grandchildren, the researchers gathered the evidence of high three-generation co-residence rates in Nanjing (43.5 percent) through surveying four kindergartens (N = 210) in Nanjing city. Of grandparents who lived apart from their adult children and grandchildren, 75 percent lived within a short distance of 5-10 kilometers. Of this group, 71.6 percent of the adult children took their children to visit the grandparents once a week. Grandparents who provided direct care to grandchildren were found to pay more attention to the physical needs (64.1 percent) of the children compared with their intellectual (18.1 percent) and character development (12.4 percent). Also, the authors asserted that grandparents did not express enough affirmation to grandchildren, and tended to deal inappropriately with misbehaving scenarios. Hence, this study painted a rather negative picture of grandparents' childcare skills and advocated that grandparents should learn better parenting skills.

Wang (2007) found three main modes of raising children in China, namely, grandparents as main caregivers; grandparents and parents as joint caregivers; and parents as main caregivers. Through a survey (N = 372), she claimed that grandparents have more negative styles of childrearing behaviors and attitudes than the parents. Wang found grandparents had more time to show love to the grandchildren and thus provided children with a greater sense of security. However, the identified negative styles included: placing less emphasis on inculcating independence; being too protective and restrictive; being overindulgent and overly child-centered. These findings hint at the possible difference in child-rearing styles between grandparents and parents. It is important to note, however, that these two studies both arrived at these findings through self-reported surveys, which could only access unidirectional dimension data from grandparents to grandchildren or compare grandparent effect with parent effect. The intricate dynamics between the parents and grandparents as joint caregivers and their relationship with the grandchildren are not reflected.

Short *et al.*'s studies (2002) hinted at grandparents active involvement with providing childcare to grandchildren together with parents. Based on the China Health and Nutrition Survey (1989 to 1993) and interview data from two counties in Hubei Province, they found that parents are less likely to be involved in caring for their children when a grandmother is present. Chinese women's participation in the labor force is one of the highest in the world. One of the reasons mothers in China are able to maintain outside work lies in the availability of alternative childcare providers. And grandmothers were identified as the most important caregiver other than the parents themselves. Short *et al.*'s work is useful in alluding to grandparents' role in providing childcare to their adult children's household. However, no in-depth observation or analysis was carried out on how the caregiving roles and housework tasks were negotiated or the challenges in their roles as joint caregivers to children.

In Guo's (2000) chapter "Food and family relations: The generation gap at the table" she acknowledged that childcare in China involves the joint effort of two senior generations of family members: parents and grandparents.

Recently there has been an emerging body of literature that examines the role of grandparents in rural areas caring for "left behind" children as their adult children migrate to cities in search of jobs (Duan and Yang 2008, Jiang 2010). Since parents are generally absent, there is no discussion of joint caregiving between parents and grandparents.

2   Contemporary Chinese childrearing: a new lens

1 For a detailed discussion of the theories that embodied the unidirectional model of parenting research refer to Holden (1997).

2 According to LeVine (2007) anthropologists are at least partly dependent on developmental knowledge from other disciplines for their assumptions about how children experience their environments – and they have often turned to psychology and psychiatry for guidance in making these assumptions plausible. For instance, Freudian theory of psychosexual stages led some ethnographers to focus their data collection on feeding, toilet training, and emerging sexuality in young children. Beginning in the 1960s, psychologists like Piaget, Vygotsky, Bowlby, and Ainsworth had their influence on anthropological studies on child-hood. However, from the beginning, ethnographers used the data they had collected in the field to criticize developmental psychology and the cultural critique of developmental theory became an established genre.

3 A caveat has to be made for the list of publications identified in CNKI. It is possible that some Chinese publications are not captured by keywords and subjects used for the search.

4 An analysis of the journal papers found from CNKI shows that not all instruments used by the studies are validated in the Chinese population. The Chinese Family Assessment Instrument developed by Shek, a Hong Kong based psychologist, and the CRPR Q sort are two scales which have been validated in the Hong Kong Chinese population.

5 For examples of validating a Western scales in Asian context refer to Koh *et al.* (2007) and Woo *et al.* (2004).

6 According to Baurmind's typology of parenting styles based on the axes of warmth and control: authoritarian style belongs to high control and low warmth; authoritative style refers to high warmth and high control; permissive parenting style, on the other hand, is high in warmth but low in control; uninvolved parents are low in both axes.

7 Chen *et al.* (2000a) commented that almost all existing studies concerning parenting styles in Chinese culture have been based on self-reports of child-rearing attitudes.

8 Chen X., a Chinese researcher based in University of Pennsylvania and his associates have been active in developmental research in China. He frequently collaborates with native researchers including Chen Huichang. His team is beginning to put in concerted efforts in investigating the impact of rapid social and cultural changes in the past two decades in China on developmental significance of social functioning (http://www.gse.upenn.edu/faculty/chen).

9 This is in line with the Kantian world view where subjectivity is seen as inevitable as the one who is observing perceives, acts on, and participates in creating his or her own reality (Becvar and Becvar 2009).

10 It has to be qualified that the unidirectional model is not merely from parents to children. As early as in the 1960s developmental psychologist Bell (1968) has asserted a reinterpretation of influence from children to parents. The child-effects approach, which provided an antidote to the then mainstream research trend, grew in reaction to the exclusive focus on parent effects. An empirical study by Rothbart and Maccoby (1966) found that both children's age and gender have an effect on parental behaviors. Later studies investigated three categories of child's traits that influenced parents' behaviors, namely: general characteristics, physical characteristics, and behavioral characteristics. In a laboratory experimental study it was found that children suffering from attention deficit hyperactivity disorder tended to drive adult males to drink more beer (Lang *et al.*, 1989). I would consider the child-effects approach as still

unidirectional in orientation instead of the bidirectional model which I am advocating.
11 These include: transaction model; goodness of fit; system; and dialectics.

3 The 4-2-1 phenomenon in Xiamen: one child, many caregivers

1 In my own family, my paternal great-grandmother emigrated from Southeastern China to Singapore after the Second World War. My ancestral home town is in a neighboring area to Xiamen in Fujian, where a branch of the Minnan 闽南 dialect, known as Chao Zhou 潮州, is spoken.
2 The *hukuo* system was implemented in the 1950s in the wake of rapid migration from the countryside to urban areas. To curb such movements, every citizen was required to register at his or her place of permanent residence. Transfer of this hukuo (registration) required official approval and was generally prohibited in cases involving moves from countryside to urban areas or from smaller to larger urban places. This status defined the claims that citizens could make on state resources. Economic reform since 1979 has led to gradual relaxation of such migration. However, the old household registration system has still not been fundamentally reformed (Tao 2009).
3 The five earliest Special Economic Zones (SEZs) were Zhuhai 珠海, Shenzhen 深圳, Shantou 汕头, Xiamen 厦门, and Hainan 海南. SEZs were set up as experimental laboratories for Deng's economic reform (Ge 1999). The SEZs were capitalist concepts coexisting with the socialist framework (Prybyla 1989). The SEZs have played a pivotal role as a window to the outside world and as a laboratory to various reform policies. Without the successful operation of SEZs, China's reforms would not have been so smooth (Ge 1999).
4 For a detailed documentation of the development of the investment environment in Xiamen SEZ see Zheng and Huang (1988).
5 Source: Xiamen Department of Statistics' official website: http://www.stats-xm.gov.cn/staanis/tjfx00292.htm
  The growth at 8 percent in 2009 however, was comparatively low when compared to other cities in China.
6 Source: Xiaman Department of Statistics' official website: http://www.stats-xm.gov.cn/stasimpcp/jmzl00260.htm
7 Source: Xiaman Department of Statistics' official website: http://www.stats-xm.gov.cn/staanis/tjfx00292.htm
8 Source released by US government: http://www.state.gov/r/pa/ei/bgn/18902.htm
9 Source: Xiaman Department of Statistics' official website: http://www.stats-xm.gov.cn/plamin/mjds00008.htm
10 Xiamen is made up of six zones namely Huli, Siming, Haicang, Xiang'an, Tong'an, and Jimei. Since the ethnographic data was collected only from the main Xiamen Island which is made up of Huli and Siming zones, only primary schools from these two zones were invited to participate.
11 There should be a caveat to this interpretation as the distribution of children's ages could be due to an overall sample limitation. Because it was a non-random sample conducted in 39 primary schools, the number of preschool-age children was naturally smaller.
12 This is different from their western counterparts where maternal grandparents, especially maternal grandmothers, are the ones commonly helping to care for grandchildren (Chan and Elder 2000, Hodgson 1992, Rossi and Rossi 1990).

4 Grandparents and parents: who is in charge?

1 When quoting a transcript, the abbreviation of the name of the participant and date of conversation between the participant and I will be stated. If an extract is taken from my field notes or field diary, the date of the entry will be given.

2 It should be clarified that although paternal Grandmother Jiang complained daily to her son about the misbehaviors of the grandson, she did not disclose much about her difficulty in coping with both childcare and housework until much later. This could be owing to the fear of being perceived by the middle generation as incompetent. Only much later, when her health deteriorated, did she bring this to the attention of her son.

3 Analyzing a 17-page transcript of one conversation I had with Grandmother Jiang the Chinese word *lei* 累(tiredness) appeared 16 times (Field notes 20/04/06). It reflected the extent of stresses and strains grandmother experienced in full-time child-minding. She lamented that her son and daughter-in-law did not appreciate how taxing childcare and performing house chores were on her.

4 Refer to Zhou and Hou (1999) for a detailed report of the life experience of children born and raised in that era in Chinese history.

5 Initially I was rather surprised with the level of disclosure the grandmothers were willing to divulge. This deep disclosure could partly be attributed to the perceived "objectivity" of the "stranger" by the participants which gave rise to the "most surprising openness – confidence which sometimes have the character of a confessional which would be carefully withheld from a more closely related person" (Simmel 1950). Also, grandmothers might not have large social networks. Having someone they deem trustworthy, yet one who will only be in the community for six months, means that there is lower risk involved, and visiting them provided them an opportunity to vent. As much as these unanticipated disclosures were invaluable in alerting me to sensitive areas that were worth attending to in the course of my participant observation of the intergenerational dynamics I needed to handle these disclosure with great care. I had to balance being empathic but not take sides so that I would avoid any kind of strained relationship with other family members, all of whom were also my research participants.

6 I have to acknowledge that encounters with the participants, especially many tearful self-disclosures by grandmothers, left a profound impression on me. It seemed that some grandparents had many pent-up feelings and talking to me was in a way "therapeutic" to them, even though this was not an intentional goal that I set out to achieve as a researcher.

7 Migrant children are not entitled to enroll into the state-run schools. Hence, the two boys studied in the Minban 民办 (civil organization) primary school that cost more than RMB3000 per child per semester. Compared with the meager combined monthly income of RMB1100 that the grandparents earned, this amount was a real burden to the family.

5 The power of little suns as agentic beings

1 According to Cummings and Schermerhorn (2003), exercise of agency and sense of agency do not necessarily go together. For instance, the authors cited the example of children from harmonious homes and those with high marital conflict. Children from latter families are more likely to intervene in interparental conflict. This action reflects the exercise of agency. However, these children are less likely to have a sense of agency about these family situations.

2 Individual resources available to adults include physical strength, control over rewards, expertise, and information. Children's individual resources on the

other hand, including social skills, rapidly increase throughout development. Relational resource is probably the most important source of children's power derived from participating in an interdependent relationship with their adult caregivers. Although children are physically weak relative to adult caregivers, they can still get adults to comply because of the resources they can draw from their relationships. Similarly, the most enduring form of parental (adult caregivers) power over children may be based not on their greater authority and strength, but on the quality of the relationship they have created with their children (grandchildren). Cultural resources consist of the constraints, rights and entitlements conveyed to grandparents, parents and children by the practice of a culture (Kuczynski 2003, pp. 15–17).

3   The Chinese birth signs are a 12-year cycle used for dating the years. These 12 animals are the rat, ox, tiger, rabbit, dragon, snake, horse, sheep, monkey, rooster, dog, and wild boar.

4   When I reflected on the fact that Mr. Wang corrected me twice during the research conversation with him, I realized the cultural difference between us and the effect of language. Although proficient in Putonghua (Mandarin) I did not notice the subtle differences in connotation between the terms *quan wei* 权威 (authority) and *wei xin*威信 (respect and trust). As a researcher I needed to maintain an open attitude to learn from the participants and even to be corrected by them. This was a valuable learning experience for conducting cross-cultural research.

5   Research efforts by Kochanska (1997, Kochanska and Aksan 1995) began to consider agency in the midst of children's compliance.

6   The plight of little suns as lone tacticians

1   Kuczynski and Lollis (2004) developed a coding scheme to sensitize researchers to children's agentic behaviors. They include: Compliance; Accommodation; Cooperative negotiation; Uncooperative negotiation; Unwilling/minimal compliance; Passive non-compliance; Simple refusal; Defiance; Covert resistance.

2   Tian Tian's difficult position can be seen in the following conversation she had with me:

Tian Tian: When they [parents] fight, there is no way for me to stop them. However, if *wai po* or *wai gong* 外婆外公 (maternal grandparents) mediate, they [parents] will try to calm [themselves] down. Without *wai gong wai po* around, I will certainly become the *shou qi bao* 受气包 (punching bag).

Researcher: Oh I see!

Tian Tian: Whenever they fought during *wai gong* and *wai po*'s absence and I tried to mediate, they would yell at me "kid stay away from adults' affairs." I feel very helpless.

Researcher: When your *wai gong* and *wai po* are around you feel safer?

Tian Tian: I should say I often felt like the punching bag [when they are not around].

3   I have a nagging feeling that western readers would consider Mr. Tian's way of disciplining the child as "abusive." This perception may color the reader's impression of this chapter. To provide a balanced view one has to understand Mr. Tian's behavior in the Chinese context. In traditional Chinese societies, parents are bestowed with the authority to take whatever punitive actions are needed to correct children. Today, many Chinese still hold the attitude that "beating is caring and scolding is loving." Many regard their children as private property (Meng *et al.* 1994, Qiao and Chan 2005, Yang *et al.* 2004). Chinese

societies are sympathetic to parents who teach and train (guan) their children by using physical punishment. In the majority of cases, even the children themselves accept the punitive behavior of their parents as necessary in disciplining them (Qiao and Chan 2005). Tian Tian's non-compliance or resistance towards her father demonstrates the child's ability to be an active agent. If Tian Tian were to comply to her father fully there would be no punishment. These parent–child conflicts arose from Tian Tian's unwillingness follow her father's instructions, despite knowing the consequences. This is, therefore, a window for unpacking the child's agency.

4   In discussing the issue of whether only-children in China are spoiled, Wu (1996) alluded to the form of extreme attention, overprotection, constant monitoring of children's behaviors, and high expectations of school performance by parents and grandparents. He posited that the "problem" lay not in the only-children but parents, grandparents, and political elites. As much as these findings were helpful in highlighting the "sufferings" of only-children, they did not treat children as agentic beings.

5   I did not ask Tian Tian's mother or grandmother to comment on her point about being the "first victim." But I suspect they would disagree with her. They may even consider this an exaggeration since they both thought that Tian Tian could outwit them, which made it unlikely that she would be the victim. However, it was real from Tian Tian's perspective.

6   According to Zheng *et al.* (2005), Chinese concepts about childrearing today still reflect the value of children in a traditional agricultural culture despite economic, educational and life-style changes in Chinese society. It is observed that Confucian influence on value of children remains a fundamental part of Chinese culture.

7   Bei Bei was only five years old. Most Chinese parents indulge their pre-school children. The onset of school pressure usually takes place when the child enters primary one at seven years old.

7 Conclusion

1   Traditionally, Chinese children grew up in large extended families usually headed by a patriarch. The power dynamics of those traditional large families were very different from the three-generational coresidence in urban China we see today.

2   Figure 7.1 shows two grandparents and two parents in the IGPC. However, I am aware that the number varies depending on family types. Some families have as many as four grandparents in the IGPC, others only have one. Similarly, for single-parent families, there will only be one parent in the IGPC.

3   This framework of unity in conflict is especially relevant in studying Chinese childrearing. Unlike the Western situation where adult children launch out and start independent nuclear families, Chinese adult children, even after forming their own nuclear family units, continue their membership in their parental family. The extended family household is viewed as a "common enterprise where members from both generations have a vested interest in maintaining its existence" (Chen 2006, p. 237). As a direction for future research it is important to determine how childrearing practices are shaped by an indigenous cultural form which has unity in purpose and unity in interdependent relationships but not necessarily unity in means in raising precious only-children.

4   There was a short phase of time where Paternal Grandmother Wang stayed with the younger couple and took care of Wei Wei when he was an infant.

5   Owing to the limitation of time and resources, I conducted my members' check through mailing key findings (translated into Chinese) to the Jiang, Wang, Tian, and Bai families together with a reply slip and paid return envelope for them to

comment. I also communicated with the families through email. For the Fu family, as they cannot read, I engaged a master's level social work student from the University of Xiamen to pay a home visit to Grandparents Fu on my behalf, to read and explain the findings to them and get their feedback.

6   For a detailed discussion on the myths and stereotypes of only-children both in the west and in China refer to Bakken (1993). According to him, a similar version of the Chinese notion of "little emperor" was also found in an article on the only-child in a 1927 issue of *Liberty*, a weekly American popular magazine. He argued that such negative character traits such as "selfish, wilful, maladjusted, dependent, timid," etc., prejudices against only-children had to do with certain forms and perceptions of social danger linked to the process of modernization.

7   These discrepancies could be partly attributed to the insensitivity in using assessment tools that are developed in the west to measure social behavior in Chinese children. For instance, in Poston and Falbo's study, they employed the 31 Attributes Checklist and asked both teachers and parents to rate whether the child has undesirable personality traits. The raters might tend to err on the side of caution to appear socially desirable.

Bibliography

Abbot, D., Zheng, F. M., and Meredith, W. (1992) "An evolving redefinition of the fatherhood role in the People's Republic of China," *International Journal of Sociology of the Family, 29,* 45–54.

Adams, G. R., Ryan, B. A., Corville-Smith, J., Normore, A., and Turner, B. (1992) "Dialectics, organicism and contextualism: a rejoinder to Lerner," *Journal of Early Adolescence,* 12, 389–395.

Ahn, J. (2010) "'I'm not scared of anything' – emotion as social power in children's worlds," *Childhood,* 17(1), 94–112.

Alanen, L. (2001) "Childhood as a generational condition: children's daily lives in central Finland town," in L. Alanen and B. Mayall (eds) *Conceptualizing Child–Adult Relations*, London: Routledge, 129–143.

Alanen, L., and Berry, M. (eds) (2001) *Conceptualizing Child–Adult Relationships,* London: Routledge/Falmer.

Andrew, S. J., Peterson, G., and Bush, K. (2004) "Assessing the validity of parenting measures in a sample of Chinese adolescents," *Journal of Family Psychology,* 18(3), 539–544.

Bakken, B. (1993) "Prejudice and danger: the only-child in China," *Childhood,* 1, 46–61.

Bates, J., Pettiti, G., Dodge, K., and Ridge, B. (1998) "Interaction of temperamental resistance to control and restrictive parenting in the development of externalizing behavior," *Developmental Psychology,* 34, 982–995.

Becvar, D., and Becvar, R. (2009) *Family Therapy: A Systemic Integration*, 7th edn, Boston, MA: Pearson.

Bell, R. Q. (1968) "A reinterpretation of the direction of effects in studies of socialization," *Psychological Review,* 75(2), 81–95.

—— (1979) "Parent, child and reciprocal influences," *American Psychologist,* 34, 821–826.

Benedict, R. (1989) *The Chrysanthemum and the Sword: Patterns of Japanese Culture*, Boston, MA: Houghton Mifflin Books.

Blumer, H. (1969) *Symbolic Interactionism: Perspective and Method*, Englewood Cliffs, NJ: Prentice-Hall.

Branco, A. U., and Valsiner, J. (1997) "Changing methodologies: a co-constructivist study of goal orientations in social interactions," *Psychology in Developing Societies,* 9, 35–64.

Bronfenbrenner, U. (1979) *The Ecology of Human Development: Experiments by Nature and Design*, Cambridge, MA: Harvard University Press.

Bugental, D. B., and Goodnow, J. J. (1998) "Socialization processes," in W. Damon (ed.) *Handbook of Child Psychology*, New York: John Wiley, 389–462.

Bugental, D. B., Lyon, J. E., Karantz, J., and Cortez, V. (1997) "Who's the boss? Accessibility of dominance ideation among individuals with low perceptions of interpersonal power," *Journal of Personality and Social Psychology*, 72, 1297–1399.

Chan, C. G., and Elder, G. H. (2000) "Matrilineal advantage in grandchild–grandparent relations," *The Gerontologist*, 40(2), 179–190.

Chao, R. K. (1994) "Beyond parental control and authoritarian parenting style: understanding Chinese parenting through the cultural notion of training," *Child Development*, 65(4), 1111–1119.

Chen, H., Li, D., Hou, J., and Chen, X. (2003a) "Maternal control strategies and the child's compliant behavior in family free play (*Jia ting you xi zhong de mu qin kong zhi ce lue yu er tong shun cong xing wei* – in Chinese)," *Acta Psychologica Sinica (Xin Li Xue Bao)*, 35(1), 84–88.

Chen, H., Zhang, Y., and Chen, X. (2003b) "Parenting practice and behavior inhibition of 2-year-old toddlers (*Liang Sui Er Tong Yi Zhi Xing Wei De Xiang Guan Fu Mu Jiao Yang Yin Su*)," *Chinese Mental Health Journal (Zhong Guo Xin Li Wei Sheng Za Zhi)*, 17(4), 244–246.

Chen, J. (2006) "When to give and why: intergenerational transfer of resources in urban Chinese families," in W. Tang and B. Holzner (eds) *Social Change in Contemporary China*, Pittsburgh, PA: University of Pittsburgh Press, 233–260.

Chen, M. L., and Zhang, M. L. (2010) "Familial child rearing enviornment and its impact on children's mental health (*Jia Ting Jiao Yang Huan Jing Dui Er Tong Xin Li Jian Kang De Ying Xiang*)," *Research on Foundational Education (Ji Chu Jiao Yu Yan Jiu)*, 2, 45–46.

Chen, X. (1985) "The one child population policy, modernization and the extended Chinese family," *Journal of Marriage and the Family* (47), 193–202.

Chen, X., and Sun, J. (2006) "Sociological perspectives on urban China – from familiar territories to complex terrains," *China Information*, 20(3), 519–551.

Chen, X., Liu, M., Li, B., Cen, G., Chen, H., and Wang, L. (2000a) "Maternal authoritative and authoritarian attitudes and mother–child interactions and relationships in urban China," *International Journal of Behavioral Development*, 24(1), 119–126.

Chen, X., Liu, M., and Li, D. (2000b) "Parental warmth, control, and indulgence and their relations to adjustment in Chinese children: a longtitudinal study," *Journal of Family Psychology*, 14(3), 401–419.

Chen, X., Wu, H., Chen, H., and Wang, L. (2001) "Parenting practices and aggressive behaviour in Chinese children," *Parenting: Science and Practice*, 1(3), 159–184.

Chow, E. N.-L., and Chen, K. (1994) "The impact of the one-child policy on women and the patriarchal family in the People's Republic of China," in E. N.-L. Chow and C. W. Berheide (eds) *Women, the Family, and Policy: A Global Perspective*, Albany, NY: State University of New York Press, 71–98.

Christensen, P., and O'Brian, M. (eds) (2003) *Children in the City: Home, Neighbourhood and Community*, London: Routledge/Falmer.

Cook, J. A. (2006) "Reimagining China: Xiamen, overseas Chinese and a transnational modernity," in M. Y. Dong and J. L. Goldstein (eds) *Everyday Modernity in China*, Seattle, WA: University of Washington Press, 156–194.

Corsaro, W. A. (1997) *The Sociology of Childhood,* Thousand Oaks, CA: Pine Forge Press.

—— (2005) *The Sociology of Childhood*, Thousand Oaks, CA: Pine Forge Press.

Crockenberg, S., and Leerkes, E. (2003) "Infant negative emotionality, caregiving, and family relationships," in A. Crouter and A. Booth (eds) *Children's Influence on Family Dynamics: The Neglected Side of Family Relationships*, Mahwah, NJ: Lawrence Erlbaum, 57–78.

Crouter, A., and Booth, A. (eds) (2003) *Children's Influence on Family Dynamics: The Neglected Side of Family Relationships*, Mahwah, NJ: Lawrence Erlbaum.

Cummings, E. M., and Schermerhorn, A. C. (2003) "A developmental perspective on children as agents in the family," in L. Kuczynski (ed.) *Handbook of Dynamics in Parent–Child Relations*, Thousand Oaks, CA: Sage, 91–108.

Cummings, E. M., Davies, P. T., and Campbell, S. B. (2000) *Developmental Psychopathology and Family Process: Theory, Research and Clinical Implications*, New York: The Guilford Press.

Damon, W. (1977) *The Social World of the Child,* San Francisco, CA: Jossey-Bass.

Damon, W., and Hart, D. (1988) *Self-understanding in Childhood and Adolesence*, Cambridge: Cambridge University Press.

Dawber, T., and Kuczynski, L. (1999) "The question of ownness: influence of relationship context on parental socialization strategies," *Journal of Social and Personal Relationships,* 16(4), 475.

De Mol, J., and Buysse, A. (2008) "Understandings of children's influence in parent–child relationships: a Q-methodological study," *Journal of Social and Personal Relationships,* 25, 359–379.

Dodge, K. A. (1983) "Behavioural antecedents of peer social status," *Child Development,* 54, 1386–1399.

Du, D., and Su, Y. (2009) "Faux pas understanding among 7 to 11 years old and its correlation with maternal rearing style (*7–11 sui er tong shi yan li jie yu mu qin jiao yang fang shi de guan xi* – in Chinese)," *Developmental Psychology and Education (Xin Li Fa Zhan Yu Jiao Yu)* (1), 14–20.

Duan, C., and Yang, G. (2008) "The left behind children in China (*Wo guo nong chun liu shou er tong zhuang kuang yan jiu* – in Chinese)," *Population Research (Ren Kou Yan Jiu),* 32(3), 15–25.

Dumas, J. E., Lafreniere, P. J., and Serketich, W. J. (1995) "'Balance of power': a transactional analysis of control in mother–child dyads involving socially competent, aggressive, and anxious children," *Journal of Abnormal Psychology,* 104(1), 104–113.

Eder, D., and Corsaro, W. (1999) "Ethnographic studies of children and youth," *Journal of Contemporary Ethnography,* 28(5), 520.

Edwards, R. (ed.) (2002) *Children, Home and School: Regulation, Autonomy or Connection?*, London: Routledge/Falmer.

Eisenberg, A. R. (1992) "Conflicts between mothers and their young children," *Merrill-Palmer Quarterly,* 38, 21–43.

Emerson, R. M. (1962) "Power-dependence relations," *American Sociological Review,* 27, 21–44.

Falbo, T. (1991) "The impact of grandparents on children's outcomes in China," *Marriage and Family Review,* 16(3/4), 369–377.

Fei, X. (1992) *From the Soil: The Foundation of Chinese Society*, Berkeley, CA: University of California Press.

Fine, G. A. (1992) "Agency, structure and comparative contexts: toward a synthetic interactionism," *Symbolic Interaction*, 15(1), 87–107.

Fong, V. L. (2004) *Only Hope: Coming of Age Under China's One-Child Policy*, Stanford, CA: Stanford University Press.

Frye, D., and Zelazo, D. (2003) "The development of young children's action control and awareness," in J. Roessler and N. Eilan (eds) *Agency and Self-Awareness: Issues in Philosophy and Psychology*, Oxford: Oxford University Press, 244–262.

Fung, H. (1999) "Becoming a moral child: the socialization of shame among young Chinese children," *Ethos*, 27(2), 180–209.

Ge, W. (1999) *Special Economic Zones and the Economic Transition in China*, Singapore: World Scientific.

Giddens, A. (1984) *The Constitution of Society: Outline of the Theory of Structuration*, Berkeley, CA: University of California Press.

Giles, J., Park, A., and Zhang, J. (2005) "What is China's true unemployment rate?," *China Economic Review*, 16(2), 149–170.

Goh, E. C. L. (2006) "Raising the precious single child in urban China – an inter-generational joint mission between parents and grandparents," *Journal of Intergenerational Relationships*, 4(3), 7–28.

—— (2009) "Grandparents as childcare providers: an in-depth analysis of the case of Xiamen, China," *Journal of Aging Studies*, 23, 60–68.

Goh, E. C. L., and Kuczynski, L. (2009) "Agency and power of single children in multi-generational families in urban Xiamen, China," *Culture and Psychology*, 15(4), 506–534.

—— (2010) "'Only children' and their coalition of parents: considering grand-parents and parents as joint caregivers in urban Xiamen, China," *Asian Journal of Social Psychology*, 13(4), 221–231.

Goodman, C. C., and Silverstein, M. (2006) "Grandmothers raising grandchildren: ethnic and racial differences in well-being among custodial and coparenting families," *Journal of Family Issues*, 27(11), 1605.

Goodnow, J. J. (1994) "Acceptable disagreement across generations," *New Directions for Child Development*, 66, 51–63.

Gordon, J. E. (1957) "The validity of Shoben's parent attitude survey," *Journal of Clinical Psychology*, 13, 151–158.

Greenhalgh, S. (2008) *Just One Child*, Berkeley, CA: University of California Press.

Guo, B., Pickard, J., and Huang, J. (2007) "A cultural perspective on health outcomes of caregiving grandparents: evidence from China," *Journal of Intergenerational Relationships*, 5(4), 25–40.

Guo, H., Ding, W., Ma, X., Wang, L., and Lin, C. (2008) "Effect of family psycholog-ical intervention on parental rearing style and personality of pupils (*Jia ting xin li gan yu gai shan fu mu jiao yang fang shi he xiao xue sheng ge xing de xiao guo yan jiu* – in Chinese)," *China Journal of School Health (Xin Li Wei Sheng)*, 29(12), 1111–1113.

Guo, Y. (2000) "Food and family relations: the generation gap at the table," in J. Jing (ed.) *Feeding China's Little Emperors*, Stanford, CA: Stanford University Press, 94–113.

Hallet, C., and Prout, A. (eds) (2003) *Hearing the Voices of Children: Social Policy for a New Century*, London: Routledge/Falmer.

Harach, L., and Kuczynski, L. (2005) "Construction and maintenance of parent–child relationships: bidirectional contributions from the perspective of parents," *Infant and Child Development*, 14, 327–343.

Harris, J. R. (1998) *The Nurture Assumption: Why Children Turn Out the Way They Do*, New York: Free Press.

Hayslip, B., Shore, R. J., Henderson, C. E., and Lambert, P. L. (1998) "Custodial grandparenting and the impact of grandchildren with problems on role satisfaction and role meaning," *Journals of Gerontology Series B: Psychological Sciences and Social Sciences*, 53(3), 164–173.

Hershatter, G. (2007) *Women in China's Long Twentieth Century*, Berkeley, CA: University of California Press.

Hinde, R. A. 1979. *Towards Understanding Relationships*, London: Academic Press.

—— (1997) *Relationships: A Dialectical Perspective*, Cambridge, UK: Psychology Press.

Hinde, R. A., and Stevenson-Hinde, J. (1988) *Relationships within Families: Mutual Influences*, Oxford: Clarendon.

Ho, D. F. Y. (1987) "Fatherhood in Chinese culture," in M. E. Lamb (ed.) *The Father's Role: Cross Cultural Perspectives*, Hillsdale, NJ: Lawrence Erlbaum.

—— (1989) "Socialization in contemporary mainland China," *Asian Thought and Society*, 14(41–42), 136–149.

—— (1996a) "Chinese childhood socialization," in M. H. Bond (ed.) *The Handbook of Chinese Psychology*, Hong Kong: Oxford University Press, 143–154.

—— (1996b) "Filial piety and its psychological consequences," in M. H. Bond (ed.) *Handbook of Chinese Psychology*, Hong Kong: Oxford University Press, 155–165.

Hodgson, L. G. (1992) "Adult grandchildren and their grandparents: the enduring bond," *International Journal of Aging and Human Development*, 34, 209–225.

Holden, G. W. (1997) *Parents and the Dynamics of Child Rearing*, Boulder, CO: Westview Press.

—— (2002) "Parental attitudes toward childrearing," in M. H. Bornstein (ed.) *Handbook of Parenting*, London: Lawrence Erlbaum, 359–392.

—— (2010) *Parenting: A Dynamic Perspective*, Thousand Oaks, CA: Sage.

Holden, G. W., and Ritchie, K. L. (1988) "Child rearing and the dialects of parental intelligence," in J. Valsiner (ed.) *Child Development within Culturally Structured Environments: Parental Cognition and Adult–Child Interaction*, Norwood, NJ: Ablex, 30–59.

Holden, G. W., and Edwards, L. A. (1989) "Parental attitudes toward child rearing: instruments, issues and implications," *Psychological Bulletin*, 106, 29–58.

Holden, G. W., and Hawk, K. H. (2003) "Meta-parenting in the journey of child rearing: a cognitive meachnism for change," in L. Kuczynski (ed.) *Handbook of Dynamics in Parent–Child Relations*, Thousand Oaks, CA: Sage, 189–210.

Hou, J., Chen, H., and Chen, X. (2003) "Children's interaction with their mothers in free play and intelligent-task-oriented play at home," *Xin Li Ke Xue*, 26(2), 244–248.

—— (2005) "The relationship of parent–children interaction in the free play session and copy modeling session with the development of children's behavioural inhibition in Chinese families (*Zhong guo jia ting zhong de qing zhi hu dong xing wei yu er tong xing wei yi zhi xing de fa zhan* – in Chinese)," *Psychological Science (Xin Li Ke Xue)*, 28(4), 820–825.

Howell, J. (1993) *China Opens Its Doors: The Politics of Economic Transition*, Boulder, CO: Lynne Rienner.

Hu, Y. H. (1995) *The Myths and Traps of Three Generations Coresidence (Shan Dai Tong Tang De Mi Shi – in Chinese)*, Taipei: Ju Liu Du Shu Dong Si.

Huang, J., and Prochner, L. (2004) "Chinese parenting styles and children's self-regulated learning," *Research in Childhood Education*, 18(3), 227–238.

Hutchby, I., and Moran-Ellis, J. (eds) (2001) *Children, Technology and Culture: The Impacts of Technologies in Children's Everyday Lives*, London: Routledge/Falmer.

Hwang, K. K. (2004) *Power Game of Chinese People (Mianzi-Zhong Guo Ren de Quan Li You Xi – in Chinese)*, Beijing: Chinese Renmin University Press.

James, A. (2001) "Ethnography in the study of children and childhood," in P. Atkinson (ed.) *Handbook of Ethnography*, London: Sage, 246–257.

James, A., and Prout, A. (1997) *Constructing and Reconstructing Childhood: Contemporary Issues in the Sociological Study of Childhood*, 2nd edn, London: Falmer Press.

Jenks, C. (2005) *Childhood*, 2nd edn, London: Routledge.

Jensen, A. M., and Mckee, L. (eds) (2003) *Children and the Changing Family: between Transformation and Negotiation*, London: Routledge/Falmer.

Jiang, Y.-C. (2010) "Rural family relationship change under the background of economy of hiring out for work and model for bringing up children left behind: a case of Tan village in Hunan Province (*Da gong jing ji bei jing xia nong chun jia ting guan xi de bian qian yu liu shou er tong yang yu mo shi yan jiu* – in Chinese)," *Northwest Population (Xi Bei Ren Kou)*, 31(3), 27–31.

Jiao, S. J., and Jing, Q. C. (1986) "Comparative study of behavioural qualities of only children and sibling children," *Child Development*, 57, 357–361.

Jing, J. (2000) "Introduction: food, children, and social change in contemporary China," in J. Jing (ed.) *Feeding China's little emperors: Food, children and social change*, Stanford, CA: Stanford University Press, 1–26.

Kim, K. W. (2006) "Hyo and parenting in Korea," in K. H. Rubin and O. B. Chung (eds) *Parenting Beliefs, Behaviors, and Parent–Child Relations: A Cross-Cultural Perspective*, New York: Psychology Press, 207–223.

Kochanska, G. (1997) "Multiple pathways to conscience for children with different temperaments: from toddlerhood to age 5," *Developmental Psychology*, 33, 228–240.

Kochanska, G., and Aksan, N. (1995) "Mother–child mutually positive affect, the quality of child compliance to requests and prohibitions, and maternal control as correlates of early internalization," *Child Development*, 236–254.

Koh, J., Chang, W., Fung, D., and Kee, C. (2007) "Conceptualization and manifestation of depression in an Asian context: formal construction and validation of a children's depression scale in Singapore," *Culture, Medicine and Psychiatry*, 31(2), 225–249.

Kuczynski, L. (2001) "Four foundations for a dynamic model of parenting," in J. R. M. Gerris (ed.) *Dynamics of Parenting*, Leuven-Apeldoorn: Garant, 445–462.

—— (2003) "Beyond bidirectionality: bilateral conceptual frameworks for understanding dynamics," in L. Kuczynski (ed.) *Handbook of Dynamics in Parent–Child Relations*, Thousand Oaks, CA: Sage, 1–24.

Kuczynski, L., and Kochanska, G. (1990) "The development of children's noncompliance strategies from toddlerhood to age 5," *Developmental Psychology,* 26, 398–408.

Kuczynski, L., and Hildebrant, N. (1997) "Models of conformity and resistance in socialization theory," in J. E. Grusec and L. Kuczynski (eds) *Parenting and the Internalization of Values: A Handbook of Contemporary Theory,* New York: Wiley, 227–256.

Kuczynski, L., and Daly, K. (2003) "Qualitative methods for inductive (theory-generating) research: psychological and sociological approaches," in L. Kuczynski (ed.) *Handbook of Dynamics in Parent-Child Relations,* Thousand Oaks, CA: Sage, 373–392.

Kuczynski, L., and Lollis, S. (2004) "The child as agent in family life," in H. Goelman, S. K. Marshall and S. Ross (eds) *Multiple Lenses Multiple Images: Perspectives on the Child Across Time, Space and Disciplines,* Toronto: University of Toronto Press, 197–229.

Kuczynski, L., and Parkin, M. (2006) "Agency and bidirectionality in socialization: interactions, transactions and relational dialectics," in J. Grusec and P. Hasting (eds) *Handbook of Socialization,* New York: Guilford Press, 259–283.

Kuczynski, L., Harach, L., and Bernardini, S. C. (1999) "Psychology's child meets sociology's child: agency, influence and power in parent–child relationships," in C. L. Shehan (ed.) *Through the Eyes of the Child: Revisioning Children as Active Agents of Family Life,* Stamford, CT: JAI Press, 21–52.

Kuczynski, L., Pitman, R., and Mitchell, M. B. (2009) "Dialectics and transactional models: conceptualizing antecedents, processes, and consequences of changes in parent–child relationships," in J. A. Mancini., and K. A. Roberto (eds) *Pathways of Human Development,* Plymouth: Lexington Books, 151–170.

Lai, A. C., and Zhang, Z.-X. (2000) "Child rearing practices in Hong Kong and Beijing Chinese families: a comparative study," *International Journal of Psychology,* 35(1), 60–66.

Lang, A., *et al.* (1989) "Levels of adult alcohol consumption induced by interactions with child confederates exhibiting normal versus externalizing behaviors," *Journal of Abnormal Psychology,* 98(3), 294–299.

Lawrence, J. A., and Valsiner, J. (1993) "Conceptual roots of internalization: from transmission to transformation," *Human Development,* 36(3), 150–167.

Lerner, R.M. (1993) "The influence of child temperament characteristics on parent behaviors," in T. Luster and L. Okagaki (eds) *Parenting: An Ecological Perspective,* Hillsdale, NJ: Lawrence Erlbaum, 101–120.

Leung, J. C. B. (2010) "Residential care services for older people in China: from state to market provisions?," *Social Development Issues,* 32(1), 31–47.

LeVine, R. A. (1982) *Culture, Behavior and Personality,* New York: Aldine.

—— (2007) "Ethnographic studies of childhood: a historical overview," *American Anthropologist,* 109(2), 247–260.

Levy, M. (1949) *The Family Revolution in Modern China,* Cambridge, MA: Harvard University Press.

Li, C. N., Ma, C. R., and Zou, H. (2006) "Relationship between parent–offspring perceptual differences of family functioning and adolescents' self-esteem (*Jia ting gong neng zhi jue de qin zi cha yi ji qi yu qing shao nian zi zun de guan xi* – in Chinese)," *Chinese Journal of Clinical Psychology (Zhong Guo Lin Chuang Xin Li Xue Za Zhi),* 6, 617–619.

Li, Y. (2003) *Grandchildren from One Grandfather (Yi Ye Zi Sun* – in Chinese), Beijing: Cultural and Arts Publishing.

Li, Y., and Sang, B. (2006). "Mother's parenting style and the development of children's theory of mind (*Mu qin jiao yang fang shi yu er tong xin li li lun fa zhan de guan xi* – in Chinese)," *Chinese Mental Health Journal (Zhong Guo Xin Li Wei Shen Za Zhi),* 20(1), 5–9.

Liang, Z., Zhang, G., Chen, H., and Zhou, B. (2007) "The relations between personal construction and school adjustment in adolescents (*Er tong qi mu qin jiao yang fang shi yu 11 sui er tong xue xiao shi ying de guan xi* – in Chinese)," *Studies of Psychology and Behavior (Xin Li Yu Xing Wei Yan Jiu),* 5(1), 36–40.

Lin, C., and Chen, Y. (2009) "Advances of China's developmental psychology in the past 30 years (*Zhong guo fan zhan xin li xue 30 nian de jing zhan* – in Chinese)," *Beijing Shi Fan Da Xue Xue Bao,* 211(1), 38–36.

Liu, B. (2006) *Families within Societal Change: Research on Contemporary Urban Families in China (She Hui Bian Qian Zhong De Jia Ting: Dang Dai Zhong Guo Cheng Shi Jia Ting Yan Jiu* – in Chinese), Chengdu: Ba Shu Shu She.

Liu, B., Chen, X., and Wang, X. (2009) "Parental rearing patterns on college students' mental health (*Fu mu jiao yang fang shi dui da xue sheng xin li jian kang de ying xiang* – in Chinese)," *Social Psychology (Shui Xin Li Xue),* 6, 739–743.

Liu, Q., Zhou, S., Yang, H., Chu, Y., and Liu, L. (2009) "A research on the parenting styles of Chinese College students (*Da xue sheng de fu mu jiao yang fang shi te dian fen xi* – in Chinese)," *Chinese Journal of Clinical Psychology (Zhong Guo Lin Chuang Xin Li Xue Za Zhi),* 17(6), 736–738.

Logan, J., and Bian, F. (1999) "Family values and coresidence with married children and urban China," *Social Forces,* 77(4), 1253–1282.

Logan, J., Bian, F., and Bian, Y. (1998) "Tradition and change in the urban Chinese family: the case of living arrangements," *Social Forces,* 76(3), 851–882.

Lollis, S. (2003) "Conceptualizing the influence of the past and the future in present parent–child relationships," in L. Kuczynski (ed.) *Handbook of Dynamics in Parent–Child Relationships,* Thousand Oaks, CA: Sage, 67–87.

Lollis, S., and Kuczynski, L. (1997) "Beyond one hand clapping: seeing bidirectionality in parent–child relations," *Journal of Social and Personal Relationships,* 14, 441–461.

Lu, Q., Chen, H., Wang, L., and Chen, X. (2002) "Parents' childrearing attitude and children's problem behaviors at two four and four years of age (*Fu mu jiao yang dai du yu er tong zai 2 4 sui jian de wen ti xing wei* – in Chinese)," *Acta Psychologica Sinica (Xin Li Xue Bao),* 1, 89–92.

Luescher, K. (2004) "Conceptualizing and uncovering intergenerational ambivalence," in K. Pillemer and K. Luescher (eds) *Intergenerational Ambivalences: New Perspectives on Parent–Child Relations in Later Life,* Amsterdam: Elsevier, 23–62.

Maccoby, E. E. (2000) "The uniqueness of the parent–child relationship," in W. A. Collins and B. Laursen (eds) *Relationships as Developmental Contexts,* Mahwah, NJ: Lawrence Erlbaum, 157–175.

—— (2002) "Parenting effects: issues and controversies," in J. G. Borkowski, S. L. Ramey and M. Bristol-Power (eds) *Parenting and the Child's World: Influences on Academic, Intellectual, and Social-Emotional Development,* Mahwah, NJ: Lawrence Erlbaum, 35–48.

Maccoby, E. E., and Martin, J. (1983) "Socialization in the context of family: parent–child interaction," in E. M. Hetherington (ed.) *Mussen Manual of Child Psychology*, New York: Wiley, 1–101.

Malinowski, B. (1927) *Sex and Repression in Savage Society*, London: Paul, Trench, Trubner.

—— (1929) *The Sexual Life of Savages in North Western Melanesia*, London: Routledge.

Marshall, M. N. (2006) "Sampling for qualitative research," *Family Practice*, 13(6), 522–526.

Mayall, B. (1994) "Children in action at home and school," in B. Mayall (ed.) *Children's Childhoods: Observed and Experienced*, Washington, DC: The Falmer Press.

—— (2001) "Understanding childhood in London," in L. Alanen and B. Mayall (eds) *Conceptualizing Child–Adult Relations*, London: Routledge, 114–128.

—— (2002) *Towards a Sociology for Childhood*, Maidenhead: Open University Press.

Mead, G. H. (1929) "The nature of the past," in J. Cross (ed.) *Essays in Honor of John Dewey*, New York: Henry Holt, 235–242.

Mead, M. (1961) *Coming of Age in Samoa*, New York: Morrow.

—— (1962) *Growing Up in New Guinea: A Comparative Study of Primitive Education*, New York: Morrow.

Meng, Q., Liu, X., and Zhang, H. (1994) "Study on the public definition of child abuse (*Er tong qu di nue dai de gong gong ding yi yan jiu* – in Chinese)," *Chinese Social Medicine (Zong Guo She Hui Yi Xue)*, 50(1), 10–13.

Miles, M. B., and Huberman, A. M. (1994) *Qualitative Data Analysis*, Thousand Oaks, CA: Sage.

Miller, P. J., Fung, H., and Mintz, J. (1996) "Self-construction through narrative practice: a Chinese and American comparison of early socialization," *Ethos*, 24(2), 237–280.

Miller, P. J., Sandel, T., Liang, C.-H., and Fung, H. (2001) "Narrating transgressions in Longwood: the discourses, meanings and paradoxes of an American socializing practice," *Ethos*, 29(2), 159–186.

Nie, Y., and Wyman, R. (2005) "The one-child policy in Shanghai: acceptance and internalization," *Population and Development Review*, 313–336.

Niu, Z., Chen, H., Wang, L., and Zhang, H. (2004) "Behavioral representations of 7-year-old children in helping situations and its relationship with parenting styles (*7 sui er tong zai zhu ren qing jing zhong de xing wei biao xian ji yu fu mu jiao yang fang shi de guan xi* – in Chinese)," *Psychological Development and Education (Xin Li Fa Zhan Yu Jiao Yu)*, 2, 17–21.

O'Reilly, K. (2005) *Ethnographic Methods*, London: Routledge.

Orleans, M., and Overton, T. (1999) "The media power of children: case studies of child–family interactions," in C. L. Shehan (ed.) *Through the Eyes of the Child: Revisioning Children as Active Agents of Family Life*, Stamford, CT: JAI Press, 287–310.

Pan, Y. K. (2002) *Family Sociology (Jia Ting She Hui Xue* – in Chinese*)*, Beijing: Zhong Guo She Hui Chu Ban She.

Pan, Y. K., and Lin, N. (2006) "The model of modernized family structure (*Zhong guo cheng shi xian dai jia ting mo shi* – in Chinese)," in Shanghai Social Science Institute Family Research Centre (ed.) *Research on Chinese Families (Zhong*

Guo Jia Ting Yan Jiu – in Chinese), Shanghai: Shanghai Social Science Press, 16–44.

Parsons, T., and Bales, R. F. (1955) *Family, Socialization and Interaction Process,* Glencoe, IL: Free Press.

Perlman, M., Siddiqui, A., and Ross, H. S. (1999) "An analysis of sources of power in chidren's conflict interactions," in R. Mills and S. Duck (eds) *The Developmental Psychology of Personal Relationships,* Chichester: John Wiley & Sons, 155–174.

Peters, C. L., Hooker, K., and Zvonkovic, A. (2006) "Older parents' perceptions of ambivalence in relationships with their children," *Family Relations,* 55(Dec), 539–551.

Peterson, G. W., and Rollins, B. C. (1986) "Parent–child socialization," in M. B. Sussman and S. K. Steinmetz (eds) *Handbook of Marriage and the Family,* New York: Plenum Press, 471–507.

Peterson, G. W., Steinmetz, S. K., and Wilson, S. M. (2003) "Cultural and cross-cultural perspectives on parent–youth relations," *Marriage and Family Review,* 35(3/4), 5–14.

—— (eds) (2004) *Parent–Youth Relations: Cultural and Cross-Cultural Perspectives,* New York: Haworth Press.

Pole, C., Mizen, P., and Bolton, A. (eds) (2001) *International Perspectives on Children's Work and Labour 2001,* London: Routledge/Falmer.

Pomfret, J. (2006) *Chinese Lessons: Five Classmates and the Story of the New China,* New York: Henry Holt.

Poston, D., and Falbo, T. (1990) "Academic performance and personality traits of Chinese children: 'onlies' versus others," *The American Journal of Sociology,* 96(2), 433–451.

Price, R. H., Choi, J. N., and Lim, S. (2007) "Beyond the iron rice bowl," in G. Lee and W. Malcolm (eds) *Unemployment in China: Economy, Human Resources and Labour Markets,* London: Routledge, 108–127.

Prybyla, J. S. (1989) "China's economic experiment: from Mao to market," in M. Bornstein (ed.) *Comparative Economic Systems: Models and Cases,* Homewood, IL: Irwin, 388.

Punch, S. (2001) "Negotiating autonomy: childhood in rural Bolivia," in A. Leena and M. Berry (eds) *Conceptualizing Child–Adult Relations,* London Routledge, 23–36.

Qiao, D. P., and Chan, Y. C. (2005) "Child abuse in China: a yet-to-be-acknowledged social problem in the Chinese mainland," *Child and Family Social Work,* 10, 21–27.

Quoss, B., and Wen, Z. (1995) "Parenting styles and children's satisfaction with parenting in China and the United States," *Journal of Comparative Family Studies,* 26(2), 265–280.

Richards, L. (2005) *Handling Qualitative Data: A Practical Guide,* London: Sage.

Riegel, K. F. (1976) "The dialectics of human development," *American Psychologist,* 31(10), 689–700.

Roopnarine, J. L., and Carter, B. D. (1992) "The cultural context of socialization: a much ignored issue," in I. E. Sigel (ed.) *Parent–Child Socialization in Diverse Cultures,* Boston, MA: Ablex, 245–253.

Rossi, A. H., and Rossi, P. H. (1990) *Of Human Bonding: Parent–Child Relations Across the Life Course,* New York: de Gruyter.

Rothbart, M., and Maccoby, E. (1966) "Parents' differential reactions to sons and daughters," *Journal of Personality and Social Psychology*, 4(3), 237–243.

Rowe, D. (1994) *The Limits of Family Influence: Genes, Experience and Behavior*, New York: Guilford.

Russell, A. G., Pettiti, G., and Mize, J. (1998) "Horizontal qualities in parent–child relationships: parallels with possible consequences for children's peer relationships," *Developmental Review*, 18, 313–352.

Sameroff, A. (1975a) "Early influences on development: fact or fancy?" *Merrill-Palmer Quarterly*, 21, 267–293.

—— (1975b) "Transactional models of early social relations," *Human Development*, 18, 65–79.

Scott, J. C. (1985) *Weapons of the Weak: Everyday Forms of Peasant Resistance*, New Haven, CT: Yale University Press.

—— (1986) *Everyday forms of peasant resistance in South-East Asia*, edited by J. C. Scott and B. J. Tria Kerkvliet, London: Frank Cass.

Shaung, H., Gu, C., and Chen, H. (2004) "Parental attribution to children's aggressive and social withdrawal (*Fu mu dui er tong he tui shuo xing wei de gui yin ji qi yu fu mu qing xu fan ying de guanxi* – in Chinese)," *Chinese Mental Health Journal (Zhong Guo Xin Li Wei Sheng Za Zhi)*, 18(10), 695–698.

Shehan, C. L. (1999) "No longer a place for innocence: The re-submergence of childhood in post-industrial societies," in C. L. Shehan (ed.) *Through the Eyes of the Child: Revisioning Children as Active Agents of Family Life*, Stamford, CT: JAI Press, 1–20.

Shen, C. L., and Yang, S. H. (1995) *Research on Contemporary Urban Chinese Families (Dandai zhongguo chengshi jiating yanjiu* – in Chinese), Beijing: Chinese Social Science Press.

Shen, C. L., Yang, S. H., and Li, D. S. (1999) *Urban and Rural Families in the Transiting Century (Shi Ji Zhi Jiao De Cheng Xiang Jia Ting* – in Chinese), Beijing: Chinese Social Science Press.

Shen, Y., and Chen, J. (2009) "The influence of family environment and peer relationship on preschooler's ToM (*Jia ting huan jing tong ban guan xi dui you er xin li li lun de ying xiang* – in Chinese)," *Studies in Preschool Education (Xue Qian Jiao Yu Yan Jiu)*, 3, 31–34.

Short, S., Chen, F., Entwsle, B., and Zhai, F. (2002) "Maternal work and child care in China: a multi-method analysis," *Population and Development Review*, 28(1), 31–57.

Simmel, G. (1950) *The Sociology of Georg Simmel*, Glencoe, IL: Free Press.

Skinner, E. A., Chapman, M., and Baltes, P. B. (1988) "Children's beliefs about control, means-ends, and agency: developmental differences during middle childhood," *International Journal of Behavioral Development*, 11, 369–388.

Smith, P. K., and Drew, L. M. (2002) "Grandparenthood," in M. Bornstein (ed.) *Handbook of Parenting*, Hillsdale, NJ: Lawrence Erlbaum, 141–172.

Stack, C. B. (1975) *All Our Kin: Strategies for Survival in a Black Community*, New York: Basic Books.

Strauss, A., and Corbin, J. (1990) *Basics of Qualitative Research: Grounded Theory Procedures and Techniques*, London: Sage.

Sun, Y. (1998) *Inculcating Healthy Character in Single Children (Pei Yang Du Sheng Zi Nv De Jian Kang Ren Ge* – in Chinese), Tianjin: Tianjin Education Press.

Tao, R. (2009) "Hukuo reform and social security for migrant workers in China," in R. Murphy (ed.) *Labour Migration and Social Development in Contemporary China*, London: Routledge, 73–95.

Tardif, T., and Miao, X. (2000) "Developmental psychology in China," *International Journal of Behavioral Development*, 24(1), 68–72.

Trommsdorff, G. (2009) "A social change and human development perspective on value of children," in S. Bekman and A. Aksu-Koc (eds) *Perspective on Human, Development, Family and Culture*, New York: Cambridge University Press, 86–107.

Trommsdorff, G., and Kornadt, H. J. (2003) "Parent–child relations in cross cultural perspective," in L. Kuczynski (ed.) *Handbook of Dynamics in Parent–Child Relations*, Thousand Oaks, CA: Sage, 271–306.

Tseng, W. S., and Wu, D. (1985) *Chinese Culture and Mental Health*, Orlando, FL: Academic Press.

Tu, W. M. (1985) *Confucian Thought: Selfhood and Creative Transformation*, Albany, NY: State of New York University Press.

Unger, J. (2000) *Urban Families in the Eighties: An Analysis of Chinese Surveys*, netLibrary, available online: http://www.netlibrary.com/Details.aspx (accessed 19 June 2010).

UNICEF (2005) "At a glance: China," available online: http://www.unicef.org/infobycountry/china_statistics.html (accessed 11 Sept 2010).

United Nations (2000) *The World's Women 1970–1990: Trends and Statistics*, New York.

Valsiner, J. (2006) "Dangerous curves in knowledge construction in psychology: fragmentation of methodology," *Theory and Psychology*, 16, 597–612.

Valsiner, J., Branco, A. U., and Dantas, C. M. (1997) "Co-construction of human development: heterogeneity within parental belief orientation," in J. E. Grusec and L. Kuczynski (eds) *Parenting and the Internalization of Values: A Handbook of Contemporary Theory*, New York: John Wiley, 227–256.

Wan, Y. (1993) *Educating the Single Children (Du Sheng Zi Nu De Jiao Yu* – in Chinese), Shanghai: East China Normal University Press.

Wang, C. J. (2004) *An Overview of the Philosophy of Traditional Chinese Family Precepts (Chuan Tong Jia Xuen Si Xiang Tong Lun* – in Chinese), Jilin: Jilin People's Press.

Wang, L. (2007) "The relations between skipped generation childrearing and the mental health of young children (*You er ge dai jiao yang fang shi yu xin li jian kang de guan xi* – in Chinese)," *China Behavioural Medicine Science (Zhongguo Xing Wei Yi Xue Ke Xue)*, 16(2), 158–160.

Wang, S., Zhang, W., and Chen, H. (2006) "Development of ego identity and its relations to parenting style and parent-adolescent communication in middle school students (*Zhong xue sheng zi wo tong yi xing de fa zhan yu fu mu jiao yang fang shi qin zi gou tong de guan xi* – in Chinese)," *Studies of Psychology and Behavior (Xin Li Yu Xing Wei Yan Jiu)*, 2, 126–132.

Wang, Z. (2003) "Gender, employment and women's resistance," in E. Perry and M. Selden (eds) *Chinese Society: Change, Conflict, and Resistance*, 2nd edn, New York: RoutledgeCurzon, 158–182.

Wank, D. L. (1999) *Commodifying Communism: Business, Trust, and Politics in a Chinese City*, New York: Cambridge University Press.

Wen, C., and Xiao, X. (2005) *The Chinese Perception and Behaviour (Zhong Guo*

Ren: Guan Nian Yu Xing Wei – in Chinese), Nanjing: Jiangsu Education Publishing House.

Werner, O., and Campbell, D. T. (1970) "Translating, working through interpreters and the problem of decentering," in R. Naroll and R. Cohen (eds) *A Handbook of Cultural Anthropology*, New York: American Museum of Natural History, 398–419.

White, T. (2006) *China's Longest Campaign: Birth Planning in the People's Republic, 1949–2005,* Ithaca, NY: Cornell University Press.

Whiting, B. B. (1963) *Six Cultures: Studies of Child Rearing,* New York: John Wiley.

Whiting, B. B., and Whiting, J. W. M. (1975) *Children of Six Cultures: A Psycho-Cultural Analysis*, Cambridge, MA: Harvard University Press.

Whyte, M. K. (2005) "Continuity and change in urban Chinese family life," *The China Journal,* 53, 9–34.

Whyte, M. K., and Parish, W. (1984) *Urban Life in Contemporary China*, Chicago, IL: University of Chicago Press.

Wicker, A. W. (1969) "Attitudes versus actions: the relationship of verbal and overt behavioral responses to attitude objects," *Journal of Social Issues,* 25, 41–78.

Wilmot, W. (1995) *Relational Communication*, New York: McGraw-Hill.

Woo, B., *et al.* (2004) "Development and validation of a depression scale for Asian adolescents," *Journal of Adolescence,* 27(6), 677–689.

Wu, D. (1996) "Parental control: psychocultural interpretations of Chinese patterns of socialization," in S. Lau (ed.) *Growing Up the Chinese Way: Chinese Child and Adolescent Development*, Hong Kong: The Chinese University Press, 1–28.

Wyness, M. G. (2006) *Childhood and Society: An Introduction to the Sociology of Childhood*, New York: Palgrave Macmillan.

Xiamen Shi Di Fang Zhi Bian Zuan Wei Yuan Hui (ed.) (2004) *Xiamen Shi Zhi* (in Chinese), Beijing: Fang Zhi Chu Ban She.

Xin, M. (2000) *Labour Market Reform in China*, Cambridge: Cambridge University Press.

Xu, H., Zhang, J., and Zhang, M. (2009) "A research summary of how family parenting patterns influence children's socialization development (*Jia ting jiao yang fang shi dui er tong she hui hua fa zhan ying xiang de yan jiu zong shu* – in Chinese)," *Psychological Science (Xin Li Ke Xue),* 31(4), 940–942.

Yan, H. (2006) *China's One-Child Policy in Need of Change*, East Asian Institute, National University of Singapore.

Yan, Y. X. (1997) "The triumph of conjugality: structural transformation of family relations in a Chinese village," *Ethnology,* 36(3), 191–213.

Yan, Y. (2003) *Private Life Under Socialism*, Stanford, CA: Stanford University Press.

Yang, C., and Hou, D. (2009) "Relationship between children's trait anxiety and parenting styles (*Zi nu te zhi jiao lu yu fu mu jiao yang fang shi guan xi* – in Chinese)," *Psychological Science (Xin Li Ke Xue),* 32(5), 1274–1275.

Yang, C., Hart, C. H., Nelson, D. A., Porter, C. L., Olsen, S. F., Robinson, C. C., and Jin, S. (2004) "Fathering in a Beijing, Chinese sample: associations with boys' and girls' negative emotionality and aggression," in R. D. Day and M. E. Lamb (eds) *Conceptualizing and Measuring Father Involvement*, Mahwah, NJ: Lawrence Erlbaum, 185–216.

Yang, H. (1996) "The distributive norm of monetary support to older parents: a look at a township in China," *Journal of Marriage and the Family,* 58(May), 404–415.

Yang, K. S. (1995) "Chinese social orientation: An integrative analysis," in T. Y.

Lin, W. S. Tseng, and E. K. Yeh (eds) *Chinese Societies and Mental Health*, Oxford: Oxford University Press.

Yang, S., Zhang, Y., and Huang, G. (2004) "A preliminary study on child abuse (*Er tong nue dai fang shi de yang jiu* – in Chinese)," *Chinese Journal of Clinical Psychology (Zhong Guo Lin Chuang Xin Li Xue Zha Zi)*, 12(2), 140–141.

Ye, W. Z. (1996) *Theory of Children's Needs: The Cost and Profits of Raising Children in China (Haizi Xu Qiu Lun: Zhong Guo Haizi De Cheng Ben He Xiao Yong* – in Chinese), Shanghai: Fudan University Press.

Ye, Y., Zou, H., and Li, C. (2006) "The developmental characteristics of adolescents' family functioning and its influence on mental health (*Qing shao nian jia ting gong neng de fa zhan te dian ji qi yu xin li jian kang de guan xi* – in Chinese)," *Chinese Mental Health Journal (Zhong Guo Xin Li Wei Sheng Za Zhi)*, 6, 385–387.

Yin, X., Hu, T., and Chen, X. (2009) "The study on relationship between self-concept and parental rearing patterns of achievers and underachievers (*Xue you sheng he xue kun sheng fu mu jiao yang fang shi zi wo gai nian de dui bi yan jiu* – in Chinese)," *Science & Technology Information (Ke Ji Xin Xi)*, 31, 175–177.

Zeng, Q., Lu, Y., Zhou, H., Dong, Q., and Chen, X. (1997) "Parenting styles and children's school adjustments (*Fu mu jiao yu fang shi yu er tong de xue xiao shi ying* – in Chinese)," *Journal of Psychology and Education (Xin Li Fa Zhan Yu Jiao Yu)*, 2, 46–51.

Zhang, W. (1997) "A comparison of parenting styles in urban and rural areas," *Pyschological Development and Education*, 13, 44–49.

Zheng, G., Shi, S., and Tang, H. (2005) "Population development and the value of children in the People's Republic of China," in G. Trommsdorff and B. Nauck (eds) *The Value of Children in Cross Cultural Perspective*, Lengerich: Pabst Science Publishers, 239–282.

Zheng, J. M., and Huang, S. Z. (1988) "The construction and improvement of the investment environment in Xiamen Special Economic Zone," in B. Brogan (ed.) *Xiamen Special Economic Zone: a Report of a Workshop*, Canberra: National Centre for Development Studies, 72–81.

Zhou, Q. (2004) "Chinese children's effortful control and dispositional anger/ frustration: relations to parenting styles and children's social functioning," *Development Psychology*, 40(3), 352–366.

Zhou, X. and Hou, L. (1999) "Children of cultural revolution: the state and life course in the People's Republic of China," *American Sociological Review*, 64(1), 12–36.

Zhou, X., and Yang, D. (2009) "A survey and analysis of family's influence on adolescents' mental health (*Qing shao nian xin li jian kang jia ting ying xiang yin su de diao cha yu fen xi* – in Chinese)," *Journal of Liaoning Teachers College – Social Science Edition (Liao Ning Shi Zhuan Xue Bao)*, 66(6), 66–67.

Zhu, Y., Webber, M., and Benson, J. (2010) *The Everyday Impact of Economic Reform in China*, London: Routledge.

Zou, H., Zhang, Q., and Wang, Y. (2005) "Research review on the relationships between family functioning and youth crimes (*Jia ting gong neng yu shao nian fan zui de guanxi de yan jiu jin zhan* – in Chinese)," *Developmental Psychology and Education (Xin Li Fa Zhan Yu Jiao Yu)*, 3, 120–124.

Zunich, M. (1962) "Relationship between maternal behavior and attitudes toward children," *Journal of Genetic Psychology*, 100, 155–165.

Index

Note: page numbers in **bold** refer to illustrations

180   *Index*

For Product Safety Concerns and Information please contact our EU
representative GPSR@taylorandfrancis.com
Taylor & Francis Verlag GmbH, Kaufingerstraße 24, 80331 München, Germany

www.ingramcontent.com/pod-product-compliance
Lightning Source LLC
Chambersburg PA
CBHW050709280326
41926CB00088B/2885

9 780415 855570